Crime, Second Chances, and Human Services

Crime, Second Chances, and Human Services

Creating a Pathway to Ordinary Life for the Convicted

Edited by
Fonkem Achankeng I
and Janet Hagen

LEXINGTON BOOKS
Lanham • Boulder • New York • London

Published by Lexington Books
An imprint of The Rowman & Littlefield Publishing Group, Inc.
4501 Forbes Boulevard, Suite 200, Lanham, Maryland 20706
www.rowman.com

6 Tinworth Street, London SE11 5AL, United Kingdom

British Library Cataloguing in Publication Information Available

Library of Congress Cataloging-in-Publication Data

Includes bibliographic references and index.
ISBN 978-1-4985-9590-2 (pbk.)
ISBN 978-1-4985-9588-9 (cloth)
ISBN 978-1-4985-9589-6 (electronic)

Contents

Preface

I am a member of the Kiwanis Club of Appleton-Fox Cities. I was present at the Friday Club meeting on May 20, 2016. On that day we had our "Inspiration Breakfast" and a few guests that I did not know. The Club president, Renee Waterman, spoke about the beginnings in 2008 of the Warming Shelter in Appleton, Wisconsin, through the building of a permanent structure in 2010. She then presented Scott Peeples, the director of the Warming Shelter, with a check for US$600.00 from the Appleton-Fox Cities Club.

Scott walked up to the podium, accepted the check, and began to speak. He began by thanking the club president, Renee Waterman, the leadership of the club, and everyone at Appleton-Fox Cities Kiwanis Club for organizing the inspiration breakfast in honor of the officials of the Warming Shelter. His brief speech focused on the growth that the shelter had experienced since 2008 and on how the shelter was already utilizing over three thousand volunteers a year. The Shelter had even recently purchased a new eleven-passenger van to transport clients and while US$600.00 once supported the shelter's "One Day at a Time" program (paying for one day of Shelter for all its residents) that cost had risen to US$1,186.00. With no wish to ask the Kiwanis Club for more money, the director went on to recognize the founding members of the club and other individuals and agencies including St. Joseph's Catholic Church and Father Leary Abler, who opened their doors to the shelter in 2008 when no one else would. He recounted with sincere gratitude how the shelter got a lot of support throughout the community but especially from the religious community and specifically from the Catholic churches in the community and showered special praise on Father Leary, pastor at St. Joseph's Catholic Church, who was also present at the club meeting as he spoke that day.

Scott continued his remarks by highlighting the mission of the Fox Valley Warming Shelter. As he put it, the shelter provides overnight temporary shelter to adult men and women who are homeless and collaborates with community resources to pave a path toward self-sufficiency. He mentioned how he explained the shelter's mission to clients at meetings two times a month, talking to clients just like he was talking to the members of the Kiwanis Club on that Friday morning. He broke it into three parts: "We are here to provide basic needs—shelter, food, shower facilities and laundry." The second part is the "we love you so much we want you to leave" part of our mission: "We connect people with jobs, housing, counseling, and alcohol and other drug services." Within that perspective, the shelter tries to use trauma-informed care, which means understanding where clients are coming from and what they have experienced in their lives that have brought them to this point.

And the third part of the shelter's mission is that the Warming Shelter is a place they don't dread coming to. "We don't want people to feel excited about coming here—the Warming Shelter is great—but we want to feel O.K. about it, too." After explaining the mission of the shelter, the director went on to describe some of its clients. "We have tough clients. Frankly, many of them aren't eligible to go to Homeless Connections because of their criminal background and/or their active struggles with drugs and alcohol." Above all, the director felt happy to share success stories too. One story was very striking from the point of view of second chance education. It was the story of William (last name withheld). He shared the following story.

> The first client I talked to when I walked into the Warming Shelter as the new director in January of 2014 was William. During my early morning tour, he sidled up to the board chair of the shelter and me and thanked us for providing a place for people who were struggling with alcoholism. When he walked away, I asked our board chair if he was a client or a staff person. In our dealings with him for the next year and a half, William always had the dual distinction of sounding extremely erudite and accomplished while struggling with mental illness, lack of motivation to work, and alcoholism. People called him "the professor," a moniker that endeared him to some and made him a source of consternation for others.
>
> He spent several months at the Warming Shelter, moved to Homeless Connections, came back to the Warming Shelter and then—by choice—spent a couple months outside during some of the coldest months of the winter of 2015. When he returned to the Warming Shelter (an igloo he had constructed for himself on private property was destroyed by authorities) we emphasized the importance of him helping himself. In the meantime, we continued to provide his basic needs: a warm shelter from the elements, food, shower, and laundry facilities. For several more months, he made very little movement. Jobs came and went and he was not able to save money to get out of the shelter. Finally, in the early fall of 2015, he became eligible for a transitional

housing opportunity at the Salvation Army's Project Home. About a week before he left, he was at the shelter when representatives of Casa Hispana/ Hispanic Chamber of Commerce came to do an evening presentation about a free welding training program at the local technical college. Now in his early fifties, William had worked in several professions, including teaching and selling insurance. He was still physically fit enough to consider a new opportunity and he decided to go for it. He started attending the twelve-week welding program and shortly afterward he moved into his new transitional home. While he had moved out of the shelter, we were kept informed and told he would be graduating with a certificate in welding and a new job he had been connected with through the program. I (Scott) attended his graduation from the program on February 29—and guess who was the class speaker! Yes, it was William. The speech was only five minutes but it was great that he thanked the Warming Shelter and the other agencies that had helped him get to that point.

I'm not sure whether William will actually get a job as a welder, but I know the experience helped him continue on a better path. William's path to success is not the linear path that society might consider for someone who is homeless. He made progress and slid backwards many times during his approximately two-year affiliation with the Warming Shelter. But, throughout it all, his days at the Warming Shelter gave him the stability he needed to get his life together and eventually embark on a new career. His path to self-sufficiency was paved by many individuals and agencies along the way. In the end, it was his personal change of perspective and dedication to change that made the difference. But the second chance from the stability of the Warming Shelter helped him get there.

William's story illustrates the fact that individuals can turn their lives around if society provides them inspiration for second chances. This story reveals that William spent several months at the Warming Shelter. Homeless Connections gave him another chance. When he returned to the Warming Shelter, the shelter still opened its doors to William. The Warming Shelter recognized his dignity as a human being and offered him yet another chance. Then, by his personal choice, William spent a couple of months outside during some of the coldest months of the 2015 winter. When he returned to the Warming Shelter after an igloo he had constructed for himself on private property was destroyed by authorities, officials at the shelter let him understand the importance of him helping himself. He finally understood the advice and went on to find help at the local technical college.

There are many Williams out there who have fallen between the cracks and many of whom have served their time in prison and are willing to gain back their lives. In the case of this William, his second, third, and fourth chance came from inspiration gained from the work of the Warming Shelter. The many Williams in our neighborhoods, communities, and societies would benefit tremendously if individuals, agencies, and communities are willing to offer them a second or even a third chance. The question remains whether, as a society, we have the will to help the many Williams out there.

Acknowledgments

The idea for this book originated from a field trip with our social issues and solutions class at the University of Wisconsin Oshkosh in spring 2014. One requirement for the class was a field learning paper. Over the semesters, our students and I visited a human services agency or institution located in the community to meet clients and officials who work there. The visit to a human services agency provided students an opportunity to further understand some of the issues studied in the class in order that students could begin a critical reflection on and understanding of why some individuals and/or groups become clients of human services practice. On the field trip, we worked under the supervision of the agency's officials to understand what goes on at each agency or institution. At the end of the field trip, students wrote a critical thinking/reflective paper. The paper was expected to include new knowledge gained at the agency by integrating relevant theories from class readings and a reflection on the needs of the individuals and/or groups studied on such learning from the field. This assignment assisted students in getting a feel of how some of the issues studied in class impacted individuals, families, groups and communities and how such issues created needs for human services practice.

Our choice for the field trip in the spring of 2014 was STEP Industries, a human services agency located in Neenah, Wisconsin. In the fall semester of 2013, my field supervision duties included one student placement at STEP Industries in Neenah, Wisconsin. I had not heard of this agency before, but because one of my students was placed at that site, I decided to look up the site in order to understand what STEP Industries did as part of the preparation for my supervision visit to the site. As I began to read about STEP Industries, I was struck by the agency's "hope for the future . . . where there was none" mission. I shared my interest in the work of the agency with Janet

Hagen, my department chair, who already knew the agency from her many years' experience in the Human Services Leadership Program at the University of Wisconsin Oshkosh.

My first conversation with the president of STEP Industries happened even before I met with my student. In my teaching in human services leadership I had focused mainly on the needs provision framework of the field. I was struck by the work of STEP Industries for many reasons. Some of these reasons included the expansion of the human services field in the way STEP Industries had done in its thinking and actions. Especially of interest to me was the fact that STEP Industries was founded to "employ recovering drug or alcoholic individuals exclusively or members of their families." This vision was particularly impressive to me within the context of an American society in which work remained essential to survival and a society where a criminal record was a problem for employment. If people could not find work because of a criminal record, in a society where there is no free meal, how could they then survive?

At STEP Industries, my students and I fell in love with a creative and innovative approach initiated by one individual to impact the lives of several people in recovery. We experienced a great story anchored on the value and place of "second chances" in a country where second chances remained difficult to come by for anyone with a criminal record. We saw this human services agency as a pioneer in that it went beyond the initial needs provision approach in the human services field to embrace an advocacy approach through creating "second chances" for groups in American society, who otherwise, would be completely written off. The target group at STEP Industries is recovering drug addicts in a society that generally treats drug addicts as criminals. This consideration may also have its place because we know that drugs and crime are close associates.

As an example of Margaret Mead's emphasis on how much change thoughtful individuals can bring to a society, the STEP Industries' case is one example of an individual with an idea stepping forward to focus on one group in our society. As the writing of this book progressed, we learned of several other such organizations around the state and the country, including WISDOM in Milwaukee, Wisconsin; Circles of Support in Appleton, Wisconsin; Halfway House or Office of Re-Entry in Newark, New Jersey; National Hire Network in Georgia, and others. Like in many of these initiatives, people with addictions and others with criminal records remained excluded and abandoned to live in the margins of society because they are blocked from getting jobs by a criminal record. And this situation does not only occur in a society where drugs and crime go hand in hand, but in a society whose members thrive on jobs and job acquisition. That is the reason I arranged a field trip with students to experientially open up to my students the idea behind STEP Industries in Neenah, Wisconsin, and the idea of "second chances" in life.

Although this book deals mainly with certain aspects of the current national life in the United States, we conceived the book idea in response to the lives of the tens of millions of Americans with a criminal record who are a core group of human services practice. The statistics show that there are up to seventy million Americans with a criminal record. By the first decades of the twenty-first century the huge numbers of people incarcerated began to force a national debate on the problem of incarceration in national life. This debate gave rise to a resurgence of the concept of "second chances" increasingly heard and becoming a familiar part of the national vocabulary especially in the Obama administration. The intent of this book therefore is to capture and build on this increasingly familiar national vocabulary especially with regard to life after prison for many clients and client groups of human services practice.

In this regard, this book explores the concept of "second chances" (Shavit, Ayalon, & Kurleander, 2004; Ross & Gray, 2005) in the field of human services as a way of expanding the thinking in the field from a traditional needs provision emphasis to include an emphasis on prevention and advocacy in the pioneering direction of STEP Industries. It explores the concept of "second chances" as a foundational theoretical construct of the human services field, one that seeks to reduce marginalization and increase inclusion. Our primary purpose in the book is to make a case for second chances not only as a part of human life in general because we all make mistakes, but to argue that the concept of second chances ought to be a foundational concept in human services theorizing. The reason for this thinking is that the concept of second chances is basic to human services philosophy and practice. Although basic to the philosophy of the field, the concept of second chances does not appear to have found a place in the traditional approach to human services theorizing as in education. In education, taking a test or an examination over or repeating a class is a basic notion whereas in the traditional approach to the human services field, many practitioners still focus mainly on services and resources provision to the needy in society. This book therefore also seeks to humanize the stories of individuals with a criminal record, a population often marginalized even though wishing to re-enter society in order to catch a glimpse of the American dream concept.

From this perspective there are many thanks to be made. My coeditor and I would like to thank all the students taught over the years in the social issues and solutions class at the University of Wisconsin Oshkosh and particularly those students in the field trip class to STEP Industries in spring 2014. We also would like to thank those of our colleagues, Diane McMillen and Melinda Kline at the Department of Human Services, Washburn University, Topeka, Kansas, and John Paulson at the University of Southern Indiana at Evansville, and others, including David Liners, director of WISDOM in Milwaukee, Wisconsin, who found merit in the idea of the book and contributed to the theoretical perspectives developed in the book. The approach of this book and many of the ideas have been explored with these colleagues in lectures and seminars, and we have benefited from their engagement with the idea of the human being to change, both sympathetic and critical.

Our colleagues at the College of Education and Human Services at the University of Wisconsin Oshkosh also provided a stimulating and supportive intellectual environment. Dean Fred Yeo did not only like the idea we were exploring but also provided the funding we needed to organize the 2015 Human Services Leadership Community Collaborative Panel on the subject of second chances. We also gained much from conversations with Alfred Kisubi and Toni House, colleagues in the department, and particularly from Alfred Kisubi's contribution of some philosophical insights into the need to search for meaning of life, the "I-Them" dilemma, emotivism v. empiricism, and individualism v. passion debate in human services.

In my case, I owe a great debt of gratitude to Penny Garcia, who supported my learning about human services with a copy of *the Introduction to Human Services* book by Edward Neikrug when she found me wondering what the field was about. I am equally indebted to others like Martin Rice and Tricia McCourt, who did not only contribute a chapter each, but represent the very idea that people can and do indeed change. Above all, I would like to thank Michelle D. Giese, the President of STEP Industries in Neenah, Wisconsin, for her leadership and collaboration and also the Kimberly Clark executive (anonymous), who gave birth to the STEP Industries' idea to provide a second chance for individuals in recovery. The Kiwanis Club of Appleton-Fox Valley and Scott Peeples, director of the Appleton Warming Shelter, also deserve special thanks for granting us the permission to use excerpts from Scott's 2016 message at the club as a contribution to this book.

Similarly, we wish to thank the editors at Rowman & Littlefield who guided us with their immense knowledge regarding the publishing trade as we worked on the manuscript. Before being directed to contact Rowman & Littlefield, we also benefitted from the helpful comments of Uli Spalthoff at Dignity Press, who very early in the proposal process, thought very highly of this book project. We owe a special debt of gratitude for his encouraging words which kept the effort alive. As he put it, "[L]ike you, I see giving a second chance a very important topic and your book certainly is in line with our work in human dignity and humiliation studies." Finally, we also owe immense gratitude to our families, whose love kept us going as we worked on this manuscript. May they find in the pages that follow some of the love they gave us.

REFERENCES

Ross, S., & Gray, J. (2005, December). Transitions and re-engagement through second chance education. *The Australian Educational Researcher, 32*(3).

Shavit, Y., Ayalon, H., & Kurleander, M. (2004). Schooling alternatives . . . *Studies in Educational Administration and Organization, 28*, 63–93.

Incarceration and American Society: An Introduction

Fonkem Achankeng

The United States has about 5 percent of the world's population, but 23 percent of the world's prisoners. From a human services perspective, we cannot ignore this situation, especially in a country where a criminal record marginalizes an individual and can close doors on getting a job, voting, going to school, getting loans or licenses, or securing a place to live (Collins, 2014). Summarizing the general attitude of Americans and prisons, Andreas Kluth (2012) stated that Americans love locking people up. They do not see any irony in loudly claiming to be the freest country in the world, while robbing more individuals of their freedom, their dignity, and their rights than any other country. Kluth added that the United States has the highest incarceration rate in the world and that we lock up 732 people out of every 100,000 while the G7 countries, lock up 96 people for 100,000. The only other country in the world that came closest to the United States is Russia with 607 people. This conservative and prevailing American attitude toward incarceration remains based on vengeance rather than on rehabilitation.

In the context of many reflections around the nation in 2015 on excessive incarceration rates in the United States, the relevance of a book on "second chances" in life struggles cannot be overemphasized. As I considered working on this book, there was almost no one who articulated the hopeful message of "second chances in life" better than Pope Francis during a state visit to the United States. Pope Francis went to see inmates at Philadelphia's largest prison and told them that "confinement was not the same thing as exclusion." Speaking before some one hundred inmates and their families in a cinder-block gymnasium at Curran-Fromhold Correctional Facility, the pontiff implored Americans to remember prisoners, who are part of his global mission to tend to the poor, the forgotten and the neglected. As he put it, "I am here as a pastor but, above all, as a brother . . . to share your situation and to make it my own." How hopeful! This message of hopefulness was not only timely, but powerful.

How can we as a society spread Pope Francis's message of hope not only to persons with a criminal record, but also to all who think anyone with a criminal record ought to be put away behind bars, forgotten and neglected as a brother or sister, neighbor, or fellow citizen? How often do we forget our own humanity and our own frailty as human beings when we see members of our families, neighbors, or other citizens as if they were less than human mainly because they made errors in life? How often do we as fellow citizens rush to condemn those in error without ever caring to reflect on what may have caused them to commit the errors, including harm to others in the first place?

Pope Francis did not think the way many in our society do. Rather, he offered an alternative perception of people with a criminal record whom he saw just as human as we all are. He demonstrated his viewpoint in two different ways. First, he reiterated that everybody can be redeemed by recognizing that "[I]n life we all get our feet dirty from the dust-filled roads of life and history." Second, he also moved forward to teach by example when he washed the feet of a Muslim woman serving her sentence in that prison at a time in the United States when Muslims were largely perceived as enemies.

Our primary purpose in this book is to make a case for second chances not only as a part of human life in general because we all make mistakes, but to argue that the concept of second chances ought to be a foundational concept in human services theorizing because the concept is basic to human services philosophy and practice. As a notion, "second chances" does not appear to have gained currency in human services theorizing especially in the traditional approach to the field, which has focused mainly on providing services and resources to the needy in society.

Many people go into the field of human services because they want to make a difference in the lives of less fortunate individuals in the society. Although students in human services come from different cultures, heritages, family backgrounds or systems, experiences, and upbringings, they all come for the same reason of gaining new knowledge and skills for a career in the field. The human services field is about impacting the lives of people and groups in need—often by providing services which are lacking. The field is about the prevention of problems rather than calling in services to try to address the disruption of lives afterwards. The third concern of the field is social action and justice. This three-pronged approach to human services envisages expanding our thinking in the field. The assumption in this approach is that "those affected by conditions that render them needy are more than victims or incompetent individuals, but only individuals that have power, abilities and other resources that can be impressively increased when linked and focused" (Homan, Shepard, & Totten, 2012). This approach in the field is positioned to play a pivotal role in bringing people together in order to change conditions that affect them. Homan, Shepard, and Totten also indicated that making a difference in people's lives certainly entails working together with service agencies to provide services, rallying to prevent problems from occurring as in community gardens to produce vegetables, or rallying for direct action as in the 99 percent or groups giving away clean syringes to drug addicts in the movement from case to cause.

In its 2014 Call for Proposals for the Midwest Organization for Human Services (MWOHS) Conference in Marion, Indiana, the National Organization for Human Services (NOHS) revisited the development of the field in order to frame the conference theme. According to the organization, human services was developed in response to the increased needs of individuals, families, and communities that resulted from deinstitutionalization, the Civil Rights movement, and the War on Poverty. Community integration, empowerment, and both social and economic justice continue to be at the core of our mission and outreach to these marginalized groups. The following groups are among those assisted by human services professionals: homeless; wounded warriors; older adults; offenders; LGBTQI; immigrants and refugees; children and families in the protective services system; persons with disabilities; victims and survivors of traumatic events; and persons with HIV/AIDS, Alzheimer's disease, substance dependence, and countless other long-term conditions. Often, the individuals are targets of anger, resentment, fear, ridicule, and apathy. Human service practitioners recognize the inherent worth of these marginalized individuals, and pursue collaborative solutions to improve the well-being and quality of life. At the core of this perception of human services, the field is still mainly focused on providing for increased needs of individuals, families and communities resulting from the issues outlined above.

The field of human services understands that human beings are complex and diverse in many ways. At a time when the field is growing exponentially, it is important to underscore the basis of our thinking, especially in the context of key concepts such as empowerment, strengths perspective and resiliency. In order to help individuals and groups with problems they face and needs they have, the field emphasizes empowerment, strengths perspectives, and resiliency. While Gutierrez (2001, p. 210) views empowerment as the "process of increasing personal, interpersonal, or political power so that individuals can take action to improve their life situations," the strength perspective "focuses on client resources, capabilities, knowledge, abilities, motivations, experiences, intelligence, and other positive qualities that can be put to use to solve problems and pursue positive change" (Zastrow & Kirst-Ashman, 2013, p. 13) of individuals and groups. The strengths perspective views every individual, family, group, and community as having strengths which can built on - however bad the situation may be. This perspective also emphasizes that every environment is full of resources that can be tapped into and that illness and struggle can both be a challenge and opportunity. With regard to resiliency, the field depends on the use of strengths to fight adversity. Resiliency is defined as "the ability of an individual, family, group, community or organization to recover from adversity and resume functioning even when suffering serious trouble, confusion or hardship" (Zastrow & Kirst-Ashman, 2013, p. 17). Resiliency according to Gutheil and Congress (2000, p. 41) is the use of strengths to cope with adversity and survive, despite difficulties.

From the standpoint of this book, everyone is, and ought to be, part of the workforce in a country that prides itself on work. As Dawn Norris (2016) pointed out, the identity of individuals is tied to work. For Norris, work is identity in the United States because who we are is what we do. How much stronger might our economy be if everyone made a contribution as a member of the workforce? How many more individuals and families could be empowered and strengthened if everyone with requisite skills and the willingness to work was allowed to work? Increasingly incarcerating people and especially young people constitutes a greater danger to our society than many are willing to acknowledge. In terms of committing crimes, studies show that one's ideology develops generally during the adolescent and post-adolescent years, and therefore is most influenced by the ideological setting in which one finds one's self at that period in life because one's ideological setting functions as the setting for identity (Linde, 1993; McAdams, 1997).

People with a criminal record should be on a pathway of returning to society, whether it is for new employment opportunities, promotion possibilities or simply for the pure pleasure of living ordinary lives. Loss of work, Norris (2016) argued, can result in loss of self and such loss of self, which Norris refers to as "identity void," can be detrimental to one's mental health in a country where work means everything. Although it is obvious that prisons and prisoners should always be part of a country's approach to the disciplining of its citizens, a good quality reform of how we perceive prisons and prisoners will be needed for a long time in the United States of America.

The contributors to this book and I trust that it will ensure a change of thinking on the futures of persons with a criminal record who serve their time and are willing and determined to return to society and truly aspire to work and be visible and active members of their families and communities. Each of the chapters that make up this book tries to understand some significant transitions in the lives of fellow human beings. The authors draw on different theories to make sense of the lives of people with criminal records. Among the different aspects they examine, we find an emphasis on the place of change with Mark Rice; Diane McMillen and Melinda Kline; David Liners;

John Paulson, Kevin Groves, and Leslie A. Hagedorn, and others focus on healing and restoration.

The case of STEP Industries is highlighted herein as just one example of many groups and organizations concerned about creative and innovative approaches to impact the lives of several individuals in recovery. In focusing on STEP Industries the book considers the agency as a pioneer, and one that went beyond the initial needs provision approach in the human services field to embrace an advocacy approach through creating "a second chance" for groups in America, who otherwise, may be completely written off. The agency tries to anchor the experience of healing and re-entry on the value and place of "second chances" in a country where second chances remain difficult to come by for anyone with a criminal record.

Some of the contributors use narrative psychology to provide the lives of individuals with unity or purpose (Habermas & Bluck, 2000; Pillemer, 1992; Singer, 1995). Michelle Devine Giese, Pearl Wright, and Tricia McCourt present their life stories as individuals who consider themselves redeemed from an earlier period of great pain in their lives. Following the narrative methodology, Tricia McCourt outlines, from a biographer's standpoint, how she found recovery and a healthier way of living from her understanding of the Three Principles (Mind, Thought, and Consciousness). In narrating their life stories, some of these contributors draw from McAdam's life story theory of identity (1993) as they focus on how the stories influence their thoughts, feelings, and behavior in terms of who they become. In his chapter, Alfred T. Kisubi discusses the constraints as well as the opportunities of passion as the earnestness, the inwardness or commitment to seeking meaning in our individual lives, as client empowerers in human services. In the chapter he argues that without passion, it is impossible to make human services education and practice meaningful to oneself as a professional in human services. Lynne M. Woehrle in her chapter focuses on what processes we use to respond to norm violations, what the restoration of community looks like and how the concept of redemption might be necessary for sustainable peace in the modern society. In the concluding chapter, Alfred T. Kisubi focuses on transfiguration using poetry.

In all, the different contributions to this book provide an interdisciplinary approach to the understanding of second chances in our society. The readings, contributed by human service professionals, social workers, historians, anthropologists, as well as sociologists and others, display the variety of theoretical perspectives and methodological approaches now competing for attention in human services research. The book will be an important reference and source of inspiration in the field.

REFERENCES

Gutheil, I. A., & Congress, E. (2000). Resiliency in older people: A paradigm for practice. In R. R. Green (Ed.), *Resiliency: An integrated approach to practice, policy and research* (pp. 40–50). Washington, DC: NASW Press.

Gutierrez, L. (2001). Empowerment theory. Zastrow, C. & Kirst-Ashman, K. K. (2013). *Understanding human behavior and the social environment* (p. 210). Belmont, CA: Brooks/Cole, Cengage Learning.

Habermas, T., & Bluck, S. (2000). Getting a life: The emergence of the life story in adolescence. *Psychological Bulletin* 126, 748–769

Hellman, L. (1993). Quoted in Landman, J. (1993). *Regret: the persistence of the possible.* New York: Oxford University Press.

Homan, M., Shephard, B., & Totten, V. (2012). Keynote at the 2012 National Organization for Human Services Conference, Milwaukee, WI.

Kluth, A. (2012). *Hannibal and me: Life lessons from history.* New York: Riverhead Books.

Kriesberg, B., & Marchionna, S. (2006, April). Attitudes of U.S. voters toward prisoner rehabilitation and reentry policies. *Focus.*

Landman, J. (2001). The crime, punishment, and ethical transformation of two radicals: Or how Katherine Power improves on Dostoevsky. D. P. McAdams, R. Josselson, & A. Lieblich (Eds.), *Turns in the road: Narrative studies of lives in transition.* Washington, DC: American Psychological Association.

Landman, J. (1993). *Regret: The persistence of the possible.* New York: Oxford University Press.

Linde, C. (1993). *Life stories: The creation of coherence.* New York: Oxford University Press.

McAdams, D. P. (1997). A conceptual history of personality psychology. In R. Hogan, J. Johnson, & S. Briggs (Eds.), *Handbook of personality psychology.* (pp. 3–39). San Diego, CA: Academic Press.

McAdams, D. P. (1993). *Stories we live by.* New York: William Morrow.

Norris, D. R. (2016). *Job loss, identity, and mental health.* New Brunswick, NJ: Rutgers University Press.

Pillemer, D. B. (1992). Remembering personal circumstances: A functional analysis. In E. Winograd & U. Neisser (Eds.), *Affect and accuracy in recall* (pp. 236–265) New York: Cambridge University Press.

Shavit, Y., Ayalon, H., & Kurleander, M. (2001). Second-chance education and inequalities in Israel. Retrieved September 23, 2014, from http://www.mzes.uni-mannheim.de/rc28/papers/shavit_etal_f.doc.

Shavit, Y., Ayalon, H., & Kurleander, M. (2004). Schooling Alternatives . . . *Studies in Educational Administration and Organization, 28*, 63.

Singer, J. A. (1995). Seeing oneself: A framework for the study of autobiographical memory in personality. *Journal of Personality, 63*, 429–457.

Zastrow, C., & Kirst-Ashman, K. K. (2013). *Understanding human behavior and the social environment.* Belmont, CA: Brooks/Cole, Cengage Learning.

Chapter One

Second Chances, Human Services, Crime, and Redemption

Fonkem Achankeng

> When people get out of jail after serving time for bloodless, victimless crimes and cannot find employment or housing or even vote, more problems are created than solved.
> —The Sentencing Project

The field of human services began with the recognition of the necessity to help individuals, families, and groups in need. The field focuses on redeeming people. This focus also includes rescuing people from mistakes they may have made in their lives. Pope Francis demonstrated this focus in human services best with his actions and words. On a state visit to the United States in 2015, for example, the pope reiterated that everybody can be redeemed. He recognized that "[I]n life we all get our feet dirty." Making mistakes is a human quality. If we made an error and fell in the gutter, we cannot stay there all our lives. Our neighbors and society ought to pull us up and out. We do this each time a car slides into a ditch. If we can pull our car or the neighbor's car out of a ditch, how can we not do the same for human beings? Pope Francis also demonstrated the human services approach to treating people when he did not only teach by word, but also by deeds. He taught by example when he washed the feet of a Muslim woman at a prison he visited in Philadelphia on his state visit. Such recognition of the fallibility of humans and the demonstration that we are each other's keeper shows that human services as a discipline anchors on the need and place of redeeming people. Redemption is about the action of saving or being saved from error.

Unfortunately, we do not, this far in the United States, always think about our neighbors in the same terms. How often do we hear that our neighbors are poor because they are lazy? How often enough have we heard that "we are all rugged individualists and we're going to take care of ourselves, not others?" How often enough must we as a society continue to blame poverty rates, crime, drugs, juvenile violence, and failing schools mainly on single parenthood as the root cause? How can we as a society not take a step back to imagine with great seriousness our rates of incarceration? The Pew Foundation reported that 1 in 100 Americans are locked up in jails and prisons. As if the picture is not troubling enough, the figures are much worse for some groups, especially young minority men where 1 in 36 Hispanic men and 1 in 15 black men are behind bars (Skolnick & Currie, 2011). How do we as a society fail to understand that "the growth of the prison system has siphoned off vast amounts of public funds that could have been used for schools, health care, and other important services that could help to prevent crime in the first place" (Skolnick & Currie, 2011, p. 323)? In her book, *The New Jim Crow: Mass Incarceration in the Age of Colorblindness*, Michelle Alexander (2012) described the misery in which ex-convicts live in America. She noted that

> The lives of convicted felons after they are released from prison are forever changed. As a result of their criminality, they are legally discriminated against in their ability to obtain housing, employment, education, and public benefits like Medicaid and food stamps. Convicted felons are prevented from voting until they pay exorbitant fines and penalties, many of which they can never fully pay. Ex-offenders are shamed in their communities, and often live in isolation and despair. Many return to crime and are re-incarcerated.

In 2013, Senator Marco Rubio (Republican-Florida) introduced legislation that would prohibit anyone with a felony or, in some cases, just a misdemeanor conviction from even applying for a navigator job. If Senator Rubio's Healthcare Privacy and Anti-Fraud Act became law, and yet another job category closed off to those with criminal records, the senator would no doubt declare it a victory for public safety. Sadhbh Walshe (2013), however, argued rightly that "[I]n truth, it would be anything but that" because "barring people with criminal records from employment is unproductive and unjust."

We may narrow this situation of our society to an attitude problem. In spite of the alarming numbers of our people behind bars, many of our citizens believe that the system is lenient with criminals even when we know our political leaders have passed punitive measures such as "three strikes and you're out" laws, which mandate twenty-five years to life sentences for criminals convicted of three felonies including possessing a small quantity of drugs. In articulating the essence of the American attitude, American dramatist, Lilian Hellman (1993) observed that "[I]t is considered unhealthy in America to remember mistakes, neurotic to think about them, psychotic to dwell upon them." From regret-averse maxims in American culture such as

"That was then, this is now," "Oh, that is history"; "Don't dwell on the past"; "Never cry over spilled milk," we are reminded that regret presents a direct affront to the optimism and future orientation of American culture. As Janet Landman (1993) put it, at some time in any adult life, the fact remains then will bleed into now, we will find ourselves thinking about—maybe even dwelling on—mistakes, and tears will fall with the spilled milk.

From narratives of some ex-convicts collected by Mark Rice (2016), Revocations Work Groups Director at WISDOM, we notice that many ex-convicts make the effort to change rather than dwell on their mistakes. One recounted, "While doing time in prison, I witnessed a system that was ballooning with predominantly young African Americans who were serving very long prison sentences . . . for drug crimes. This was troubling to me." Another interviewee stated, "When I was released, I was thinking what could I bring to the public that could help them understand what prison was like, what it looks like in a cell." A third interviewee had this to say, "I spent a lot of time destroying and hurting. Today I have the opportunity to clean up and heal. My past helps me see the truth."

These examples indicate eloquently that people can change; that people who have made errors in life can seek redemption. Such people deserve to be redeemed by their community and the greater society. As a society we should not only change our attitude toward guilt and punishment, we should also be concerned about those things we need to do to transform the regret, guilt and despair of individuals who have committed offenses, and particularly individuals who have done serious harm to others.

The main concern here is what we need to do as a society to change this attitude and to transform the regret, guilt, remorse and despair of individuals who, after committing errors and paying for the errors, would like to be given a second chance. Two other related questions are also important here. What has made our society reluctant to provide such individuals the second chance they seek? In other words, how does society help or hinder such a process? How does the US culture influence our perception of people with a criminal record? How do guilt, suffering, and imprisonment combine to transform a person's ethical stance in the world? The third and last concern in this chapter relates to the field of human services and the concept of second chances as a foundational principle of the field.

SECOND CHANCES AND HUMAN SERVICES

The notion of "second chances" originally developed in education focuses on the idea that "through an organized structure an individual can actualize an opportunity missed or failed the first time around" (Shavit, Ayalon, & Kurleander, 2001, p. 2). According to Yogev (1997, p. 469), the philosophy underpinning second chance education is that "errors made by the selection mechanisms of the educational system or by individuals who terminated their own educational career could be corrected at a later stage." Other researchers in the area of youth transitions have also articulated the same reasoning regarding the complexities of youth transitions (Steinberg, Dornbusch & Brown, 1992; Rumberger, 2001; Ross & Gray, 2005). As Ross and Gray (2005) have pointed out, "the notion of 'second chance' is strongly supported by recent theories of transition in the field of youth studies research. The traditional, linear, unidimensional models based on age or school–to–work transition are considered inadequate as they fail to capture the complexities of youth transitions in the post-modern era. Recent views of youth transitions as multidimensional, circular processes are gaining prominence. They include other kinds of transition such as moving away from home, movement from one relationship to the next, changes in life styles and transitions from single to parental status (p. 104).

At a time when the human services field is growing exponentially, I received a correspondence on April 29, 2016, from Sara El-Amine, executive director of Organizing for Action, a group working for President Barack Obama. The message was a request for me to join the efforts being deployed by the president to give formerly incarcerated individuals a second chance. It was a call for me to join the "call for a criminal justice system that lives up to our values." The entire message read:

> It's National Reentry Week, a time when we shed a light on the resources needed to help those who were formerly incarcerated get another shot to join their communities in a positive way. In America, we believe in second chances—that even if you make a mistake that lands you in jail, if you serve your time, you can still earn a second chance at the American Dream.
>
> At least, that's the way it's supposed to work. But our criminal justice system is broken. Every year, more than 600,000 Americans get released from prison ready to make a new start, only to be met with often insurmountable obstacles. Getting a job, finding affordable housing, and getting access to both health care and education are all significantly harder. For too many, the system is rigged to fail.
>
> Our system is not supposed to make it easier to revert back to criminal behavior than to become a productive member of society, but it often does. Preventing relapses into crime is one of the most fundamental priorities of criminal justice, but with the system set up as it is today, too many Americans end up trapped in a cruel cycle of poverty and crime that weakens our communities.
>
> That's why President Obama's administration consistently took steps to make our system fairer, smarter, less expensive, and more effective. From reducing barriers to employment, to increasing access to education for formerly incarcerated individuals, the president continued to do what he could, where he could. But that was not enough. Some members of Congress had already been working on the issue, but if we are going to break down the very real

barriers that stand in the way of citizens returning to society to become positive members of their communities, we need more of their colleagues to come to the table and pass a bipartisan criminal justice reform bill.

This message came when the writing of this book was already at an advanced stage. Equipped with the learning about the need for second chances in life as advocated for by Iowa senator Tom Harkin, the ongoing reflection on the challenge of the American Association for Colleges and Universities and the Department of Education to rethink the approaches to civic engagement became more evident to me. In particular, I thought of the call by former health and human services secretary Kathleen Sebelius for "better training and a push for evidence based practices" in human services. As I reflected on how to tailor the training of students toward "producing informed, engaged, open-minded, and socially responsible professionals with a commitment to competence and effectiveness" in service provision, prevention and social action, the idea for a book on "second chances and human services" became obvious. In "an era of increased suffering and decreased caring" notably in relation to a population living in the fringes of society because they are blocked by a criminal record, this book will enhance the educational needs of students and professionals for greater practitioner effectiveness in human services.

This book aims to highlight the notion of "second chances" in a society where getting a job is essential to survival. The central question then is what happens to all with a criminal record, who find themselves invisible as a result of being trapped in situations that block them in the fringes of society. In examining "second chances" as a concept, the book argues in agreement with Wade F. Horn, an assistant secretary at the Department of Health and Human Services, who recognized that those on the margins of our society are not just crushed, but also hurt.

In constructing an expanded conceptualization of human services in the twenty first century, a conceptualization which challenges the preparation for practitioner effectiveness in "an era of increased suffering and decreased caring" (Homan, Shephard, & Totten, 2012), the book seeks to capture the concept of "second chances" as a major foundational concept in the theory and practice of human services. As a concept, "second chances," refers to the idea that "through an organized structure individuals can actualize an opportunity missed or a first time failure" (Shavit, Ayalon, & Kurleander, 2001, p. 2). "Second chances," long understood and practiced in education whereby many students are given a second and even a third and a fourth chance to take a class or repeat a test, has not been fully implemented in human services theory and practice. This concept is absolutely essential to the foundation of Human Services, as part of our focus on the human condition has not been adequately explored in human services theorizing. The concept of second chances ought to rightly belong foundationally to human services consider-ing the human services field as one focusing on the human condition.

It is in this regard that Alfred Kisubi in his approach to human services theorizing in the chapter on passion, affirms clearly how we need science in human services to understand reality, which is seen as fleeting. For him, change is the essence of helping and changing people through helping is empowering them to grow. His conception of the field does not only focus on the client and the place of second chances in empowering individuals need-ing help, but also on the helper. In the helping interaction, he suggests, the helper and the helpee should mutually treat each other as unique individuals who have idiosyncratic needs and values.

STRUGGLING WITH THE PREDICAMENT OF CRIME

In her book, *The New Jim Crow: Mass Incarceration in the Age of Color-blindness*, Michelle Alexander (2012) observed that "[A]ll people make mis-takes . . . All of us violate the law at some point in our lives. In fact, if the worst thing you have ever done is speed ten miles over the speed limit on the freeway, you have put yourself and others at more risk of harm than someone smoking marijuana in the privacy of his or her living room. Yet there are people in the United States serving life sentences for first-time drug offenses, something virtually unheard of anywhere else in the world." It is now esti-mated that more than one out of every three Americans passes through the criminal justice system. Since 2002, the United States has had the highest incarceration rate in the world. Over ten million children have parents who were imprisoned at some point in the children's lives. And prison terms are lengthening: for example, those released from state prisons in 2009 served sentences an average of 36 percent longer than those released in 1990—costing state taxpayers an extra \$10 billion, mostly for nonviolent offenders. A burgeoning for-profit prison industry has arisen, for which human bodies are the inventory that keeps the dollars flowing.

In addition to incarceration rates, the effects of incarceration on families, lengths of sentences and the profits in prison projects, we need to be con-cerned about how the criminal feels. Janet Landman (2001) posited that crimes result in an overwhelming sense of shame in the individuals who commit crimes. The shame-induced act that makes the criminal want to flee from society brings with it other enormously distressing psychological pun-ishments, including a sense of profound alienation, regret, guilt, remorse, panic, apathy, and suicidal despair. If we know of anyone who has been convicted—a family member, a friend or a neighbor—we all understand how many of them feel about the error(s) they committed.

The people who struggle with crimes could be very close to you. As some observers have stated, it could be your niece or nephew. Or even your son or daughter. It might even have been you, many years ago. Good people make dumb mistakes, especially when they're young. Maybe a neighbor's mailbox is intentionally damaged. Maybe an item is stolen from a high-end department store. Maybe a small quantity of marijuana is shared among a group of college students. Any of these situations can result in the filing of criminal charges. The convicted offender may be sentenced to pay fines, perform community service, complete a term of supervised probation, or even serve jail time. Society's debt must be paid, but at some point, all aspects of the court matter are finished and the person is expected to reenter productive life. It is not so easy. According to a source on Wisconsin Public Radio on May 14, 2014, about seven thousand people are released from prison every year and most of these people go back to prison because of lack of jobs.

The vast majority of convicted folks will one day reenter society. But as many people are finding out, a criminal conviction can close doors on getting a job, going to school, voting, getting loans or licenses, or securing a place to live (Collins, 2014). In New York, for example, Rick Collins hinted that "up to 60 percent of people with criminal records remain unemployed one year later." Blocking workers with criminal records from getting jobs hurts the economy and reduces public safety by turning potentially productive citizens into taxpayer burdens . . . or into recidivists who slip back into crime to earn a living for themselves and their families. Nearly nine out of ten New Yorkers who violated probation or parole were unemployed at the time. "Making dumb mistakes is human and no human group ought to be abandoned in the fringes of society because of a mistake in life" (Collins, 2014).

REDEMPTION

Redemption is defined as "the action of saving or being saved from sin, error, or evil."

There is no provision for expungement—the removal or sealing of a criminal record—in the federal courts. A federal conviction involving any type of crime, however nonviolent or out-of-character, will dog you until the day you die. Can we as a society think differently? Can we think about the redemption of people with criminal records as some in human services are doing, including STEP Industries and WISDOM?

Reforming society's attitude toward people with a criminal record is not only rewarding for such individuals by helping to rebuild their humanity, and their self-esteem, and by providing opportunities for a decent living, but also changing that attitude is enormously rewarding to the entire society. We all should, as Pope Francis recalled, remember that "being part of that effort, all of us are invited to encourage, help and enable the rehabilitation of persons with a criminal record. Let us all as a society give them a hand in getting back on the right road, a hand to help them rejoin society. Such work, the pontiff noted, "benefits and elevates the morale of the entire community." This approach to redeeming individuals was uppermost in the mind of John H, the anonymous founder of STEP Industries. His idea was, that "employing the drunks could help them establish a good work record, improve their self-esteem and help them learn how to work again so that they would be employable, and after a period of time, move on to other employment or even return to school if they so wished." This idea that individuals who have made errors can be redeemed is a fabulous second-chance opportunity for such individuals.

Many in our society do not yet seem to be where the anonymous founder of STEP Industries was when he developed his idea about redeeming individuals with a criminal record. As Americans probably love locking people up they continue to claim that the only danger prisoners face is from each other. For many in this category prisoners are really bad people. Indeed, they claim that prisoners are people who have no respect for themselves, their neighbors, or for the rules and so not worthy of redemption. For people in this group, prisoners can be difficult to live with, without question, but that cannot be avoided. Prison, they claim, is for bad people. It is to keep bad people away from good people so that the bad people can't hurt the good ones (Kluth, 2012).

Why would this view persist when, according to Barry Kriesberg and Susan Marchionna (2006) in February 2006, a national public opinion poll about American attitudes toward rehabilitation and reentry of prisoners into their home communities showed that striking majorities favor rehabilitation as a major goal of incarceration for prisoners convicted of nonviolent crimes, such as drug or property offenses? And that is not all. By the results of the Zogby poll, the public appeared to recognize that current correctional systems in the United States do not help the problem of crime because prisoners face enormous barriers to successful reintegration to the community. The public also appeared to recognize that rehabilitative services ought to be provided as a means of reducing crime.

Redemption is and should be a core principle of human services. Songwriter John Legend (quoted in Visser, 2015) put it well in the context of the incarcerated when he advocated for life after prison. According to Legend, "we can ask employers to choose the best candidates based on job skills and qualifications, instead of tossing their applications because of past convictions." How can we as a society fail to imagine that the vast majority of convicted individuals have to reenter society one day when it is now estimated that more than one out of three Americans passes through the criminal justice system? My concern is on how many in American society help or hinder the idea and process of redeeming individuals in this society who have committed errors, served their time in prison and are willing to change. Is there anything in US culture that influences the thinking that guilt, suffering, and imprisonment do not combine in transforming the ethical stance of individuals with a criminal record?

Pope Francis's action at a prison in Philadelphia remains a good display of the humanity of the Muslim woman whose feet the pontiff washed, especially at a time in the United States when some were quick to label and castigate Muslims. In a way, Pope Francis was advancing the lesson that we all struggle with the predicament of crime. It was an example the pope used to warn humanity about our desire to judge others rather too quickly without pausing to understand what may have caused the individuals in prison to commit offences. The judgmental attitude of some about others, which remains a hallmark of American society, deserves to be changed. As a society, we must be more concerned about the conditions that lead people and young people especially to commit offences rather than focusing mainly on the offences and the punishments prescribed for such offences. I argue in agreement with Martin Luther King Jr. (1963), against resting content with the superficial kind of social analysis that deals merely with effects and does not grapple with underlying causes. For King, we only need a heart full of grace . . . a soul generated by love. Like Pope Francis, Martin L. King Jr. urged us "never to be afraid to do what's right, especially if the well-being of a person is at stake." Many in American society are yet to be convinced that prisoners must at some point be brought back into society. Some continue to view prisoners as outcasts, with no hope of atoning and changing and playing a productive role in society. We seem to ignore that this situation accounts for the fact that we continue to experience the world's highest recidivism rate of 70 percent in California, for example. We also seem to ignore the fact that the inability of an individual to work in an American society which prides itself on work can result in loss of self or identity void of mental health problems (Norris, 2016).

If we ignore these facts and situations, it is important also to consider the American culture in terms of regret and its cure. In articulating the essence of the American attitude toward regret, Lilian Hellman (1993) observed that "[I]t is considered unhealthy in America to remember mistakes, neurotic to think about them, psychotic to dwell upon them." From regret-averse maxims in American culture such as "That was then, this is now," "Oh, that is history"; "Don't dwell on the past"; "Never cry over spilled milk," we are reminded that regret presents a direct affront to the optimism and future orientation of American culture. As Landman (1993) put it, at some time in any adult life, the fact remains then will bleed into now, we will find ourselves thinking about—maybe even dwelling on—mistakes, and tears will fall with the spilled milk. Many Americans may be regret-averse because they may think of themselves as rugged individualists who do not need others to take care of themselves, but they need to recognize that as a diverse society, all members of the society cannot be the same and cannot have the same abilities.

According to the Associated Press, President Barack Obama asked Congress in a policy speech in Newark, New Jersey, on November 3, 2015, to "ban the box—shorthand for prohibiting the government and its contractors from asking job applicants about criminal histories on applications." As D'Almeida (2015) put it, "[T]he president called on Congress to take a lead from those states, cities, and private companies that have already chosen to ban the box, by considering bipartisan legislation that would outlaw the practice for federal hiring, including hiring by federal contractors.

By the time President Obama requested this policy reform, nineteen states from every region of the United States had already implemented these "fair chance" laws, according to a database compiled by the National Employment Law Project (NELP) and more than one hundred cities already had similar laws on the books. New York City's Fair Chance Act, for example, passed by its City Council in June 2015 kicked in on October 27, 2015, effectively opening new doors for the estimated 2.5 million residents there with criminal records. The question remained, however, whether the New York example would be replicated in other cities across the nation.

As I embarked on writing this chapter, the question also remained whether Congress would take up the reform requested by the president and succeed in providing "second chances" to individuals with criminal records as a force for good. From this standpoint, and considering the guilt, and suffering of imprisonment, we must agree with McAdams and Bowman (2001, p. 6) about the need for redemption after much pain.

The main focus in this chapter is about what we need to do as a society to transform the regret, guilt, remorse and despair of individuals who, after making errors and paying for the errors, would like to be given a second chance. The second concern is about why many in our society remain reluctant to provide such individuals the second chance that many may seek and deserve. The third and last concern in the chapter relates to why the field of human services is yet to own the concept of second chances as a foundational principle of the field.

REFERENCES

Alexander, M. (2012). *The new Jim Crow: Mass incarceration in the age of colorblindness*. New York: The New Press.
Collins, R. (2014, May 13). The importance of second chances. *Huffington Post*. May 13.
D'Almeida, K. (2015, November). Obama calls on Congress to "ban the box" on criminal records. *RH Reality Check*.

Gutierrez, L. (2001). Empowerment theory. In Zastrow, C. & Kirst-Ashman, K. K. (2013), *Understanding human behavior and the social environment* (p. 210). Belmont, CA: Brooks/ Cole, Cengage Learning.

Hellman, L. (1993). Quoted in Landman, J. (1993), *Regret: the persistence of the possible.* New York, NY: Oxford University Press.

Homan, M., Shephard, B., & Totten, V. (2012). Keynote at the 2012 National Organization for Human Services Conference, Milwaukee, WI.

Kluth, A. (2012). American attitudes toward prisons. Retrieved from https://andreaskluth.org/ 2009/08/13/american-attitudes-toward-prisons/

King, M. L. (1963). Letter from a Birmingham jail. Retreived from https://www.mtholyoke. edu/acad/intrel/mlkbirm.htm

Landman, J. (1993). *Regret: The persistence of the possible.* New York, NY: Oxford University Press.

Landman, J. (2001). The crime, punishment, and ethical transformation of two radicals: Or how Katherine Power improves on Dostoevsky. In Dan, P., McAdams, Ruthellen Josselson, and Amia Lieblich (Eds.), *Turns in the road: Narrative studies of lives in transition.* Washington, DC: American Psychological Association.

Linde, C. (1993). *Life stories: The creation of coherence.* New York, NY: Oxford University Press.

McAdams, D. P. (1997). *The stories we live by: Personal myths and the making of the self.* New York, NY: Guilford Press.

McAdams, D. P., & Bowman, P. J. (2001). Narrating life's turning points: redemption and contamination. In Dan P. McAdams, Ruthellen Josselson, and Amia Lieblich (Eds.), *Turns in the road: Narrative studies of lives in transition.* Washington, DC: American Psychological Association.

Norris, D. R. (2016). *Job loss, identity, and mental health.* New Brunswick, NJ: Rutgers University Press.

Obama, B. (2015). Breaking the cycle of incarceration. Rutgers Law School, Newark, New Jersey.

Ross, S., & Gray, J. (2005, December). Transitions and re-engagement through second chance education. *The Australian Educational Researcher, 32*(3): 103–140.

Rumberger, R. (2001). Why students drop out of school and what can be done. Paper prepared for the conference Dropouts in America: How Severe is the Problem? Harvard University, January 13, 2001.

Rice, M. (2016, April). Keynote presentation, 3rd Annual Human Services Leadership Community Collaborative Panel, University of Wisconsin Oshkosh.

Skolnick, J. H., & Currie, E. (2011). *Crisis in American institutions.* Boston, MA: Allyn & Bacon.

Shavit, Y., H. Ayalon, & M. Kurleander. (2001). "Second-chance Education and Inequalities in Israel." Retrieved September 23, 2004, from http://www.mzes.uni-annheim.de/rc28/papers/ shavit_etal_f.doc.

Steinberg, L., S. M. Dornbusch, & B. B. Brown. (1992). Ethnic differences in adolescent Achievement, *American Psychologist, 47*, 723–729.

Visser, N. (2015, December 28). A just society is not one built on fear or repression or vengeance or exclusion but one built on love: Quotes by John Legend in 2015. *Huffington Post.*

Walshe, S. (2013). Ex-convicts should not be stigmatized into unemployment. *Al Jazeera America.* Retrieved from http://america.aljazeera.com/opinions/2013/11/employment-ex-convictsbanboxjobscriminalrecord.html.

Yogev, A. (1997). Second chance education and alternative routes. In L. Saha (Ed.), *International Encyclopedia of the Sociology of Education.* New York, NY: Pergamon.

Zastrow, C., & Kirst-Ashman, K. K. (2013). *Understanding human behavior and the social environment.* Belmont, CA: Brooks/Cole, Cengage Learning.

Chapter Two

Changing the Trajectory of Life

Diane McMillen and Melinda Kline

It is way too easy to get caught in the downward cycle of thinking. A thought "I'm not good enough" leads to a feeling "I'm *worried* about this interview," which leads to a behavior "afraid to try," which results in "doing poorly" in the interview. Which leads to another thought, "I'll never get a job" which leads to feeling "discouraged," which leads to a behavior "giving up" and results in more "failure" . . . and the cycle continues. The really big problem that occurs with this line of thinking is the illusion that there is *any* truth in that initial thought "I'm not good enough," which is really nothing more than a passing thought we innocently think and then accept as truth.

INTRODUCTION

This chapter describes an understanding, and approach to human services practice, premised on exciting new insights about everyone's innate health, potential for well-being, and access to wisdom. This understanding changes the very foundation upon which helpers stand and allows practitioners to remain connected to their own well-being as they reach for the health and wisdom that resides in those they hope to help. This Inside-Out model of prevention and intervention, also referred to as a "3 Principles Approach" has energized our profession. This approach recognizes mental health as human's "default setting," it's our natural state and we are always, automatically, trying to get to that state of health. When people gain this understanding, they find a new perspective, and it profoundly changes the direction of their life.

For too long now the helping professions have been influenced by the medical model which is rife with expectations of disease and deficits and focuses on the pathologies and the problems that people face. The consequence of this orientation is that the people who are being served by helping professionals buy in to these notions and think they are that diagnosis or the sum total of the problems they face. This situation can have a devastating impact on the mental and emotional state of people, their belief in themselves, and their willingness to try to change. In addition, when we, the helping professionals, view those in need of services based mainly on their problems, deficits, or diagnosis, it gravely shapes our approach to helping.

Although still not the dominant paradigm, there are a growing number of practitioners who operate from a resiliency focused, strengths-based, empowerment perspective which can completely change the nature of the helping relationship and dramatically impact the outcomes for the consumers of services. It is a movement away from a helping philosophy that views those in need as sick or broken and in need of curing or fixing. Rather, the approach focuses on perceiving those we serve as innately healthy and capable, people who have merely lost their way. In the same way that we can support our natural immune system with good nutrition and rest to help our body fight disease, we help people strengthen their psychological immune system by understanding better how their mind works. It is an approach that truly gives people a second chance!

THE PHILOSOPHICAL FOUNDATION

The essence of the Inside-Out approach is premised on the belief that everyone is born with an innate capacity toward health. Every individual is naturally resilient, and designed to "bounce back" from even the most challenging situations and circumstances. Although Sydney Banks had a spontaneous insight that gave rise to his understanding and resulted in his articulation of the Three Principles (which will be fully described later in this chapter) there is a firm foundation in several streams of academic thought and research that also support this perspective. In Social Work, for instance, there are a growing number of practitioners and researchers who advocate for a Strengths Perspective. Dennis Saleebey (2009) and many others (Anderson, Cowger, & Snively, 2009; Blundo, 2009; Clark, 2009; Fast & Chapin, 2000; Kisthardt, 2009; Rapp & Goscha, 2006; Weick, Rapp, Sullivan, & Kisthardt, 1989; etc.) have written extensively about the strengths perspective, which is a clear alternative to the deficit and problem oriented approach that typifies traditional social work practice.

These social workers engage in a collaborative process with the people they serve and everything they do is premised on "seeing" and amplifying the client's strengths, working with each of them to overcome their insecurities and inhibitions, and helping them accomplish their goals and manifest their dreams. According to Saleebey (2009), "It is an approach honoring the innate wisdom of the human spirit, the inherent capacity for transformation of even the most humbled and abused" (p. 1). At its most fundamental level it is an effort to point helping professionals toward seeing and thinking about the health and the capacity of individuals, rather than focusing only on identified problems and struggles. This is a fundamental shift that ignites hope, sees possibilities, and transforms the helping relationship into a dynamic partnership.

In psychology, with the leadership of Martin Seligman and Mihaly Csikszentmihalyi (2000) there have been numerous researchers (Compton & Hoffman, 2013; Keyes, 2007; Peterson, 2009; Siang-Yang, 2006; Snyder & Lopez, 2002; etc.), who promoted the idea of Positive Psychology. This approach has stepped away from the idea of simply treating mental illness and instead has its focus on enhancing mental health. The therapeutic aim is to increase positive feeling and behavior rather than focus on the negative thoughts and difficult aspects of life. Seligman and Csikszentmihalyi (2000) summed up this approach with their statement, "We believe that a psychology of positive human functioning will arise, which achieves a scientific understanding and effective interventions to build thriving individuals, families, and communities" (p. 13). Professional helpers in various fields have taken to heart Seligman and Csikszentmihalyi's (2000) message that "psychology is not just the study of pathology, weakness, and damage; it is also the study of strength and virtue" (p. 7). This message supports our clarion call to action in terms of changing our approach to human services.

And moving even closer to the heart of our approach is the work of Bonnie Benard (2004), Emmy Werner (1999) and many others (Benson, 2007; Benson, Galbraith & Espeland, 1998; Henderson, 2003; Marshall, 2000; Wolin & Wolin, 1993; etc) whose research on resiliency and protective factors mirrors our perspective. Their research directly challenged the "risk factors" approach that has been the dominant focus of social services. Although Benard, Henderson, Sharp-Light, and Richardson's (1996) redefinition of resiliency as "an innate self-righting and transcending ability within all children, youth, adults, organizations, and communities" (p. 4) seems a monumentally important shift in thinking, this definition still appears to represent a minority view in the field, at least in terms of practice. To hold a strengths perspective or to see humans as innately resilient in no way ignores or denies the injuries that can occur if one grows up in an abusive home environment, or lives in a violent, crime infested neighborhood, or suffers marginalization and/or oppression, or makes a big mistake in his/her life that results in incarceration. These are very real challenges. However, these researchers were fascinated with the folks who grew up with high numbers of risk factors yet ended up overcoming the challenges and living happy, productive lives.

These pioneering practitioners/researchers questioned the value of the predominant risk-based focus and led the chorus of voices and a plethora of research suggesting that we are all born with innate resiliency as part of our genetic makeup (Benard, 1991) and possess a self-righting capacity (Werner & Smith, 1992) as part of our natural tendency. With this foundation, and the knowledge that we do *not* have to build resilience in people, they come with it as standard equipment, helping professionals can reach for that innate health and wisdom people possess. Again, both the consumer and the practitioner are well served by these strength and resiliency based approaches. As practitioners, we are more effective in establishing helping relationships and facilitating change when we see strengths, assets and resiliency and work from a perspective that promotes health and empowerment for all people. And the clients we serve are strengthened and empowered by being treated with the dignity, respect and confidence in their abilities; energy is ignited, hope is restored, and their lives change for the better. This reciprocal, respectful, and empowering helping relationship is the essence of the Inside-Out or 3 Principles approach. In addition, this understanding provides a firm foundation, a healthy center, for helpers to navigate the many systems and multiple obstacles those systems can present and provide true opportunities for second chances and new beginnings for people who have a criminal record.

A NEW UNDERSTANDING

It is the goal of the helping professions to facilitate change in individual lives, as well as in the neighborhoods, communities, and ultimately, at least for some of us, our world. But what do we really know about how this occurs? What is it, really, that sparks individual and community change? Without disregarding the need and the importance of effective social services, available resources, efforts to improve our schools and neighborhoods, and so forth, if people are unwilling or unable to take advantage of these resources, they are of little use in our efforts to facilitate change. How do we help people change the trajectory of their life? This is the question that has haunted many a helping professional as we work side by side with people who sincerely want their situations and circumstances to be improved but are overwhelmed and stuck. It certainly was a question that intrigued Dr. Roger Mills when he was executive director of one of the first community mental health centers in Eugene, Oregon, in the early 1970s. It troubled him that the deinstitutionalization movement seemed to be failing, and that the mental health system did not seem to be actually helping people. Mills, like most helpers, wanted to do something that would make a difference for people.

More than chronically treat illness, he wanted to promote mental health in order to free people from suffering.

He found his answer when he met Sydney Banks (1998) and he proved the point that change was not only possible, but probable, when he implemented this inside-out approach in low-income housing projects in Miami, Florida. Mills entered Modello, a community riddled with violence, drug addiction, gangs, school failure, and more, with hope and optimism. Although anyone could easily have been overwhelmed by the range and intensity of problems this community faced, he absolutely believed in what he had seen, and personally experienced, as a result of his association with Sydney Banks. Mills, although initially skeptical, had several personal deep insights that profoundly changed his life. And, he was confident that when others were exposed to this inside-out approach, they too would experience insights, uncover the innate health that exists in all of us, and it would change their lives. Although initially Dr. Mills encountered a great deal of resistance from the social services providers already in place and attempting to serve the community, their skepticism and occasional outright hostility subsided as big changes in the community began to occur. This chapter is not the place to detail this amazing story, but the remarkable turnaround of this community is chronicled in *Modello: A Story of Hope for the Inner-City and Beyond* (Pransky, 2011). However, it is worth noting research documented that in the three years after Mills introduced this inside-out approach, for the 150 families and 650 youth served by the program, household use or selling drugs dropped from 65 percent to less than 20 percent; the overall endemic crime rate decreased by 70–80 percent; the teen pregnancy rate dropped from 50 percent to 10 percent; school dropout rates dropped from 60 percent to 10 percent; endemic child abuse and neglect decreased by more than 70 percent; households on public assistance went from 65 percent to negligible; and the parent unemployment rate dropped from 85 percent to 35 percent (Pransky, Mills, Sedgeman, & Blevens, 1997).

INNATE HEALTH AND RESILIENCE

Given these jaw-dropping changes in rates of crime and violence, teen age pregnancy, school drop-outs, and so forth, the obvious question is, "what occurred here?" What did Dr. Mills and his staff do that facilitated such remarkable change? First and foremost, they understood the 3 Principles put forward by Syd Banks, and they functioned from the Inside-Out themselves. They believed everyone has within him or herself a natural state of health that can be directly accessed via wisdom and/or "common sense." Mills and his staff had complete confidence that all people have this natural capacity, whether they knew it or not, and their approach was directed toward reveal-

ing and uncovering people's innate health. Despite whatever unsavory behavior they might encounter when working with the residents, they radiated
the health within themselves, and constantly reached for the health they knew
exists in all humans.

The staff all modeled living in health and well-being. They understood
how fear and insecurity can cause angry and defensive behavior, and when
residents acted/reacted in insecure ways, they did not take that personally.
The helpers used natural avenues, such as parenting classes, community
activities, individual counseling, and so forth, as opportunities to teach residents about how their moods affected their thinking and how their thoughts
kept them stuck and covered their natural health and access to wisdom. As
Dr. Mills described in the beginning, "The reason things are the way they are
down there is that people who live there don't think they can do any better.
They've been conditioned because of their upbringing or their experience
with society or whatever they have learned in their lives to think that is the
best they can do" (Pransky, 2011, p. 20). As the residents continued to
experience the genuineness of the helpers and were treated with respect and
dignity, they allowed their self-talk or "thinking" to quiet down and made
room for a deeper wisdom to come into their awareness, a shift occurred on a
deep level, and their lives changed.

And secondly, the foundation of these astonishing changes and what
makes this an inside-out approach, is that they focused on helping people
understand the inner workings of the human mind and how we are all creating reality moment by moment with our creative power of Thought. This idea
of the power of Thought (with a capital T), comes from an understanding that
is now most often called the 3 Principles (formally called Heath Realization
and Psychology of Mind, also referred to as "a principle-based understanding" and "state of mind"). Sydney Banks had a spontaneous and profound
insight related to three underlying principles that explain human psychological functioning. He did not formally name the wisdom he had come to understand, he simply called it Mind, Thought, and Consciousness, and these
constructs form the foundation for this inside-out approach (Banks, 1998). It
is Banks's unwavering belief that these three principles are always working
in harmony to give people their moment by moment mental/emotional experience of life and the behaviors that follow. His use of the word "principle" is
very appropriate because this word means "a law or a fact of nature that
explains how something works or why something happens" (Merriam-Web-
ster). A good example we can all relate to is the principle of gravity. People
do not have to believe in gravity or be able to explain how it works for it to
impact them. It is a force of nature that tethers them to earth whether they
know about it or not. Banks asserted the same is true of the Three Principles;
that all behavior is determined by the interplay of Mind, Thought, and Consciousness. And it is Pransky's (2003) assertion that people's lack of aware-

ness of this truth, and their innocent misuse of the gift of Thought is what gives rise to most of the psychological and social problems we face. As Pransky (2003) stated, "When people are connected to or aligned with what might be called their "spiritual essence" or their "innate health" or wisdom (or any number of other terms people may use) they do not engage in problem behaviors" (pp. 14–15).

THE PRINCIPLES

The words *Mind*, *Thought*, and *Consciousness* are trying to describe something that is formless, thus precise, concrete descriptions are tricky and cannot fully capture the essence of these gifts. And in reality, a solid, specific definition is not nearly as important as what the principles are pointing to in terms of helping us understand our power to create our reality. Pransky (2003) very briefly summarized these principles as "Mind refers to the Universal, formless energy or intelligence behind life, the life force that is the source of all things. Thought, in essence, is the power to create. Consciousness, in essence, is the power to experience" (p. 77). Thus, Mind is the creative energy of the universe and the pure life force of humanity. It is the power source that allows to think, create, and experience life. When we are connected to Mind we are in touch with our wisdom. It is when we are "in" our wisdom that we feel secure, loving, satisfied and happy. When we feel confident, we have good ideas and make decisions that allow us to live in health and well-being.

However, we live in a Thought created world, and too often our thinking takes us away from our health. As was demonstrated in Modello, and other projects that have replicated this model, practitioners know that all people, despite their problematic behavior, have wisdom and are merely acting on their unhealthy thoughts (we will elaborate on this more later in the chapter). The important thing to understand is that every experience we have is a product of our own thoughts. It is why two people can be in the very same situation at the very same time and have two very different experiences of what is happening! How is it that two friends can go together to the same movie, one walks out thinking it's the best movie she ever saw, and the other is aghast and thinking it was the biggest waste of money of her life? Each friend is affected by their individual process of thinking which is made of their personal ideas, beliefs, and interpretations. There is a continuous stream of mental activity resulting in their separate and unique experience of the movie. We are walking talking thinking machines who have an average of seventy thousand thoughts a day that pop into our heads. We are constantly thinking and many times thoughts come in and go out of the mind so quickly we are not even aware of *what* we are thinking. That is why it is so important to know *that* we are thinking, and that it is our thoughts that are creating our experience of reality, not the event in the outside world.

Consciousness is our ability to experience life, and this *awareness* is what makes our thoughts seem real. Thoughts and Consciousness are inextricably intertwined and work together to give us the experience of whatever we are thinking. We feel it through our senses and we are convinced that whatever we are thinking is "real" and it affects us emotionally and behaviorally. All I have to do is think about fresh, hot, chocolate chip cookies coming out of the oven and my mouth begins to water. There are no cookies in my outside world, only the thought of cookies. Yet, that thought, combined with Consciousness, has given me this "real" experience and I am salivating in anticipation of a cookie. Consciousness brings our thoughts to life. It is how we get a feeling from our thoughts, and without it we would be incapable of experiencing anything. As Ami Chen Mills-Naim (2005) described, "Consciousness is like the hot water you add a bag of tea in a cup to make hot tea. Every thought is a different flavor, like tea bags are different flavors. Consciousness is the water you add to the cup which 'wakes up' the flavor of your thoughts" (p. 15).

So if you have a thought of being mistreated by your boss at work, you have a feeling of anger. If you have a thought of how lucky you are to have such a great best friend, you have a feeling of love. Every feeling we have is a product of a thought. Even if a thought went by so quickly, we were not aware we were thinking, the feeling is the indicator that we are thinking! This is a very valuable mechanism to be aware of, because when we have a feeling that is giving us discomfort, anger, fear, frustration, whatever it might be, the feeling is our "indicator" to check our thinking. Much like the warning light on the dashboard of our car indicating that we need to stop for fuel, our feelings are the gauge that lets us know we need to stop and check our thinking.

PRACTICING FROM THIS FOUNDATION

We firmly believe individual and community change is possible when people are pointed in the direction of their innate health and helped to see how our thinking shapes our perspective and creates our subjective reality. Changing individual lives, communities, and the world does not come from the external environment and any attempt to "fix" people. Change happens within. If human services professionals want to spark positive change, focusing on the problems and dissecting all the things that are wrong only keeps us stuck in the problem. Helping professionals desperately need to shift their attention to possibilities and reach for people's capacity and strengths. This is how we inspire and motivate people to dream and help them set pathways to their goals.

Imagine how differently the world might look if we, as human services professionals, viewed people as healthy and whole and capable and reached for that health when people come into our office and our lives? The idea of applying the 3 Principles is based on strengths and empowerment, but it goes even deeper. People are not defined by their problems, deficits, diagnosis, or by the crimes they may have committed. We know that all people already have exactly what they need to have a happy life. If, as practitioners, we reach for that innate health and wisdom, we can "wake up" that wisdom within and people will respond. If we point people towards their innate capacity (towards health as opposed to staying focused on their problems) and teach them about Thought, the results will be amazing. Pranksy (2011) shares a very insightful story about a woman in his study named Maria who articulates her experience by explaining "...seeing my health instead of my disease, that was very, very helpful" (p. 135). And yes, because most people *think* their problems or circumstances are caused by external events and that other people *make* them feel and act the way they do, we need to teach them about Thought. When people "see" that it is actually their own thinking that gives them their experiences, and that they are the creator of their feelings, everything changes. Our work is in helping them see this or uncover this simple truth.

UNPACKING THE UNDERSTANDING

What does this look like in terms of what we actually do with people? When applying the 3 Principles to our work in human services, it is useful to consider the following ideas: innate health, being present, quiet mind, seeing the innocence in others, wisdom, and deep listening. Understanding and ap-plying these concepts that underpin this approach is helpful in terms of our work in the field and pointing others (clients and colleagues) in the direction of understanding the 3 Principles and living in well-being.

Innate Health

The idea of innate health takes the Strengths Perspective to the next level. Innate health implies exactly what it sounds like. We, as human beings, have a birthright to psychological wellness. It is inside each and every one of us and is how we are meant to be. At a very deep level, this is our essence and it could be described as pure love. On a very basic level it can be described like a beach ball floating on top of the water, attempts to sink the ball by several hands pushing down are thwarted when the hands get out of the way, the beach ball bounces effortlessly up to the surface. It is a place of peace, wholeness, wellness and warmth.

Seeing a person's innate health is a way of looking past his or her differences and seeing their wholeness and similarities. Reaching for the health and wholeness within someone and knowing with confidence that it resides there within each person no matter what is going on externally totally changes the helping dynamic because our focus is on strengths and possibilities, not problems. Again, it is by design that each human has this resiliency and no person is an exception. It may be helpful to consider our physical design and how healing occurs. If we scratch or cut ourselves, our body heals. It takes longer if we pick at it or continually reopen the wound, but our body has the ability to heal and be whole again. It is the same with our mental/psychological health. We have the ability to heal and return to our natural state of health.

When our Human Service practice in grounded in the 3 Principles, we become experts at identifying and "fanning the flame" of this human resiliency. It is our job to point our clients in this direction. Pointing them inward towards their own strengths and innate health places the honor and responsibility of their success and happiness in their own hands. It is very freeing for the helper and hopeful for the client. The simple act of seeing their innate health (from a place of innate health within the helper) illuminates their resiliency and provides an opportunity for growth and forward momentum. Clients experience more independence and empowerment and feel honored in the helping relationship.

Being Present

Being present with another human being, being *truly* present, is a gift to both the client and the helper. This phrase describes a state of holding sacred space and allowing the moment to unfold. The helper has the opportunity to create this safe space and offer the client his/her full attention and awareness.

As human beings we are often caught up in reviewing the past or projecting into the future. If you think of this in terms of everyday life, you can easily find examples. Let's say you are in the shower and going about the business of having your shower and getting yourself ready for the day ahead. While washing your hair, you may mentally be reviewing your "to-do" list. You imagine yourself dropping off the children to day care and driving to work and reminding yourself of the meetings you are charged with leading. Next, you may land upon thinking of the last staff meeting and how that went and the unsavory interaction you had with your boss. You have gone over this same conversation no fewer than ten times and each time wishing you had said this or that instead of what you did say. Recalling this conversation you find yourself feeling upset once again and redirect your thinking back to planning what you will say when you encounter your boss today. You become so caught up in this mental trip between future and past that you get out of the shower and realize you've forgotten to rinse the conditioner from your hair. You have completely missed out on being present in the current moment.

Many may refer to mindfulness or meditation in terms of being present. These are practices that may be helpful in reminding us to be present. It is helpful to use one's five senses to stay in the present and just "be." What does this moment look like, sound like, taste like? How does it feel? What does it smell like? Our senses can ground us in the current moment but they can also take us to another place and time. It is recommended that when we notice we have drifted away from the current moment that we simply allow that noticing to enter our awareness and then gently come back to the current moment in time. After all, this is a common occurrence for all humans and there is no reason to scold ourselves or be harsh, we simply notice it and in the noticing we can return to being present effortlessly.

These ideas are all related and interrelated. The more time we can spend being present the more centered we are in our innate health. We notice it. It comes into our awareness. When we allow ourselves to be present with a client, we also notice their innate health and resiliency and the easier it is to assist them in uncovering their health and well-being. Being present in also conducive to having what may be referred to as quiet mind.

Quiet Mind

Human beings experience an estimated sixty to seventy thousand thoughts per day according to the Laboratory of Neuro Imaging (LONI). These are not always unique thoughts as we tend towards having habitual thought and often think the same ones over and over. Some thoughts we pay no attention to and others we hold on firmly to and these thoughts become our beliefs. Our most healthy and creative thoughts seem to surface when we are experiencing a time of calm or quiet mind.

Brain scientists tell us that the brain is best able to access its executive functioning (highest level and most creative level of thinking) when we are relaxed and tranquil. This is also true in terms of interacting with (helping) others and our professional performance in relation to clients. If we continually try to "work" our intellect to find an answer, we may overlook wisdom and the path to true freedom for ourselves and the clients we are serving.

It may be helpful to consider the metaphor of our desire for a quiet mind being like an ocean. Our thoughts and emotions may resemble the churning of the ocean's surface. The chaos and stress of life may leave us feeling tossed about and at times even "shipwrecked" if you will. We may be caught up in waves of anxiety, fear, anger, or fatigue. However, deep below the surface lays a depth of peace and tranquility untouched by the storms raging on the surface. Our journey towards a quiet mind is directed inward rather than seeking any external solution.

It is from this center of peace and tranquility that each of us has access to what we call wisdom. According to Sydney Banks (1988), "Wisdom is divine nourishment for the soul; it is a God-given intelligence before the contamination of form or personal thought" (p. 105). It is from this quiet place that the path to wisdom becomes illuminated. The helper is best able to assist the clients by being in this state of health and wisdom themselves and modeling it for the client by simply being present with them. The beauty is in the unfolding of truth and that every answer a person seeks lies within them in the essence of who they truly are. It becomes evident that the helper does not need to provide an answer for the client or direct them towards anything outward, that the answer to each question lies within them and realizing this can help them become more equipped to live a full and healthy life regardless of circumstance.

Wisdom

Wisdom is available to each and every one of us at any moment in time. Wisdom surpasses intellect and may be described as *knowing* on a different, deeper level, instinct, common sense, or intuition. We sometimes describe wisdom as being a still, quiet voice much like a Native American flute while our habitual thinking is more like a marching band! We must first quiet the marching band in order to hear the sweet voice of wisdom.

"Everyone in this world shares the same innate source of wisdom, but it is hidden by the tangle of our own misguided personal thoughts" (Banks, 1998, p. 17). In a large group of people, ask the group to take a deep breath, relax and get quiet and then, point to themselves. Participants will do as told and they will inevitably point to themselves with an index finger pointing to their chest or their heart. Human beings instinctively know that the essence of who we are resides within our body at a heart level and not at a brain level. No one ever points to their head, they point towards their heart. And yet we often live our lives as if we reside full time in our heads (in our thinking). Our wisdom, too, resides at a deeper level within.

Seeing the Innocence

When we talk about "seeing the innocence" in people, we are talking about seeing past their behavior to their inner health and wisdom. We understand the motivation behind every behavior lies in thought. When a person has a thought and believes that thought (which is how we all operate) they may behave in a way that we do not prefer. Yet, if we understand the 3 Principles we know that we can't take their behavior personally. They are doing their very best at the level of thinking they are aware of at the time. They are psychologically innocent.

Some may speak of this concept as forgiveness because it feels like forgiveness. It feels freeing to release resentment and judgment. Seeing the innocence in others feels similar. Seeing the innocence in both you and in others is a way to cultivate compassion and patience as well as peace and unity with others and self. We may want to refer to it as having grace.

Each of these words or concepts assists in pointing us toward the 3 Principles: Mind, Consciousness, and Thought. When we experience these concepts and allow this understanding to impact our lives it can be transformative, both personally and in the lives of the clients we serve. A critical medium of this transformational experience within a relationship is known as deep listening. Deep listening refers to a very special kind of listening that involves quieting judgment and ego and allows for true communication and transcending above words and roles.

THE ART OF DEEP LISTENING

In the field of human services and social work, communication is acclaimed as the key element in the helping and/or clinical process. Interpersonal communication is offered at the university level and much practice is dedicated to perfecting ones active listening skills. However, the 3 Principles offer a paradigm for listening that is unique and profoundly different from active listening. Deep listening is a way of being truly present with another human being. It is non-violent and non-judgmental. The helper holds space for their client and allows the client to communicate their struggles openly. The helper becomes deeply fascinated in what the other individual has to communicate. This listening could be described as "listening with the heart" rather than the ears or the intellect.

Deep listening presents a unique perspective for using communication as a vehicle to create space and a path for an individual's wisdom (their intuition or ability to solve every problem) to arrive. When a person is allowed to articulate their story, their struggle, to a person who is deeply listening, the answer to the situation they are dealing with seems to naturally emerge from within. The art of deep listening is designed to absorb the helper in an experience of taking in all that is being said and felt. This may include the spoken words but leans more towards simply "being with" as opposed to "doing for" or "fixing," This method of listening is beneficial not only for clients who need a "second chance" but for anyone with whom we are in relationship and hoping to improve communication and depth of that relationship.

To further understand this concept of deep listening it is helpful to consider an example of communication that does not include deep listening. The next time you find yourself in a restaurant or public gathering, take notice of the individuals around you and notice if they are listening to each other or if they are simply waiting for their chance to speak. Become aware that some are not very good at waiting for their turn and will likely talk over others or use other tactics to make their voices heard. You may also notice that some friends seek commonality when listening to you and will listen just long enough to relate to the story and then respond with their similar story (or often relay details that are somehow worse than your situation—as if it is a competition for suffering).

The exception you may notice at a restaurant or other public place is if you have opportunity to observe a couple who are in love or falling in love. They appear to be fascinated with each other and take turns truly listening, deep listening, to one another. They are interested, curious, as to what the world looks like through each other's lenses. They want to know, *really* know, how their new love views the world.

Without practicing deep listening skills, many individuals are unable to separate their own interests and needs from the interests and needs of others. They tend to listen with bias and judgment and often find themselves wondering about and trying to formulate their reply without fully hearing the message being delivered. They are likely to interrupt the conversation or misunderstand the intent of the speaker. They have yet to develop the ability to hear "past" the words or listen for the feelings coming out between the lines. They are often prepared to either argue or debate the idea or try to repeat the information back to seek clarity or put the idea into their own words, often altering the true intended meaning.

By contrast, deep listening, means that the listener is quiet, on the inside and out. They are open-minded, nonjudgmental and genuinely interested in absorbing all that is being said, unsaid, intended, and felt by the speaker. Deep listening creates an environment, a synergy, between two people that encourages honesty and wisdom. Deep listening generates empathy, trust, support and wisdom. It has been called an ancient healing art. It is rooted in both mindfulness and storytelling. The practice of deep listening has the ability to unlock innate wisdom, weaken fear and awaken strength within each individual. Through the deep listening experience we may become overwhelmed with a sense of connectedness—connectedness to each other, to our own spirit within and to the energy flowing through us, around us, between us and the energy *that is us*.

As helpers, we are quick to present solutions and what we believe are great ideas for growth and development for the clients we are working with. When helpers create a peaceful, nonjudgmental space for clients to share their thoughts, the opportunity exists for their wisdom to surface. As deep listening continues, the opportunity for wisdom to emerge is great. The help-er is free to coach from the sidelines rather than attempting to solve the problems or "fix" the situation. Perhaps a question will "bubble up" and beg to be asked. This question will direct the client to delve deeper inside to find the answer. These questions are known as "vertical" questions to describe the direction the excavation of the dig for the answer is taking. The client under-stands that the answer is not external but buried inside them.

A MONKEY TRAP

There is a story (folklore) that involves the humane monkey traps of Indone-sia. The story of the monkey trap lends itself well to examining the traps we set for ourselves as humans and is especially thought provoking in terms of judging and self-judging that happens with and to persons who have experi-enced legal prosecution.

The story tells that in these rural communities of Indonesia, the hunters wanted to design a humane trap for the monkey(s) who were damaging their crop and threatening their family's food supply. They simply bore out a coconut by drilling a small hole in the side. They filled the coconut with monkey treats, banana, seeds, nuts, etc. The hole, of course, was just the right size. It was big enough for the monkey to reach his hand in, but small enough to keep him trapped once he grabbed the goodies waiting inside. The coconut was then tethered to a tree or a stake and secured.

Once the monkey grabs a handful of his desired eats and tries to run off with the goodies, he finds himself trapped. He may begin to panic and thrash about but refuses to let go. It is obvious to the onlooker, that at any point, the monkey could free himself by releasing his fist. He could drop the goodies, slip his hand free, and run home to safety. One might say that he is trapped by his own fear and greed or what we may refer to as his thinking. This is not unlike humankind and the stubborn commitment that we each participate in our own "traps" in our thinking and perception. At any time we have the power to free ourselves, but because we refuse to release whatever thought or benefit we get from the current situation, we remain trapped. We may not *see* the "trap" when we are caught up in it. We may point fingers or blame others.

While watching a monkey struggle in this described trap, it would appear obvious to onlookers who might begin to chant, "Let go! Let go!" The monkey just can't see it. The same is true for us at times, we just can't see it. We don't see that it is the thought or belief we are clinging to so desperately that is actually the trap. It is our own thinking that is to blame for causing our suffering or misery. The letting go, for the monkey, and for us, requires some kind of a shift in perception, seeing the situation through a different lens or from a different angle.

In terms of second chances, it may be helpful to identify the trap known as thinking and invite our clients to shift their perception of self. Keep in mind that not one of us is perfect or without mistakes. Imagine for a moment the worst thing you've ever done in your whole life and now imagine that everyone knows about it, family, friends, coworkers, everyone. Perhaps it was published in the newspaper, on television, and/or put on social media. While you have that image fresh in your mind, ask yourself if this is the only event that defines who you are. Should you be judged for your entire life based on this mistake?

Luckily, the knowledge of our worst mistakes is fairly limited to ourselves and maybe our closest friends and loved ones. Hopefully, they choose to love and accept us in spite of our shortcomings and mistakes. Hopefully, we have also learned to have grace with ourselves and don't allow our worst mistake to define our entire life or worthiness. Graduates of our so-called justice system may not be so lucky. They have often suffered public humiliation and various violations of privacy. They have new labels that invite judgment and ridicule from family, friends, and the community. They have been labeled based on the mistakes they have made rather than their strengths or positive qualities that also play a part in the definition of who they are.

Again, the real trap is when these individuals begin to judge themselves harshly and define themselves by their mistakes and shortcomings. As helpers, we have been taught to look at the person beyond the problem and look for strengths and at the value of the human being who lies beneath the bad behaviors. We are not immune however to the concentration on mistakes and focus on problems, and can become jaded. This is a reminder to consider thinking about your worst mistake and the scenario presented here. Is it fair to define this person by any one thing that they have done? Consider their strengths and their potential. Deep listen to them and create an environment that opens traps and provides hope for a brighter future. In terms of second chances, it may be helpful to identify the trap known as *thinking* and invite our clients to shift their perception of self.

A COURSE CORRECTION

We have provided the conceptual framework and articulated the foundation for this Inside-Out approach to human services known as the 3 Principles. Now we will conclude this chapter with some final thoughts about working with people who are facing the very real challenges and obstacles that occur upon exiting prison with a felony record. There is nothing more important for this chapter to convey than the idea that people must, and more importantly can transcend that label and not let the word "x-con" describe how they think of themselves. Much like the Scarlet Letter, if people internalize that label, it can affect their entire life, potentially leading to an unrealized life of dissatisfaction and disappointment. If we as helpers operate from the firm foundation the 3 Principles give us, we can point people inward, to their innate health. We can help them see how their thinking is creating their moment by moment experience of reality, and seeing this can change the trajectory of their life. If they see this, their being emanates, "I may have committed a felony, but that is not who I am" and living that thought can change everything for them.

Nothing stated in this chapter disregards the VERY real struggles people do face upon exiting prison and attempting to re-enter society, those challenges exist. We live in a society that does not offer a clear and unobstructed path to a meaningful and productive life for people with a prison record. There are a multitude of obstacles that must be faced, overcome, and removed. We do not deny the reality of the difficulties that people face. Our society seems to have forgotten the original intention of the penitentiary. The word comes from the Latin *paenitentia* and means "repentance." A penitentiary is a place we send people with the idea that they are punished, are repentant, and are released and given another chance. It is however, sadly clear that 'punishment' in the form of negative public attitudes, limited job opportunities, unsafe living conditions, etc. continues beyond incarceration. It is easy to see how "x-cons" can feel like they are still in prison. Thus, it is imperative that helping professionals help people "see" they can be free from that label. They will remain "in prison" if they adopt that mental identity of "x-felon" or "x-convict" to describe who they are, and it will be the prison of their own mind.

Inevitably they will have moments of being reminded of their past, we all have those moments. Understanding the true nature of Thought does not spare any of us the intrusion of unwanted thoughts, they happen. But the power of this inside-out understanding is in knowing that we have a choice about which thoughts we entertain. This understanding also does not overcome the human condition that we have "bad moods" and low states of mind. This part of life still exists, but when we see if for what it is, and we know we cannot trust low mood thinking, we have confidence that a higher state of mind and a much better feeling will come. If people understand 3 Principles they can live in the freedom of their "thought world" and the greater community will see that radiant being, that confident "can do" person they were always meant to be. This creates opportunities, when we think it, we create it. We can help people move from chaos to clarity, and in clarity we can more easily see the steps we can take to improve our life. Living Inside-out, being in innate health is *the* hope for people with a felony record; otherwise they will continue to live in the prison of their mental activity and self- identity.

So, do you have the cloud of "felon" over your head, or do you radiate health and well-being? The answer to this question has implications far beyond the individual. One of the beauties of this Inside-out understanding is how it ripples out. We see evidence of this understanding ripples out in multiple public housing programs (Pransky, Mills, Sedgeman, & Belvins, 1997), schools (Marshall, 2005), juvenile correction facilities (Singh, 2003), substance abuse treatment facilities (Banerjee, Howard, Mansheim & Beattie) and correctional settings and prisons (Kelley, 1990, 1993) to name only a few. It is our contention that when people who carry the ascribed label of "felon" but live in their health and emanate resilience, optimism, and well-being, it is palpable. People (employers, property managers, neighbors, etc.) can see and feel that solid citizen in front of them. It is a healthy state for the individual to live in, but it also influences the community.

When the health of the individual is evident, not only does the employer want to help the individual, but that employer is faced with examining the frame of reference they hold about "x-cons." People often begin to question their preconceived notions about "the others" when they are confronted with individuals who do not fit their stereotype. Changing minds is tricky business. There is no doubt that facilitating a change of heart and mind of someone who fears the idea of giving a person with a felony record a job (or supporting them moving into the neighborhood) can be challenging. However, the fear is rising because they do not know the person. If they encounter a human being in his or her health and radiating the resilience and well-being that is the natural state, health connects with health and thinking calms down. This is how this understanding ripples out, and social change happens. We firmly believe that this holds true when addressing the challenges for people who are exiting prison, and we see hope for this population and health for the greater community as the STEP Industries' example demonstrates. Our firm conviction that such change is possible is aptly summed up by the sixth-century Chinese philosopher, Lao-tse.

> *If there is radiance in the soul, it will abound in the family.*
> *If there is radiance in the family, it will be abundant in the community.*
> *If there is radiance in the community, it will grow in the nation.*
> *If there is radiance in the nation, the universe will flourish.*

REFERENCES

Anderson, K., Cowger, C., & Snively, C. (2009). Assessing strengths: Identifying acts of resistance to violence and oppression. In Saleebey (Ed.). *The strengths perspective in social work practice,* (5th Eed.) (181–200). Boston, MA: Pearson Education, pp. 181–200.

Banks, S. (1998). *The missing link.* Renton, WA: Lone Pine Publishing.

Benson, P. (2007). Connecting resiliency, youth development, and asset development in a positive-focused framework for youth. In N. Henderson, B. Benard, & N. Sharp-Light (Eds.), *Resiliency in action: Practical ideas for overcoming risks and building strengths in youth, families, & communities.* Ojai, CA: Resiliency in Action, Inc.

Benson, P., Galbraith, J. & Espeland, P. (1998). *What kids need to succeed: Proven, practical ways to raise good kids.* Minneapolis, MN: Free Spirit Publishing, Inc.

Blundo, R. (2009). The challenge of seeing anew the world we think we know: Learning strengths-based practice. In Saleebey (Ed.). *The strengths perspective in social work practice,* (5th Eed.) (24–44). Boston, MA: Pearson Education, pp. 24–44.

Clark, M. (2009). The strengths perspective in criminal justice. In Saleebey (Ed.). *The strengths perspective in social work practice,* (5th Eed.) (122–175). Boston, MA: Pearson Education, pp. 122–175.

Compton, W. C., & Hoffman, E. (2013). *Positive Psychology: The Science of Happiness and Flourishing.* (2nd ed.). Belmont, CA: Wadsworth Cengage Learning.

Fast, B., & Chapin, R. (2000). *Strengths case management in long term care.* Baltimore, MD Health Professions Press.

Henderson, N. (2003). Hard-wired to bounce back. In N. Henderson (Ed.), *Resiliency in action: Practical ideas for overcoming risks and building strengths in youth, families, and communities* (2nd Eed.). Ojai, CA: Resiliency in Action, Inc.

Henderson, N., Benard, B., & Sharp-Light, N. (1999). *Resiliency in action: Practical ideas for overcoming risks and building strengths in youth, families, & communities.* Ojai, CA: Resiliency in Action, Inc.

Keyes, C. L. (2007). Promoting and protecting mental health as flourishing: A complementary strategy for improving national mental health. *American Psychologist, 62,* 95–108.

Kisthardt, W. E. (2009). The opportunities of strengths-based, person-centered practice: Purposes, principles, and application in a climate of systems integration. In Saleebey (Ed.). *The strengths perspective in social work practice,* (5th Eed.) (47–70). Boston, MA: Pearson Education, pp. 47–70.

Marshall, K. (2005). Resilience in our schools: Discovering mental health and hope from the inside-out. In D. L. White, M. K. Faber, & B. C. Glenn, (Eds.). *Proceedings of the Persistently Safe Schools 2005* (128–140). Washington, DC: Hamilton Fish Institute, George Washington University.

Marshall, K. (2000). Experiences implementing resilience/health realization in schools. Minneapolis, MN: University of Minnesota, National Resilience Resource Center.

Mills-Naim, A. C. (2005). *The spark inside.* Auburn, WA: Lone Pine Publishing.

Pransky, G. S., Mills, R. C., Sedgeman, J. A., & Blevens, J. K. (1997). An emerging paradigm for brief treatment and prevention. In L. Vandercreek, S. Knapp, & T. J. Jackson, (Eds.). *Innovations in Clinical Practice: A Source Book* (Vol. 15) (76–98). Sarasota, FL: Professional Resource Press.

Pransky, J. (2003). *Prevention from the Inside-Out.* Bloomington, IN: Author House.

Pransky, J. (2011). *Somebody should have told us: Simple truths for living well* (3rd ed.). British Columbia, Canada: CCB Publishing.

Pransky, J. (2011). *Modello: A story of hope for the inner city and beyond.* Terrace, BC: CCB Publishing.

Pransky, J. (2003). *Prevention from the Inside-Out.* Bloomington, IN: Author House.

Peterson, C. (2009). Positive psychology. *Reclaiming Children and Youth* 18(2): 3–7.

Rapp, C. A., & Goscha, R. J. (2006). *The strengths model: Case management with people with psychiatric illness.* New York: Oxford University Press.

Seligman, M., & Csikszentmihalyi, M. (2000). "Positive Psychology: An Introduction" *American Psychologist* 55(1): 5–14.

Siang-Yang, T. (2006). Applied Positive Psychology: Putting Positive Psychology into Practice. *Journal of Psychology & Christianity*, 25(1), 68–73.

Signh, N. (2003). Summative evaluation report ATOD program. Minneapolis, MN: University of Minnesota Center for Applied Research and Educational Improvement.

Snyder, C. R., & Lopez, S. (2002). *Handbook of positive psychology.* New York: Oxford University Press.

Weick, A., Rapp, C., Sullivan, W. P., & Kisthardt, W. (1989, July). A strengths perspective for social work practice. *Social Work,* 350–354.

Werner, E. (1999). How children become resilient: Observations and cautions. In N. Henderson, B. Benard, & N. Sharp-Light (Eds.), *Resiliency in action: Practical ideas for overcoming risks and building strengths in youth, families, & communities.* Ojai, CA: Resiliency in Action, Inc.

Werner, E., & Smith, R. (1992). *Overcoming the odds: High-risk children from birth to adult-hood.* Ithaca, NY: Cornell University Press.
Wolin, S., & Wolin, S. (1993). *The resilient self: How survivors of troubled families rise above adversity.* New York: Villard Books.

Chapter Three

The Blooming Lotus

*Wounded Healers and
Their Aspirations to Give Back* [1]

John Paulson, Kevin Groves,
and Leslie A. Hagedorn

Many people who have experienced issues in their lives, and who often have received services from various behavioral health and social service programs and providers to help address and resolve those issues, often decide later to become helping professionals themselves. Informed by their struggles with their own past challenges such individuals use the energy of their past suffering as a motivation to serve and benefit others (LeBel, Richie, & Maruna, 2015; Zerubavel & Wright, 2012).

Two metaphors from the wisdom of Asian traditions seem very fitting when describing such individuals. The first is the archetype of the Bodhisattva. Bodhisattvas are characters who represent the perfection and personification of certain attributes, such as compassion and wisdom. The Bodhisattva of compassion, for example, is an entity which represents a commitment to not only connect with the suffering of all beings, but also to alleviate it. Stories of these beings include accounts of them bravely traveling into "hell realms" of great suffering to rescue beings still stuck there from continued torment. A defining characteristic of Bodhisattvas is also their commitment to postpone their own spiritual awakening and liberation until all other beings are liberated as well (Tirch, Silberstein, & Kolts, 2015).

Images of these Bodhisattvas often depict them seated on a lotus throne. The lotus blossom is another metaphor used to represent life. In order for the beautiful lotus to bloom, it must first struggle through the dirt at the bottom of the pond and rise through the muddy waters to reach the surface. This struggle to the surface is seen as necessary for the development of the lotus because ultimately it can only finally bloom into all its beauty and majesty once it has first drawn nourishment from the mud that once covered it and held it down (Frederic, 1995).

Each individual that has pushed through the mud of his or her own past struggles has been nurtured and shaped by those experiences, and those experiences have allowed him or her to blossom into the beings she or he are today. Those who have finally bloomed through the muds of addiction, domestic violence and other murky terrains and who now also commit to travelling back into those hell realms to alleviate the suffering of those still stuck compassionately illustrate the Bodhisattva-nature that exists in all humans. Their persistence and success in the presence of and despite such adversity is both inspiring and motivating, and such attributes should be honored and celebrated by the helping professions.

Sadly this is not always the case. All too often individuals with a criminal history who pursue education and employment face significant challenges. The first of these challenges is how their history may affect their ability to even be admitted to universities or to certain academic programs. In helping profession programs, for example, these exclusionary policies are often guided by principles of "gatekeeping," or defining and deciding who should be allowed into the profession. If and when admitted to universities, individuals with a criminal history may encounter difficulties while in school with acclimating to educational standards and successfully completing program expectations, especially supervised experience while in school referred to as either field placements or internships. Field placements can be difficult, if not impossible, for individuals with histories of offenses to secure since many agencies prohibit program staff with past offenses. Even after they graduate they will continue to encounter hardships in securing employment and obtaining advanced licensure and credentialing in the profession.

Significant changes need to be made and more needs to be done in reforming policies and practices regarding individuals with histories of legal offenses who want to pursue education in the helping professions. Doing nothing, or even worse actively excluding individuals with these histories, does an unfortunate disservice to all involved. First the profession would lose out on caring, dedicated workers who can significantly impact and improve not only the lives of clients, but also inform and reform professional practices based on their own personal experiences. More importantly, for the helping professions to exclude these individuals would also contribute to the on-going systemic oppression of this population. This rejection further excludes individuals with a criminal record from the community and interferes with their ability to rebuild their lives, and this time the marginalization would be coming from the very people and professions who have committed to help them. This chapter explores the issues with gatekeeping practices, admissions standards and challenges that students with a criminal justice history face in education and employment. It offers suggestions for how these practices can be reformed and how educators in helping profession programs can best support this population.

SETTING THE STAGE

Who can, or should, become a helping professional? Who should be kept out of the helping professions, and how should that be determined? These questions are central to the helping professions, the educational programs that train the next generation of professional helpers, and students who pursue education and training to work in the helping professions.

In this chapter the term "helping professions" is used broadly to describe those disciplines involved in providing direct care and services to assist individuals with either psychosocial, behavioral health or general healthcare needs. While this term will most often be used here to refer more specifically to the particular professions of human services and social work, it also includes the important, additional helping professions of counseling, psychology, marriage and family therapy, and even professions in the medical field, such as physicians, nurses, and other allied medical disciplines.

Each of these professions has the unique privilege of working with fellow human beings in need, and each uses its knowledge and skills to intervene with the various challenges and difficulties that the recipients of care experience and for which they present for services. The provision of these services exposes the professional helper to very intimate information about the recipients of care, including details about sensitive health conditions they may have, including histories of trauma and abuse, and personal information about finances and assets.

Helping professionals ask about and come to know information about their clients that the clients may never have shared before, not even with their family or friends. The helper may come to learn that unbeknownst to the rest of the client's family that they were sexually molested by an older relative for years, or that they have an addiction to pain medications that they had not disclosed yet. The client may also confide in the helper about his or her struggle with issues he or she fears may alienate him or her from others, such as issues over sexual orientation, gender identity, or whether or not to abort an unplanned pregnancy. The professional helper may even need access to clients' personal identifying information, including social security number, bank accounts, tax returns, or even their legal status to help them qualify for benefits.

The exposure of such intimate information leaves clients in a very vulnerable and disadvantaged position. In order to protect the physical and psychological well-being of clients each helping profession has established a code of ethics to guide its practitioners on how best to serve clients while also maintaining the integrity and safety of all involved, including clients, the professional, the profession and the greater society. Each code addresses priorities and limits with regards to such issues as protecting the confidentiality of clients' identities, the fact they are receiving services, and relevant details about them and their care, avoiding dual relationships where clients can be harmed, and for professionals to not practice while impaired or outside the scope of their training (NASW, 2008; NOHS, 2015).

Developing and later identifying with a professional identity begins with the formal education and training of future practitioners. While historically many social services have been, and continue to be provided by volunteers without formal education or training over the past several decades there has been a growing emphasis on requiring those who work in certain capacities and settings to be professionals that have formal training and a specific level and type of postsecondary degree (Neukrug, 2012).

Students pursuing an education program and degree that will one day allow them to work in the social service or behavioral health fields face a variety of options and decisions, even after they have decided what major they wish to pursue. The first has to do with whether the institution is open or limited enrollment. Limited enrollment colleges and universities require students to meet certain standards, such as Grade Point Average (GPA) or scores on standardized tests, whereas open enrollment institutions tend to accept all applicants regardless of past performance. The second consideration is the level of degree being sought. Some students will pursue only a two year associate degree, while others will use their two year degree to move towards obtaining a bachelor's or master's degree. Within the helping professions this decision is an important one because certain positions and certain types of work are restricted to those who hold a specific degree (bachelor's or master's). A third consideration is whether or not a discipline-specific program is limited enrollment, even if the university is not.

These postsecondary educational programs are seen as a source not only of helping students to acquire discipline-specific content related to the knowledge and skills they will utilize in working with clients, but also as the platform for helping students to develop an identity as a helping professional and a commitment to adopt process-based priorities for how to engage and best serve clients in an ethical manner. Considering the sensitive nature of the needs addressed by the helping professions, caution is given to who enters the field, and these educational programs are seen as the entry point for helping to determine if trainees have the emotional and psychological qualities necessary for working effectively with vulnerable and disadvantaged populations.

GATEKEEPING

"Gatekeeping" is a term that is used to describe the practice by which professions establish standards and processes for determining whether or not trainees possess the skills, qualities and attributes expected by the profession. While many professions utilize gatekeeping processes, such practices are seen to be an important and necessary component of human services and social work educational programs, as well as for the various helping professions generally. This necessity is due to the honor that helping professionals have in serving underrepresented and under-resourced populations. Such work imbues a sense of duty to provide high quality, competent services while also protecting the individuals being served. Although the task of gatekeeping is seen as a necessary one, there continues to be significant disagreement about defining standards and determining who should be responsible for deciding whether or not trainees are an appropriate fit for the profession (Elpers & FitzGerald, 2013; Miller & Koerin, 2001; Sowbel, 2012).

While the field of Human Services has always paid attention to the role of gatekeeping, much more has been written on the topic in social work publications than in the human services literature. This is most likely due to the fact that many human services programs at the associate and bachelor's degree levels are open enrollment while most accredited Bachelor of Social Work (BSW) and Master of Social Work (MSW) degree programs accredited by the Council on Social Work Education (CSWE) are limited enrollment, meaning that each requires certain standards be met to gain admission. These standards can include the completion of a certain number of credit hours and particular prerequisite courses, providing letters of recommendation, and completing criminal background checks. This admission process is often considered the first step in the gatekeeping process. Although the standards may be different for human services and social work, both disciplines share many overlapping core values and practices. An overview of practices related to social work, then, is also relevant to human services. This parallel is strengthened by the fact that often students who complete a two-year degree in human services at a community college later pursue an advanced degree in social work (Rose, 2015).

One of the primary challenges in the social work literature with regards to gatekeeping is deciding at what point in the developmental process it should primarily occur. As mentioned previously often the initial point of gatekeeping is at the admission process, whether that be to the school generally, or to the program specifically, or both. A second point of screening typically occurs when students enter field placements or internships. Some argue that professors and educational institutions should not determine fit for the profession and that gatekeeping should occur once students complete their education and enter the field through seeking employment and eventually trying to secure either licensure or certifications, thus placing gatekeeping responsibility on employers and licensure boards. Despite disagreements over which of these should be emphasized, it is obvious that each serves as a progressive gate in the process. Another challenge to defining gatekeeping is determining what criteria should be used or emphasized. Some authors argue that more objective academic standards, such as grade point average and courses completed, should be used, while others advocate for more values-based criteria related to the candidate's maturity, attitude, and behavior (Elpers & FitzGerald, 2013; Miller & Koerin, 2001).

Most processes will utilize a combination of the two, highlighting the challenge that educational programs face in walking the line between developing knowledge versus professional qualities and priorities. Some faculty members are reluctant to focus on strengthening the sense of professionalism in students, seeing their role solely as an academic one. Such educators are more likely to favor utilizing academic standards in determining admission while deferring gatekeeping processes to employers and boards. This reluctance sadly does a disservice to students, as many social service employers state that in addition to technical knowledge they want professionals who are honest, trustworthy, have a sense of integrity and commitment, are willing to learn and accept feedback and who conduct themselves in an ethical manner. Most employers also rely on helping profession programs to produce candidates who have already developed these attributes while in training, as opposed to workers not beginning to develop them until after they have been hired by an agency (Elpers & FitzGerald, 2013; Evenson & Holloway, 2003).

A primary gatekeeping practice for determining if a student's skills and behaviors meet professional standards is field education, where trainees are required to work under supervision and complete a required number of contact hours in one or more field placements or internships (Sowbel, 2012). Although field education is often seen as a final proving ground in the educational process for determining the student's fit with the profession, utilizing field education as a screening process can backfire if field instructors are not committed to the general principle of gatekeeping. There may be several reasons that they are not willing to adopt or support such practices. Field supervisors may have received very little, if any, training on what standards are expected, and the priority of emphasizing professionalism may not have been addressed or emphasized in their field instructor training either. Other field supervisors may avoid giving students poor performance or professionalism scores out of concerns for how low ratings of students might affect the agency's relationship with the university or out of fear for how low ratings may negatively affect the student's future (Miller & Koerin, 2001; Sowbel, 2012).

Despite the challenges in delineating and applying standards, the practice of gatekeeping persists because educational programs and field placements are seen as the primary screening process for removing individuals that are not appropriate to work as helping professionals. This practice often places educators in a difficult position of having to balance the dual roles of being responsible for students while also being responsible to agencies, the profession and to protecting the recipients of services. A goodness of fit between the candidate and the profession is seen as requiring both technical knowledge and attitudes, as well as priorities and behaviors that reflect the ethical and professional standards likely to safeguard clients and communities (Miller & Koerin, 2001).

WHEN PAST FELONS WANT TO BECOME PROFESSIONAL HELPERS

As mentioned previously people often desire to become professional helpers and come to the helping professions out of their own histories of suffering with and success in resolving their past issues. These individuals are commonly referred to as "wounded healers." They may have previously experienced emotional health difficulties, such as depression, anxiety, trauma or addiction, or they may have experienced very adverse circumstances, such as abuse, neglect, poverty, or histories of dysfunctional family dynamics. Some may have been removed from and placed outside the home or required to receive services from the school system or community agencies. Such individuals remember the caseworker who was cold and rude, and they aspire to be different. They remember the therapist or residential aid who cared and went the extra mile for them, and they aspire to emulate them. Informed by their experiences and their interactions with various agencies and helping professionals they now desire to give back, to help and support others in need, as they were helped and supported (Corey & Corey, 2015; Zerubavel & Wright, 2012).

Often the tumultuous histories of these wounded healers included substance use and other behaviors that led to them acquiring a criminal record along the way. Many of these offenses resulted directly from the purchasing, possessing, producing, transporting, distributing, or being under the influence of substances. Other charges resulted from committing crimes to support their use, such as theft or forgery, while still others stemmed from acting in misguided ways while intoxicated, such as being violent toward others or property. While incarcerated or maintained by community corrections they often were required to participate in rehabilitative services, including addiction treatment, involvement in twelve-step recovery, and other psychotherapeutic or vocational services. As with other wounded healers they may also aspire to serve others and give back (LeBel, Richie, & Maruna, 2015; Zeru-bavel & Wright, 2012).

However they aspire to serve others, the challenge these wounded healers face is the weight of their legal histories. Determining who should or should not be allowed into the helping professions creates a significant issue with regards to students who have a history of legal offenses, especially a history of felony or felonies. Significant discussion continues to occur within the helping professions with regards to how this dynamic should best be ad-dressed, and there is still strong disagreement as to whether or not students with a criminal history can, or should become helping professionals.

While the arguments and issues raised in this ongoing debate have been varied, two central themes continually arise regarding students in the helping professions with a criminal history. The first concern focuses on trying to predict whether or not such students pose a continued threat to society, including most importantly, being a threat to the safety and welfare of cli-ents. In addition to posing a possible threat to clients there has also been concern that such students might pose an on-going threat to fellow students, to the university, to agencies where they may intern, or generally to the profession. A second concern raised has also been about determining even if such students are no longer considered a threat whether or not their criminal history will prevent them from being able to secure field placements, em-ployment or licensure and credentials. If it is determined that they will not be able to be gainfully employed and engaged in professional activities, then admission to and completion of a degree in the helping professions seems of little utility (Leedy & Smith, 2005).

Some authors, most notably Magen and Emerman (2000), have argued for closed gate policies within the helping professions, especially within social work, towards students with a history of felony. They suggest that students with a history of felony should not be admitted to social work programs or be allowed to become professional social workers under any circumstances. The authors base their rationale on the dual ethical expecta-tions social workers have to protect and promote. With regards to protection they see it as the social work profession's charge to protect all involved in the provision of social work services, including clients, practitioners, agencies, the profession and the greater society. They insist that the potential threat and risk posed by those with a history of felony to re-offend is too great to chance, and therefore they should be denied admission to the profession. They also highlight social work's ethical expectation to promote high quality care and the integrity, image and reputation of the profession, all of which they suggest would be tarnished by allowing those with a history of felony into the ranks.

Others see such inflexible policies as ineffective and inappropriate. Scott and Zeigler (2000), for example, consider such rigid approaches that allow no room for exceptions or discretion as doing a disservice not only to the profession, but also to the candidates who have significantly changed their lives and who want to utilize their passion for the betterment of others and themselves. They see this failure to recognize the successful changes that people have made as standing in opposition to the core values of the helping professions. Instead of blanket denial policies they suggest that programs establish specific general admission policies while also considering candidates with a history of past legal offenses on a case-by-case basis. When reviewing these candidates on a case-by-case basis they suggest synthesizing multiple sources of information with regard to the candidate's legal history, including giving consideration to the nature and number of past offenses, the amount of time since the offense, and the outcome of rehabilitative services, such as how they did while on probation or what treatment programs they completed.

Establishing objective guiding principles and practices for assessing candidates with a history of legal offenses and making decisions about whether or not to admit them has proven to be an elusive task. Some programs have sought guidance from the literature on standardized decision-making matrices and algorithms. Other programs have sought to integrate statistics on recidivism rates for particular offenses as a means for predicting the likelihood that candidates may reoffend. Using recidivism data to guide decision making, however, has been heavily questioned and criticized. A primary concern in using such data is the inherent limitation in accurately predicting future behavior based on past offenses. Even if one could say that the general recidivism rate for a particular offense, such as battery, was sixty percent that still would not indicate that everyone with such a history would reoffend. This limited ability to predict also holds true for recidivism rates related to more specific characteristics, such as individuals of a particular gender, age, race, or a combination of these. It also would not support being able to correctly or definitively determine whether or not an individual candidate who had committed that offense was likely to reoffend (Leedy & Smith, 2005).

Recidivism data, while informative, also fails to serve as an effective predictor because it cannot take into account other mitigating factors that can reduce the likelihood of recidivism, such as personal transformation, degree of social support or the effective utilization and completion of rehabilitative services. Recidivism data can also be of questionable utility because racial minorities are known to be overrepresented in crime statistics. The use of such data in determining program admissions and denials, therefore, could also result in and contribute to the continued perpetuation of oppression and discrimination (Adler, Mueller, & Laufer, 2012; Leedy & Smith, 2005).

Many institutions and programs have also turned to conducting criminal background checks as a tool in this process. While at first it would seem that reviewing such reports would be a very definitive aide, there still exists several issues with using such checks. There can be significant differences between what offenses appear on reports, depending on the source of the history and whether it is a federal, state, or local check. Reports can also vary depending on how long ago the offenses were committed, as well as where they were committed and the thoroughness and policies of those jurisdictions in recording and reporting offenses. The lack of reliability and vast discrepancies between different reports can lead to an unfortunate disparity in how such reports are utilized. This is especially problematic given data showing that university personnel often receive little to no training on how to best use and interpret such reports (Custer, 2013).

Regardless of what information is requested or required students with a history of legal offenses are regularly subjected to more extensive screening and scrutiny when applying to college than students without such a history. Custer (2013) provides an account of a woman who applied to the university where he works. The lady was required to write a narrative describing the circumstances of her past legal offenses as part of the admission process. This student had been convicted of two separate felonies, aggravated assault and theft, approximately eleven years prior to her applying to the university. She was never incarcerated for her offenses but was sentenced to probation. Her probation was eventually terminated early due to her successfully complying with and completing all probation requirements. Since then she had even completed some courses at another institution.

The admissions committee at this institution still felt uneasy about her history. The commission asked her to write a second narrative further explaining the nature and circumstances of her past offenses. The applicant wrote back and expressed her frustration over being repeatedly asked to account for events that had occurred over a decade ago. In a poignant comment to the admissions committee she stated, "[This experience] has made me understand that there will always be individuals, institutions, jobs and in this case [the university] that will always make it harder for the disadvantaged to live productive and meaningful lives" (p. 18). This woman never completed her enrollment, and it is unclear if she ever went on to continue her education at another institution. Experiences like this one lead Custer and others to the conclusion that such invasive and investigative admission processes are repressive and contradict the core values of higher education. He insists that such practices are likely more detrimental to the educational and psychological well-being of applicants than they are useful to universities (Custer, 2013).

Rose (2015) articulates the specific challenges that human services students with this history face in completing their education and entering the profession. In an observation similar to Custer's she argues that continuing one's education and obtaining a postsecondary certificate or degree has long been identified as a protective factor that reduces the likelihood of recidivism. She therefore considers policies and practices that prevent or prohibit individuals with a criminal history from attending universities and advancing their education to be both incredibly ineffective and short sighted.

In outlining the obstacles that human services students face, Rose (2015) goes on to propose the possibility that such students may face a "glass ceiling" or "brick wall" in pursuing their educational and professional dreams. Many human services programs require students to complete field placements in order to graduate and students with a history of past legal offenses often encounter difficulties in finding agencies that will accept them for placements. Even if they are able to complete their degree this still does not ensure viability in the field. Many human services programs at community colleges, which historically have been open enrollment, have now established articulation agreements and pathways with universities, including with limited enrollment schools of social work. A student with a criminal history might have been able to successfully complete one program while not being admitted by another. Rose goes on to iterate that regardless of the type or level of degree a student with a criminal history might obtain they still may never be able to find employment or receive state licensure or other credentials, thus preventing them from being part of the profession.

THE NEED FOR BETTER
STANDARDS AND SOLUTIONS

Our society can, and must do better in assisting its citizens with a history of legal offenses, including and especially those with a history of felony. We need to offer and improve services and resources that will allow a suitable and substantial path forward in life. Advocates have long drawn attention to the deplorable ways that this society generally treats individuals with a history of felony, excludes them from opportunities and avenues of advancement, and basically tarnishes their identity and brands them with what many commentators have termed "The Scarlet F" for "Felon" (Flaska, 2014). As this is true in society generally it is unfortunately equally as applicable in the specific realm of the helping professions.

To borrow Rose's metaphors it is necessary for professions such as human services and social work to help aspirants with a legal history to break through the glass ceiling and tear down the brick wall. The following suggestions and recommendations are offered as ways that faculty, field instructors, practitioners, academic programs and institutions and the professions generally can advocate for students with a criminal history.

Recommendation One:
Roll Out the Welcome Mat

Those with a history of legal offenses are sadly very accustomed to being seen and treated differently by others, including by institutions and systems. Despite having completed their sentence they likely have continued to be denied opportunities. They may have eagerly pursued employment only to find that employers either will not hire them or that the only ways they can secure employment are to accept jobs that do not pay a livable wage or to intentionally lie on their application. They may not be able to find housing due to not being able to rent in certain complexes or locations. They might even be denied certain public benefits and entitlements. Many have even been rejected or abandoned by their families and friends.

Additionally students with a history of legal offenses, especially felony, often experience problems with returning to school. They likely feel anxious about even applying and experience self-doubt about whether or not they should even return to school or if they could even be successful if they did. For those who overcome this angst and muster the courage to apply, their application for admission is often denied or subjected to further scrutiny because they indicated they had a history of felony. By having to identify themselves as "felons" they may also be treated poorly by admissions staff. Sadly this stigma may continue to be true even when they are finally engaged by advisors or faculty in their helping profession program who may have negative attitudes towards those with a criminal history and see them as unfit for the profession. They are left feeling discouraged, devalued, and unwelcomed not only by the university, but also by the profession.

While it should not be acceptable for university personnel in general to treat individuals with a criminal history this way, it seems incredibly odd and unfortunate that faculty members in helping profession programs would as well, but students with legal histories have experienced such treatment. The helping professions, including human services and social work, are built on a foundation of respecting and advocating for the individuals they serve, of enhancing their sense of autonomy and self-determination, and to instilling hope, especially with populations prone to social injustice. Students with criminal histories, in addition to being discriminated against, often present with a variety of past or current needs, including housing, unemployment, trauma, addiction, and other behavioral health issues. These psychosocial needs are all ones with which helping professionals routinely intervene.

Case managers or vocational counselors might even have been the ones to encourage their clients to return to college and advance their education. Why would it seem good to encourage clients seek advanced education and employment, just not if that meant wanting to become a "professional," and especially not a "helping professional?" If individuals with a history of felony are even allowed to work again should they only be allowed or able to work very low-skilled manual labor or service-oriented jobs, ones that sadly often offer very little pay and even fewer benefits? This dynamic is one that unfortunately can persist even among helping professionals, whether consciously or unconsciously, where the "helpers" still see themselves as different, separate from, and possibly even better than "clients" who are in need of and receiving services. Social services and therapeutic interventions become something that "those people" do, but not the well-balanced, educated, righteous professional helper (Kottler, 2010).

For a profession to treat its "clients" one way and its "students" and future "colleagues" another seems incredibly misguided. Scott and Zeigler (2000) in building their case for not excluding individuals with a history of felony from the social work profession comment, "If we [as helping professionals] believe in the capacity of people to grow and learn from their mistakes, having made mistakes should not in and of itself shut the doors to the profession" (pp. 410–411). This powerful sentiment is echoed by Rose (2015) who states, "The fundamental concept of social justice for marginalized groups and the promotion of an individual's capacity to grow and change are central to human service ethics" (p. 584). It seems necessary and beneficial, then, for social work and human services educators to commit to engaging students with a history of felony and other offenses with a sense of respect, dignity and encouragement. Instead of creating a closed and hostile environment educators and programs can work to help these individuals to feel valued and welcomed.

Besides being of virtue and benefit in and of itself, such welcoming engagement seems important because, contrary to the views and opinions of some, individuals with a history of their own personal struggles who have received and experienced various services, and who have successfully overcome their challenges are often exactly the type of worker that can benefit clients and the helping professions. Many times these individuals become some of the most sensitive and effective practitioners. Informed and motivated by their own experiential wisdom, they bring an increased ability to relate to clients, as well as powerful insights and a passion for helping others that should be honored.

Recommendation Two:
Sit Down for a Chat over a Cup of Coffee

While it is important not to be negativistic towards students with a felony or overly pessimistic about their future in the profession, it is also necessary not to deny or ignore the difficulties they are likely to face with completing their training and securing employment in the field. The conversation about these potential obstacles needs to occur, and the earlier in the process it occurs the more it allows students to predict and prepare for the difficulties they will experience (Scott & Zeigler, 2000). Academically these conversations include the before mentioned challenges of gaining admission to certain programs and securing field placements at certain agencies or with certain vulnerable populations, such as children or older adults. Once they complete their education the next challenge includes finding employment, as certain agencies or programs may not hire those with a history of felony, or even if so they will be subjected to more extensive screening than other candidates. This can be especially true for agencies or programs that receive grants or other funding that excludes or severely limits the presence or involvement of those with a history of felony. Even if the practitioner is able to obtain employment, they will face additional struggles with obtaining licensure from states or certifications from national organizations. Throughout this conversation faculty, advisors and mentors can not only help students to identify these obstacles, but they can also offer to be resources and sources of support. Early on they can encourage students to nurture relationships with a variety of teachers, supervisors and others who may eventually be needed to write letters of recommendation in their support.

During this early conversation and throughout their path towards professional employment it is essential for faculty and trainers to encourage individuals with a history of legal offenses to be increasingly open and honest about their past. Most people might automatically assume that those with a criminal history would naturally lie about or conceal their past because "that's just how criminals are," but rarely is this the case. More often individuals with a criminal history are not forthcoming about their past because when they do disclose their past they are judged, criticized, looked down on, and are subjected to oppression and discrimination.

While it is understandable given these painful experiences that such individuals would not want to be forthcoming about their past, it becomes necessary because each of the helping professions has core values related to honesty, integrity, and transparency. Being found to have concealed a past is, in actuality, more likely to result in being denied admission, field placement, or employment than is acknowledging such a history from the beginning.

Often students are reluctant to discuss their past because all that seems to be focused on is their history of misfortunes, mistakes, and regrets, which are unpleasant to acknowledge, let alone discuss. It is important that students receive the message that honestly acknowledging the past and being open to discussing it conveys that they are committed to transparency while also allowing the opportunity to highlight the student's strengths, successes, and the positive changes they have made since their offenses and how their life now is much different from what it was before.

Discussing past issues also allows for an assessment of how successfully any past issues which might have contributed to their legal offenses, such as addiction or behavioral health conditions, are actively being managed. If someone is continuing to significantly struggle in these areas, they may not be in a place as of yet to best be able to consistently serve others in a professional capacity. These conditions can not only interfere with their educational success, but can also impair their ability to work in the field and can endanger the safety of clients.

This discussion illustrates that there is a shadow to every point of light. While an individual's experiences from his or her own history are some of his or her greatest assets, they can unfortunately also be some of his or her most significant liabilities. Sometimes students who come from their own history of struggles assume that because they have "been there" that they do not require formal education or professional skills. While having "been there" does offer one a very unique and privileged perspective, it does not always ensure that they will automatically be able to relate to or understand the experiences of others. Having a past history of needs can make some workers more patient and understanding, but it can also possibly make them more impatient and confrontational. This increased demandingness may especially be true when clients continue to struggle with the same or similar issues they did, or with clients who just do not seem to be "getting it" or "trying as hard" as they themselves did and now believe others should (Corey & Corey, 2015). This automatic prediction on the part of clients, and some professionals, that only one who has "been there" can truly help comes from a sense of fear that those who have not experienced such circumstances will ultimately not understand or will criticize, judge, or reject. While this is a natural and understandable worry, it is not accurate that effective intervention can only come from one who has experienced those exact circumstances. As one colleague succinctly stated, "who would you rather have fix your leg, the doctor who has broken his leg a hundred times or the doctor who has set a hundred broken legs?"

Engaging and talking with students early on helps ensure that they are maintaining changes in their life and managing any conditions that may jeopardize their academic or professional success. It also helps support their coming to make sure that they are building on their past experiences as opposed to relying on them. More than having "been there" is someone who has "been there and come back" and who now has additional skills and resources to help serve as a guide for others. Compassion and wisdom are often referred to as the two wings of the phoenix that rises from the ashes; without both the bird cannot take flight. The painful experiences of the past cultivate the concern and regard in wounded healers, and professional education helps to provide knowledge and skills that develop wisdom. Author Joseph Goldstein (1993) states, "compassion feels the suffering . . . and wisdom understands what to do" (p. 130).

Recommendation Three:
Break Out the Placards and Petitions

Individuals with a criminal history, especially history of felony, are a marginalized group that often does not have a voice. While these individuals generally need advocates, this is especially the case in the helping professions. Here faculty, field instructors, and professional organizations can advocate for and help create increased opportunities. This advocacy can occur on the micro, mezzo, and macro levels of practice.

MICRO-LEVEL ADVOCACY

In addition to the previously mentioned micro-level advocacy of faculty members being generally engaging and encouraging towards students with a criminal history, faculty can also actively encourage the success of these students in the classroom and in their respective educational programs. Often students with criminal histories who return to school are slightly older than others in their program. This reflects a delay in starting or resuming their education due to time lost while struggling with their difficulties and dealing with the repercussions of those in the criminal justice system. Because of their age and their histories they may feel out of place, and faculty can work to help them feel more accepted and integrated in courses and the program. They can also try to connect these students to peers in their cohort.

Another challenge such students might experience is in the time between when they were last in school as "students" and current coursework. They may not be as prepared to manage course loads, homework, note taking and study skills as they once were, and they may find it hard to adjust to being a student once again. Some of these students experienced educational difficulties in the past, either academically or behaviorally, which might have impaired their academic performance or progress, or resulted in them dropping out of school. These issues may resurface once the person returns to school. Educators can continue to monitor the academic performance of these students and intervene early and consistently if problems present. It is advisable for faculty to monitor performance not only in discipline-specific courses but also in other required or elective general education courses and to maintain collaborative relationships with those faculty as well so that all who are in contact with these students can coordinate to support the success of such students.

Another issue that can arise is behavioral concerns. Some of these students, if they have experienced periods of incarceration, might experience challenges being in classrooms and around others again. They come to find that behaviors which were expected in prison communities and that even helped them to successfully survive their incarceration are now discouraged and punished in classrooms and academic communities. This dissonance creates adjustment issues. Given the role of authority assigned to faculty some students with a history of incarceration or having been on probation or parole may react negatively to faculty if they see them as similar to authority figures they have encountered previously in the criminal justice system, such as judges, probation officers, and prison guards. Human services faculty can continue to support and encourage these students by monitoring their attendance and behavior in the classroom, intervening early when issues arise while also socializing these students to the behavioral and performance standards expected both in the classroom and in the profession. To assist with both academic and behavioral needs faculty can encourage students to access supportive services and can link them to tutoring, counseling and other social services when and where those are available.

MEZZO-LEVEL ADVOCACY

When networks of resources and services are either not available or not well coordinated, faculty can engage in mezzo-level advocacy by working with programs and organizations to create more opportunities. This may include establishing centers for student success or making sure to identify providers, whether they be tutors, advisors, or counselors who are more sensitive to the needs of this population and more receptive towards working with them. This can also include reminding all involved that even if students do reoffend that it should not lead to an overgeneralization that "most" or "all" students in the helping professions with a criminal history will. This situation can be challenging because often the immediate reaction of faculty members and other university personnel when a student with a criminal history reoffends is one of embarrassment and concern for how the student's arrest will affect or reflect on their program or institution, especially if the offense was severe or the arrest was highly publicized. This is typically followed by recommendations that further restrictions and limitations be placed on all students with a history of legal offenses.

Inevitably it will occur that programs with students with criminal histories in them will encounter times where either students reoffend or when they might be dismissed from field placements due to performance or behavioral issues. Caution should be applied here because while it is entirely possible that individuals with past convictions can commit new offenses or be dismissed from field placements, it is also true that students without histories of legal charges can commit crimes, be arrested, or be excused from internships due to acting inappropriately or unethically. These concerns are unfortunately true for all students and programs, regardless of whether the students involved have any history of legal charges. There is currently no empirical indication within the human services or social work literature that students with criminal histories either commit legal offenses while in school at a higher rate than other students or that they experience more behavioral or performance issues during field placements or are dismissed from placements at a higher rate than for those without such histories.

Perhaps the most important mezzo-level advocacy in which faculty can engage is collaborating with agencies to establish field placements receptive to students with a criminal record, especially past felony convictions. Certain agencies, because of the work they do or because of their philosophical or spiritual values, are more receptive to accepting those with a criminal history. These relationships are important ones, and faculty and field instructors can help direct students with criminal histories towards these agencies and these opportunities. During this process such students can also be connected to current professionals in the community with this history who have successfully entered the field despite their past charges. These interactions and mentoring relationships can not only offer students a sense of hope that they too can be successful, but it can also provide the students with perspective on the specific obstacles that person faced when trying to complete school and find employment. Another potential area of mezzo-level advocacy could also be working with agencies and employers on the selection of background checks and how those reports are used.

MACRO-LEVEL ADVOCACY

Faculty members, practitioners and the various professional organizations, such as the National Association of Social Workers (NASW) and the National Organization for Human Services (NOHS) that represent the helping professions can all continue to advocate and lobby for policy reforms. All involved can lobby for better laws with regards to arrest and sentencing guidelines, as well as making changes to laws that restrict access to employment, education or resources for those with a history of felony or other offenses.

Perhaps the most targeted and focused issue for how macro-level advocacy may benefit students in the helping professions with a criminal history is in increasing support for and access to expungement opportunities. While the technical nuances of this process vary, expungement generally allows individuals an avenue to have past charges either removed from their record or to be able to legally say they do not have a particular charge or offense on their record. While these opportunities and initiatives continue to expand, unfortunately they are still limited, both in number and in accessibility. In some areas such opportunities do not even exist, and even if the opportunity exists individuals may still have little to no knowledge of their existence. Even when these opportunities are known and available many still have trouble accessing them due to the significant financial expense associated with seeking expungement.

Obviously each level of advocacy is important and interdependent. A summary of these principles and guidelines is presented in box 1 (see box 1). These dynamics, both the struggles and successes of students with a criminal history, are illustrated by the following example of Mary.

MARY

Mary experienced significant and repeated traumas throughout childhood and began using drugs and alcohol as a teenager to cope. Her use lasted several years into early adulthood, and during this time she received multiple legal charges, including both felonies and misdemeanors. Mary eventually decided to get help for her addiction. She first completed a residential addiction program and then an outpatient treatment program following her discharge. While she was completing this outpatient program in the community she decided to stay in a supportive living facility for women in recovery. She additionally completed a twelve-month program there and since has maintained several years of sobriety.

While in early recovery she decided to pursue a career in the helping professions. She wanted to give back and help others overcome issues with addiction, trauma, and other challenges just as she had been helped with these issues by the professionals she encountered in her various treatment programs. Mary began school at an open-enrollment community college. She was honest and transparent about her history of addiction and past legal offenses from the beginning. She majored in human services and after completing her associate degree with honors she applied to a traditional university with a limited enrollment social work program.

Mary was initially denied admission to the university because of indicating on the application that she had a history of felony. Her denial occurred without her even being given the opportunity to speak with anyone regarding the decision or her circumstances. In her denial letter from the Dean of Students it outlined the various university personnel and committees that had met and been involved in making this decision, and the letter encouraged pursuing "other educational options," including specifically suggested she consider attending the community college from which she had just graduated.

With encouragement from her family and friends she persisted. She requested a face-to-face meeting, and appealed her denial. She was eventually allowed to enroll on a probationary basis. She also gained admission to the social work program, but she was repeatedly told it would be difficult, if not impossible, for her to obtain field placements, employment, and licensure because of her criminal history. A faculty member in her social work program even told her, "I can't believe they would even admit someone like you to this program."

Despite encountering such pessimism there were several faculty members and practitioners in the community who were extremely supportive of her and willing to advocate on her behalf. Mary successfully secured a field placement with an agency that was willing to work with her despite her criminal history, and she eventually graduated with her Bachelor of Social Work degree. After graduation she found employment as a case manager at an agency that provided addiction services. Mary also secured admission to a graduate program and is completing coursework while she continues to work.

Mary was also able to get connected to a legal organization that helped her pursue expungement for her past offenses. This process was a laborious and time-consuming one, as it involved several different charges, several different types and levels of charges (both misdemeanors and felonies), in two separate jurisdictions. This expungement would not have been accessible to her financially without the generosity of the legal organization assisting her on a *pro bono* basis. All of her past charges were expunged, and this expungement will successfully aid her as she pursues state licensure as an addiction counselor.

Mary and others like her demonstrate that reform and transformation are possible, and that when provided with adequate support and opportunities people with a history of felony can, and do, succeed. While not every seedling will eventually bloom, given the right causes, conditions and circumstances a vast number of these lotus blossoms will. It is the responsibility of the rest of us, educators, practitioners, policymakers, family members, friends and fellow citizens alike, to make sure that we do our best to tend to and nourish all these beautiful blooming lotuses in the water garden.

NOTE

1. This chapter was expanded from a previous article by the authors titled "Advocacy in Action: Supporting Human Service Students with a Criminal Justice History."

REFERENCES

Adler, F., Mueller, G. O. W., & Laufer, W.S. (2012). *Criminology* (8th ed.) New York, NY: McGraw Hill.

Corey, M. S., & Corey, G. (2015). *Becoming a Helper* (7th Ed.). Belmont, CA: Brooks/Cole.

Custer, B. D. (2013). Admission denied: A case study of an ex-offender. *Journal of College Admission*, (219), 16–19.

Elpers, K., & FitsGerald, E. A. (2013). Issues and challenges in gatekeeping: A framework for implementation. *Social Work Education, 32*(3), 286-300. doi: 10.1080/02615479.2012.665867

Evenson, T. E., & Holloway, L. L. (2003). Promoting professionalism in human service education. *Human Service Education, (23)*1, 15–24.

Flaska, K. (2014). The scarlet letter "F". Retrieved from http://etikallc.com/the-scarlet-letter-f/

Frederic, L. (1995). *Buddhism: Flammarion iconographic guides.* New York, NY: Flammarion.

Goldstein, J. (1993). *Insight meditation: The practice of freedom.* Boston, MA: Shambhala.

Kottler, J. A. (2010). *On being a therapist* (4th ed). San Fransisco, CA: Jossey-Bass.

LeBel, T. P., Richie, M., & Maruna, S. (2015). Helping others as a response to reconcile a criminal past: The role of the wounded healer in prisoner reentry programs. *Criminal Justice and Behavior, 42(*1), 108-120. doi: 10.1177/009385481455029.

Leedy, G. M., & Smith, J. E. (2005). Felony convictions and program admissions: Theoretical perspectives to guide decision making. *Journal of Social Work Values and Ethics, 2*(1). Retrieved from http://www.socialworker.com/jswve/content/view/16/34.

Magen, R. H., & Emerman, J. (2000). Should convicted felons be denied admission to a social work education program? Yes! *Journal of Social Work Education, 36,* 401-414.

Miller, J., & Koerin, B. (2001). Gatekeeping in the practicum: What field instructors need to know. *The Clinical Supervisor, 20*(2), 1–18.

National Organization for Human Services (NOHS). (2015). Ethical standards for human service professionals. Retrieved from http://www.nationalhumanservices.org/ethical-standards-for-hs-professionals.

National Association of Social Workers (NASW). (2008). Code of ethics of the National Association of Social Workers. Retrieved from www.socialworkers.org/pubs/code/default.asp.

Neukrug, E. (2012). *Theory, practice, and trends in human services: An introduction.* Belmont, CA: Brooks/Cole.

Paulson, J., Groves, K., & Hagedorn, L. A. (2016). Advocacy in action: Supporting human services students with criminal justice histories. *Fitness for the Human Services Profession: Preliminary Explorations* [monograph]. Council for Standards in Human Services Education Monograph Series, 40–54.

Rose, L. H. (2015). Community college students with criminal justice histories and human services education: Glass ceiling, brick wall or pathway to success. *Community College Journal of Research and Practice, 39*(6), 584–587.

Scott, N., & Zeiger, S. (2000). Should convicted felons be denied admission to a social work education program? No! *Journal of Social Work Education, 36,* 401–414.

Sowbel, L. R. (2012). Gatekeeping: Why shouldn't we be ambivalent? *Journal of Social Work Education, 48*(1), 27-44. doi: 10.5175/JSWE.2012.201000027.

Tirch, D., Silberstein, L. R., & Kolts, R. L. (2015). *Buddhist psychology and cognitive-behavioral therapy: A clinician's guide.* New York, NY: Guilford Press.

Zerubavel, N., & Wright, M. O. (2012). The dilemma of the wounded healer. *Psychotherapy, 49*(4), 482-491. doi 10.1037/a0027824

Chapter Four

People Can Change

Experiences of Formerly Incarcerated Leaders

Mark Rice

People returning home from prisons and jails face many barriers to success-ful reentry into society. These individuals face different forms of discrimina-tion that are often based on assumptions that they will continue to engage in illegal conduct after being released. However, a growing body of research suggests that if we provide formerly incarcerated people with certain kinds of support, we can greatly decrease the likelihood that they will be reincarcerat-ed. Several cases of individuals who have been involved with Project RE-TURN, WISDOM, and EX-incarcerated People Organizing (EXPO) provide evidence that people with conviction histories can not only change but can become key leaders of social movements and organizations. In this chapter, I draw from public statements of these leaders as well as newspaper articles and organizational materials to demonstrate their transformations. In addi-tion, I share parts of my life story to add further evidence that people can change.

INTRODUCTION

The reentry of people returning home from jails and prisons has become an increasingly important issue in recent years as imprisonment rates in the United States have reached unprecedented levels. More than sixty-five mil-lion people in the United States now have arrest or conviction records (Rod-riguez and Emsellem, 2011). Each year, more than 600,000 people return home from prisons (Carson and Golinelli, 2014). These individuals face several barriers to successful reintegration into society. Petersilia (2003, p.

19) suggests that "a criminal conviction—no matter how trivial or how long ago it occurred—scars one for life." Legal scholar Michelle Alexander (2012) contends that the discrimination faced by people who have been convicted of crimes in recent decades is similar in many ways to the discrimination faced by African Americans during the Jim Crow era in the south.

Several studies document the failures and struggles of people coming home from correctional facilities, but few studies examine the experiences of previously imprisoned individuals who become important community leaders. One recent study demonstrates that about half of formerly incarcerated persons return to prison within three years of release (Durose, Cooper, and Snyder, 2014). Many people who have been incarcerated successfully make the transition back into the community and become involved in advocacy work. However, LeBel (2009, p. 167) notes that "[t]here is a paucity of literature on formerly incarcerated person's support for and/or involvement in advocacy-related activities."

This chapter examines the personal transformations of formerly incarcerated people in Wisconsin. Their stories demonstrate that members of this group can not only change but can become key leaders of social movements. The narratives also illustrate the need for penal system reform in Wisconsin. I include several brief stories in this chapter, but, unfortunately, I could not provide detailed narratives due to space constraints. This limits my ability to effectively integrate the narratives with the aggregate data I provide.

Although a small group of previously imprisoned scholars known as convict criminologists conduct research on carceral system issues, people who have not experienced incarceration conduct nearly all of the studies in this area. Richards and Ross (2003, p. 10) claim that "[m]ost academic criminologists fail to penetrate and comprehend the lived experience of defendants and prisoners, or are simply misinformed." Convict criminologists and their supporters argue that people with records should contribute more frequently to this field (Richards, 2013). Gonnerman (2004, p. 10) contends that scholarly and professional conversations about reentry "usually leave out the voices of former prisoners, relying instead on statistics." However, she believes that "the true story of America's exodus of ex-cons cannot be told only with numbers" (Gonnerman, 2004, p. 10). This chapter addresses the concerns raised by Gonnerman and convict criminologists by examining the voices and stories of formerly incarcerated leaders in Wisconsin.

INCARCERATION IN WISCONSIN

Although Wisconsin imprisons people at a rate below the national average (Carson, 2014), a comparison of its penal system with Minnesota's reveals the ineffectiveness, inefficiency, and unfairness of Wisconsin's system. Wisconsin, which has a population, political culture, financial capacity, racial demographics, and crime rates similar to Minnesota, regularly incarcerates individuals at a higher level and consistently spends much more on corrections (Bureau of Justice Statistics [BJS], 1990; BJS, 2003; Wald, 2008; "The Cost of Corrections," 2010). Wisconsin currently incarcerates people at nearly twice the rate of Minnesota, (Carson, 2014) and spends more than twice as much on corrections (Mitchell and Leachman, 2014). One recent report suggests that "[i]f Minnesota incarcerated at the same level as Wisconsin, taxpayers would need to add 24 prisons and increase the state prison budget by $419.5 million annually" ("Doing What Works," n.d.). The estimated amount does not include the cost of building the additional prisons ("Doing What Works," n.d.).

Wisconsin has one of the most racially unjust penal systems in the United States. Mass incarceration has had a particularly harmful impact on African Americans in the state. Although Black people constitute just six percent of the residents in the state, nearly half of the individuals in state prisons are Black ("Office of Justice Assistance," 2008). Wisconsin incarcerates Black men and Native American men at higher rates than any other state (Pawasarat and Quinn, 2013). Minnesota imprisons Black men at less than half the rate of Wisconsin. (Pawasarat and Quinn, 2013). Wisconsin imprisons many Black men for relatively minor offenses. About half of all Black people that the Department of Corrections (DOC) sent to prison over the last fifteen years did not get convicted of new crimes (Wisconsin Department of Corrections Presentation, 2015). Instead, public officials imprisoned these individuals for what we call crimeless revocations. A crimeless revocation occurs when the Department of Corrections reincarcerates a person on probation, parole, or extended supervision for violating a rule of supervision that does not involve a new crime. Furthermore, the Wisconsin Sentencing Commission produced a report in 2007 which demonstrates that racial disparities in imprisonment rates emerged largely because judges sent a higher percentage of African Americans to prison for drug offenses (Doedge, 2007).

Mass incarceration disproportionately affects some communities in Milwaukee. One out of two Black men in their thirties who reside in Milwaukee County has spent time in Wisconsin prisons (Pawasarat and Quinn, 2013). Wisconsin imprisoned nearly half of these individuals for drug offenses (Pawasarat and Quinn, 2013). The high rate of imprisonment among people in the 53206 zip code in Milwaukee, where 95 percent of residents are African American, illustrates the unfairness of the system. Over 60 percent of the men in this zip code have spent time in state prisons (Quinn, 2007).

BARRIERS TO SUCCESSFUL REENTRY

Several elements can influence how well people returning from incarceration adjust to life on the outside. Important factors include employment, housing, social support, and education. Individuals who suffer from addiction or mental illnesses face unique reentry challenges.

Obtaining a job is a huge obstacle to successful reintegration for many people. Numerous studies demonstrate that previously imprisoned individuals who obtain employment return to prison at lower rates (LaVigne, Visher, and Castro, 2004; LaVigne, Brooks, and Shollenberger, 2007; Rossman and Roman, 2003; Visher and Courtney, 2007; Visher, Debus, and Yahner, 2008; Yahner and Visher, 2008). However, less than 40 percent of formerly incarcerated persons are employed one year after release (Petersilia, 2003; Travis, 2005). Individuals who have been convicted of felonies are legally prohibited from working in many professions (Love, Roberts, and Klingele, 2013). In Wisconsin, people with conviction histories can potentially be ineligible to work in over seventy different professions ("Civil Consequences of Conviction," 2012). Furthermore, formerly incarcerated persons face barriers to jobs that they are not legally prohibited from obtaining. Many employers are reluctant to hire people with records (Holzer, Raphael, and Stoll, 2004) and most employers still include the box which inquires about conviction and arrest history on the initial application (Fishman, 2014). Devah Pager (2007), a Harvard sociologist, completed a study which suggests that employers tend to call back applicants with past convictions at much lower rates, particularly if they are Black.

Finding a place to live after returning from incarceration can be an obstacle to successful reentry for some individuals. Previously imprisoned people who find stable housing are less likely to recidivate (Metraux and Culhane, 2004; Roman and Travis, 2004; Thompson, 2008; Visher and Courtney, 2007). Although most people initially stay with family members after being released, (LaVigne et al. 2004; Nelson, Deess, and Allen, 1999; Solomon, Visher, LaVigne, and Osbourne, 2006) others are not as fortunate. Previously incarcerated individuals face a lot of discrimination in housing markets so if they cannot stay with family members or friends, they often become homeless (LaVigne, Shollenberger, and Debus, 2009; LeBel, 2012; Thacher 2008). Austin and Irwin (2000, p. 156) suggest that over a quarter of people returning from imprisonment "eventually end up on the streets."

Substance abuse is a significant issue for most people returning home from incarceration. While approximately two thirds of all people in prisons and jails in the United States suffer from addiction to drugs, only a little over 10 percent of these individuals receive treatment for their conditions while they are imprisoned ("National Center on Addiction and Substance Abuse," 2010). Formerly incarcerated persons who use drugs shortly after returning to communities return to prison at higher rates than those who do not (La-Vigne et al., 2004; Visher et al. 2004; LaVigne et al., 2007). Although drug treatment programs can reduce recidivism rates and drug use (LaVigne et al. 2009; LaVigne et al. 2007; Visher and Courtney 2007; Visher et al. 2004; Seiter and Kadela, 2003; Inciardi, Martin, and Butzin, 2004; Prendergast, Hall, Wexler, Melnick, and Cao, 2004), few previously imprisoned people continue to participate in treatment programs on the outside (Winterfield and Castro, 2005).

In response to the large number of crimes driven by addiction, Wisconsin has implemented a program known as Treatment Alternatives and Diversion (TAD). The TAD program diverts people with substance abuse problems who get arrested for low-level crimes from incarceration and connects them to treatment and support. Evaluations of the program demonstrates that it enhances the health of participants, reduces recidivism rates, save taxpayers money, and reduces levels of imprisonment (Van Stelle, Goodrich, and Kroll, 2014).

A lack of social support increases the likelihood that a person will return to prison. People returning from prison who maintain strong family relationships tend to recidivate at lower rates (Hairston, 1988, 2003; LaVigne et al., 2004, LaVigne et al. 2009; Nelson et al. 1999; Sullivan, Mino, Nelson, and Pope, 2002; Visher and Courtney 2007). However, many individuals do not have anyone they can rely on to provide support during the reentry process (LaVigne et al. 2009).

Although numerous studies demonstrate the benefits of providing educational opportunities to incarcerated individuals, they have been ineligible to receive Pell grants since 1994. The Obama administration restored Pell grant eligibility to a small number of incarcerated individuals in 2015 (Schwartzapfel, 2015). Research suggests that people who complete college courses while they are imprisoned are more likely to find jobs and less likely to return to prison for new crimes after being released (Gerber and Fritsch, 1993; "U.S. Bureau of Labor Statistics," 2015; Steurer, Smith, and Tracy, 2001; "RAND Corporation," 2014).

Many people returning home from jail or prison must deal with problems associated with mental illnesses that they suffer from. These individuals are much more likely to experience incarceration than the general population. About one out of every two individuals with mental illnesses has been arrested (Solomon and Draine, 1995; Walsh and Bricourt, 1997) and many of them have been imprisoned dozens of times (Osher, Steadman, and Barr, 2003). Although media accounts often portray these individuals as violent and dangerous, they normally get arrested for minor misdemeanors (Cuellar, Snowden, and Ewing, 2007). Although more than half of people in jails and state prisons and nearly half of individuals in federal prisons have some sort of mental health problem (Kim, Becker-Cohen, and Serakos, 2015), less than

20 percent of these people receive professional mental health treatment (James and Glaze, 2006). More than half of Black persons in jails and state prisons have a mental health problem (Osher, D'Amora, Plotkin, Jarrett, and Eggleston, 2012). This is a particularly important issue because of the over-representation of Black people in the penal system.

People who suffer from mental illnesses face many challenges. Approximately 75 percent of individuals who have disabling mental conditions are not employed (Draine, Salzer, Culhane, and Hadley, 2002). These people are much more likely to become homeless than the general population. Around half of homeless individuals have suffered from mental illness at some point in their lives (Caton et al., 2005). Individuals with mental illnesses who have past convictions face even greater obstacles to finding employment and housing.

In response to the increasing criminalization of those who suffer from mental illnesses, many jurisdictions have started to implement mental health courts. These courts focus on solving the problems of people with mental illnesses who have been charged with crimes by linking them to treatment programs and support in the community instead of immediately incarcerating them (Almquist and Dodd, 2009). Evaluations of mental health courts suggest that they can reduce recidivism rates, increase rates of participation in treatment programs, enhance the mental health of participants, and save taxpayers money (Almquist and Dodd, 2009). In 2008, Eau Claire County implemented the first mental health court in Wisconsin (Abrahamson, 2012). This court has saved the county money and helped people stay out of jail (Kelley, 2010). Only two other counties in Wisconsin have implemented mental health courts (NAMI Wisconsin, 2013).

THE EMERGENCE AND EVOLUTION OF
THE REENTRY SOCIAL MOVEMENT

A little over a decade ago, formerly incarcerated people in different parts of the United States began to organize to end the structural discrimination they face because of their conviction and arrest histories. In 2004, All of Us or None, an organization led by people with records, organized an event in Oakland, California, that gave hundreds of previously imprisoned individuals' opportunities to speak about the discrimination they experienced in front of dozens of politicians and local leaders (Toney, 2007). During this summit and other similar events, All of Us or None leaders decided to start a ban the box campaign which aimed to reduce employment discrimination against people with past convictions and arrests. Since the launch of this campaign, more than one hundred cities and counties and nineteen states have banned the box (Rodriguez and Nehta, 2015). Around the same time, people with past convictions in Rhode Island began to organize to restore their voting rights. Open Doors, a nonprofit organization that supports people with records, led this effort (Owens, 2014).

Toney (2007) examined organizing efforts of formerly incarcerated persons in New York, California, and Washington, DC, and concluded that a national reentry social movement has begun to emerge. He argues that this new movement is a grassroots movement characterized by high-level reframing efforts and a scarcity of resources (Toney 2007). Toney did not examine any organizations in the south or midwest, but the organizing efforts of organizations in the south like The Ordinary People Society (T.O.P.S.) in Alabama and Voice of the Ex-Offender (VOTE) in Louisiana, which are both led by formerly incarcerated persons, provide further evidence that a nationwide movement led by people with records has emerged (Cleggett, 2008; "Voice of the Ex-Offender," 2015).

Organizations like JustLeadershipUSA (JLUSA) and EX-incarcerated People Organizing (EXPO) in Wisconsin, which focus on developing the leadership capacity of formerly incarcerated individuals through training programs, have begun to emerge. The mission of JLUSA is to empower "people most affected by incarceration to drive policy reform" (JLUSA, 2015). EXPO has a similar mission. Michelle Alexander believes JLUSA "will be viewed . . . as a true game changer: the moment in the emerging movement when formerly incarcerated people finally had a chance to be heard, to organize, and to influence policy in major ways" (JLUSA, 2015). I describe EXPO in further detail below.

THE IMPACT OF ADVOCACY WORK
ON FORMERLY INCARCERATED PEOPLE

Some research suggests that participating in advocacy work can improve the psychological well-being of previously imprisoned people and help them desist from crime. Maruna (2001) studied the experiences of formerly incarcerated people in England. Some of these individuals were still committing crimes and others had begun to desist from crime. The study suggests that the group which desisted from crime found purpose in their lives (Maruna, 2001). Maruna (2001, p. 13) found that this group emphasized "the desire to make some important contribution to their communities" (Maruna, 2001 p. 13). He argues that to desist from crime, formerly incarcerated people "need to develop a coherent, prosocial identity for themselves" (Maruna, 2001, p. 7). A key part of developing this new identity often includes taking on leadership roles that enable these individuals to help others (Maruna, 2001). LeBel (2009, p. 183) examined how advocacy work affected previously imprisoned persons in New York and found that this work can help them develop pro-social identities and give "their lives purpose and meaning." LeBel (2009, p. 183) argues that this activity "appears to help transform formerly incarcerated persons from being part of the problem into part of the solution."

WISDOM, EXPO, AND PROJECT RETURN

WISDOM, a network of faith-based organizations in Wisconsin, launched the 11x15 campaign to end mass imprisonment in Wisconsin in 2012 (Langemo, 2012; "WISDOM," 2015). The campaign aimed to reduce Wisconsin's prison population in half by the end of 2015, but the state's prison population did not significantly decline during this period ("State of Wisconsin Department of Corrections," 2015). A group of formerly incarcerated individuals, local task forces, and workgroups that focused on different aspects of penal policy helped to coordinate the campaign ("The Sentencing Project," 2014). WISDOM achieved victories when legislators decided to increase funding for the state's Treatment Alternatives and Diversion program on two separate occasions (Mayer, 2014). Moreover, the campaign affected several other reforms in the state. Since the campaign began, Wisconsin has reduced the use of solitary confinement, expanded its transitional jobs program, and increased the rate of people being released on parole (Hall, 2015a; Halsted, 2015; "Public Policy Institute," 2015). In addition, a bill that would move some seventeen-year-olds out of the adult system had wide bipartisan support by late 2015 (Vielmetti, 2015). On November 3, 2015, WISDOM kicked off the next phase of its reform campaign with an event in Madison, Wisconsin. This phase of the campaign will be called ROC Wisconsin: Restoring Our Communities—Moving Beyond 11x15 (ROC Wisconsin, 2015a).

EX-incarcerated People Organizing (EXPO) is a group of formerly incarcerated people who drive WISDOM's campaign to end mass incarceration. The organization aims to influence current conversations about the carceral system and people who have experienced incarceration. EXPO also aims to restore people with records to full participation in the life of their communities. Members of this group have led organizing efforts around issues like revocations, TAD, solitary confinement, housing, and transitional jobs. EXPO currently has active chapters in Milwaukee, Madison, and Eau Claire and plans to develop chapters in Wausau, Green Bay, Racine, and Kenosha ("ROC Wisconsin," 2015b; "Ex-Prisoners Organizing," 2015). All EXPO members attend two-day and weeklong leadership training programs conducted by WISDOM and the Gamaliel Network. In June of 2015, 18 individuals completed the first ever weeklong leadership development training program for EXPO members at Marquette University (Mayer, 2015). Eighty people have participated in the two-day trainings ("ROC Wisconsin," 2015b).

Although individual EXPO leaders had previously taken leadership roles in campaigns on particular issues, the entire group had not taken on an issue collectively until the summer of 2015. During the training program, EXPO members decided the first issue the group would collectively organize around would be ban the box. The organization joined a national effort that aimed to get President Obama to issue an Executive Order to ban the box for federal jobs and federal contractors. Jorge Renaud, a community organizer with the Center for Community Change in Washington, DC, attended the training and helped to coordinate the effort. EXPO members initially reached out to state and local elected officials throughout Wisconsin and asked them to call on President Obama to issue an Executive Order to ban the box. Dozens of these politicians supported our effort. In July, three EXPO leaders joined formerly incarcerated leaders from across the nation to participate in a ban the box rally in front of the White House and meet with some of President Obama's policy advisors. In addition, EXPO leaders educated, organized, and mobilized communities across Wisconsin. On November 2, 2015, President Obama banned the box for federal jobs ("The White House Office of the Press Secretary," 2015).

Project RETURN is a nonprofit organization in Milwaukee that aims to "help men and women leaving prison make a positive and permanent return to our community" ("Project RETURN," 2015). Several of the agency's board members and staff members help to lead WISDOM's ROC Wisconsin Campaign. The organization has provided services to numerous EXPO members. The agency has helped many people successfully reintegrate into communities. The recidivism rate for people Project RETURN helps to find jobs is under 5 percent ("Helping Men and Women," 2015).

STORIES OF EXPO LEADERS

The stories of the EXPO leaders included in this chapter illustrate how reducing barriers to successful reentry can help formerly incarcerated persons succeed. Moreover, their stories suggest that engaging in advocacy work might help previously imprisoned people desist from crime. None of these individuals have returned to prison since becoming involved in the 11x15 campaign. Obtaining employment, educational opportunities, peer support, family support, substance abuse treatment, and mental health treatment played important roles in helping these individuals succeed. All of the people discussed in this chapter have moved beyond conventional success to become key leaders in a movement to transform Wisconsin's penal system.

The narratives I include below put human faces on several of the topics included in the literature review. The first seven stories below put human faces on the aggregate data I included above on racial inequalities in the carceral system. I share brief summaries of the experiences of six Black men and one Black woman. The first four stories illustrate how the war on drugs negatively affected the lives of four Black men. The following three narratives highlight the issues of racial profiling, solitary confinement, and housing. The final two stories demonstrate how addiction and mental illness negatively impacted the lives of two individuals.

The story of EXPO leader Jerome Dillard provides a strong example of how formerly incarcerated persons can change over time. His case also illustrates the failure of the war on drugs. Instead of connecting Jerome to treatment in the community for a drug addiction he suffered from, public officials forced him to spend years in federal and state prisons for behavior associated with this addiction. Since being released, Jerome has not only desisted from crime but has become a significant leader in the reentry field. Over the past thirteen years, he has served numerous nonprofit and governmental agencies that provide support to formerly incarcerated individuals ("Statement of Jerome Dillard," 2015). In 2008, Dane County honored Dillard with its Dr. Martin Luther King Jr. Recognition Award. Kathleen Falk, who served as Dane County Executive at that time, said "[s]imilar to Dr. King, Jerome gives people hope and keeps their optimism alive. His pioneering work to help former inmates succeed in the community is critical to those who come across obstacles in the way of their hopes and dreams" ("Madison and Dane County Announce," 2008).

Jerome's time in prison was a formative experience in his life. Dillard says that:

> [W]hile doing time in prison I witnessed a system that was ballooning with predominantly young African-Americans who were serving very long prison sentences, 10, 20, 30 years for drug crimes. This was troubling to me, seeing so many of us as young men losing the prime of their lives to the criminal justice system. It was while doing my time and making these observations that I decided to work hard to never return. ("Statement of Jerome Dillard," 2015)

Dillard's case shows the importance of having social support and of finding meaningful employment during the reentry process. Jerome believes that "peer support directly aided in the success of . . . [his] recovery with regard to mental health and substance abuse." ("Statement of Jerome Dillard," 2015). In response to a question about barriers to successful reentry during his testimony in 2015 in front of the Senate Homeland Security and Governmental Affairs Committee, Dillard said "I too came home facing barriers. The fact is I had support. I had individuals who kept me encouraged. . . . I was fortunate to be able to obtain living wage employment about a year and a half after being out. That was helpful because after 13 years, I finally got a tax return" ("Oversight of the Bureau of Prisons," 2015).

The story of EXPO leader William Harrell, who was raised in the 53206 zip code of Milwaukee, demonstrates the failure of the war on drugs as well. Harrell was one of the many Black men in this community that Wisconsin officials incarcerated because of involvement with drugs. He originally started using drugs and alcohol after separating from his girlfriend while he was in college. Harrell said, "Satan got his grips on me, and he pulled me in" ("William Harrell Testimonial," 2015). William said that he "probably needed some type of cognitive intervention" (Leichenger, 2014). However, instead of connecting him with community-based treatment for his addiction to drugs, the Wisconsin Department of Corrections incarcerated William for several years for crimes driven by his addiction. He overcame his addiction with the help of Project RETURN and through what he calls a "spiritual awakening" (Leichenger, 2014).

After his release from prison, William founded a group called Table of the Saints (TOTS). He explains that TOTS "is a group of brothers who were once incarcerated and upon release continued to fellowship in the Lord. We started fellowshipping in prison, and we continued after we got out" ("William Harrell Testimonial," 2015). TOTS became a 501(c)(3) nonprofit organization in 2014. The mission of Table of the Saints is "to help those who were incarcerated to make a positive transition into community and family life" ("Table of the Saints," 2015). Several women are now members of the group. Harrell said:

> When brothers do get in prison, it's not a coincidence that they find the Lord, because He finds them. He's there waiting for them to come in and repent. And that's what we did. We went in and we repented. And, ever since we've been holding, really, accountability groups and bible studies and we've been going out doing speaking engagements. ("William Harrell Testimonial," 2015).

In addition to his work with TOTS, William has been a key leader of Project RETURN and WISDOM's 11x15 campaign. Harrell, a person who has been served by Project RETURN, has served as a board member for the agency since 2010 ("Project RETURN Summer 2015 Newsletter," 2015). William has helped to lead EXPO's efforts to ban the box. Furthermore, Harrell, who spent many months in solitary confinement while he was incarcerated, has helped to lead efforts to reform solitary confinement practices in Wisconsin (Coursen, 2014).

The story of EXPO leader Charles Hampton, provides further evidence of the harm that the war on drugs has caused to Black men. The Wisconsin DOC imprisoned Hampton for nearly a decade because of a drug offense. Hampton, a founding member of Table of the Saints, has become an important leader in the reentry field since his release in 2010. TOTS gave Charles "a purpose, [and] a desire to help change the community for the better" ("Project RETURN Summer 2015 Newsletter," 2015). Charles joined Project RETURN's board at the same time as William Harrell and still serves as a board member today. Hampton says, "[i]t is a joy to come into the [Project RETURN] office, to see the hope generated by the work of the staff, to see a client begin to see themselves as somebody of worth and talent. That is what I love the most about what we do. I am most proud that I am blessed to be a part of this" ("Project RETURN Summer 2015 Newsletter," 2015). In addition to his work with these organizations, Charles has been a key leader of EXPO's campaign to ban the box (Mikkelson, 2015).

The story of EXPO leader Rodney Evans illustrates how difficult the reentry process can be for people with substance abuse problems. Wisconsin public officials imprisoned Rodney for a nonviolent crime when he was seventeen years old. This experience and his addiction to drugs contributed to behavior that caused Rodney to be periodically incarcerated during the following two decades. Although Evans did not get convicted of new crimes, the Department of Corrections sent him back to prison several times for violating technical conditions of supervision. ("Project RETURN Spring 2015 Newsletter," 2015; "Annie E. Casey Foundation," 2011).

Project RETURN played a central role in helping Rodney turn his life around. The organization helped Evans find a job soon after he reentered the community at the age of thirty-seven. Additionally, Project RETURN provided him with a drug treatment program as well as programs focused on parenting, fatherhood, and relationships. This assistance helped Rodney support his wife and ten children and break his pattern of recidivism ("Project RETURN Spring 2015 Newsletter," 2015; "Annie E. Casey Foundation," 2011). Evans said, *"[b]efore Project RETURN, I was truly on a downward spiral." Without this agency, Rodney believes that he "would be dead or in an institution"* ("Annie E. Casey Foundation," 2011).

Over the last five years, Rodney has been involved in advocacy work. He regularly speaks about his experience with the reentry process at community organizations. In 2010, Evans joined Project RETURN's board, and he has served as Board President since 2013 ("Project RETURN Spring 2015 Newsletter," 2015). In addition, Rodney chairs WISDOM's seventeen-year-olds workgroup which aims to keep seventeen-years-olds out of the adult prison system. Evans has spoken about his experience of being a teenager in the adult prison system at hearings in front of state legislators ("Joint Committee on Finance Public Hearing," 2015). Rodney hopes that Project RETURN will become "a force in the social justice arena in our city" ("Project RETURN Spring 2015 Newsletter," 2015).

EXPO leader Brian Osei, a young Black man who grew up on the north side of Milwaukee, has experienced the racism of Wisconsin's penal system.

One day during the summer of 2008, Milwaukee police officers racially profiled him. *While Brian was driving to a barbershop, he made eye contact with a police officer. Osei said "[a]t that point, I know I was profiled[.] . . . I had a nice care with nice rims on it that I earned legit from working, and some people figure that when you live in a certain area, you can only get something like that illegally"* (Causey, 2014). The officer turned on his siren and followed Brian. He eventually pulled over. Another officer arrived shortly after this and ordered Osei to put his window down. Brian rolled the window down a little, and the officer proceeded to break the window with his baton a few moments later. Osei chose to drive away because he was scared. He said, "I was just trying to get to safety[.] . . . If I got beat up, I wanted somebody to see it" (Causey, 2014). The police eventually caught Osei as he tried to walk into a friend's house. During the arrest, the officers pointed their guns at Brian. He believed that they were going to kill him. While speaking about this incident at a church in Milwaukee, Osei said "to see an individual just hate you and treat you a certain way because of your color man, it is disturbing" (Causey, 2014).

Public officials incarcerated Osei for this incident, and a judge convicted him of a felony that was later reduced to a lesser charge after he completed community service. Brian fought the case for two years. During this period, he experienced employment discrimination. Osei said that *"the hardest thing for him was not being able to provide for his daughter. I had to go out there and cut grass and shovel snow and help people move to try to make an honest dollar because I knew hustling was going to get me in jail and I didn't want to go that route"* (Causey, 2014). After three years of unemployment, one of Osei's friends introduced him to the transitional jobs program. Brian said that he *"thanks God for that"* (Causey, 2014).

During his testimony at the state capitol in December 2014, EXPO leader and Project RETURN case manager Andre Brown spoke about Osei's experience with this program. Brown said, *"Brian took full advantage of the transitional jobs program and has been employed at Project RETURN for three years because of this transitional jobs program"* ("WISDOM 11x15 Blueprint," 2014). Brown added that *"this is something that is working. This is an ally to reentry. Transitional jobs is something that is needed. . . . If you give someone a job, they're not going back to jail"* ("WISDOM 11x15 Blueprint," 2014).

EXPO leader Talib Akbar has used his experience with solitary confinement to help transform policy in Wisconsin. DOC administrators sent Talib to solitary confinement several times during the twenty years he spent in the Wisconsin prison system. At one point, DOC officials forced Akbar to stay in solitary for nearly an entire year. Talib said his time in solitary confinement *"took a toll on his mind"* (Hall, 2015b). Akbar believes his lack of education and a mental illness that he suffers from were underlying problems that contributed to the behavior that resulted in his incarceration ("For the Record," 2015). While he was in prison, Talib drew a picture of a solitary confinement cell that he was in. WISDOM used this picture to create a replica cell that has been displayed at the state capitol and other locations throughout Wisconsin ("For the Record," 2015). This cell, which also includes sound effects similar to what a person would hear, helps people understand what it is like to be in solitary confinement. Akbar regularly speaks about his experience in solitary to help raise public awareness of the potential harm that it can do.

The advocacy and organizing work of Talib and numerous other WISDOM members helped to change solitary confinement policy in Wisconsin. In 2015 the DOC announced that it will be limiting the amount of time individuals can stay in solitary confinement to three months. The DOC previously could force people to stay there for up to 360 days for many common offenses. Cathy Jess, a DOC administrator, said, *"[t]hings change, the pendulum swings with corrections, and depending on the public's opinion and how laws get passed and different things."* (Hall, 2015a). Jess's comment suggests that WISDOM's efforts to change public opinion are having an impact in Wisconsin. However, Wisconsin's new policy still enables corrections officials to engage in what is considered torture by international standards. The United Nations warns that forcing an individual to stay in solitary confinement for more than fifteen days can be considered torture ("United Nations General Assembly," 2011).

EXPO leader Na'Zeeya Bey developed a passion for helping formerly incarcerated people who experience homelessness because of her own experience with homelessness and incarceration. Na'Zeeya shared her story during testimony at the state capitol on December 10, 2014. She spoke briefly about her struggle with mental illness and being detained for revocations, but she focused mostly on housing. Na'Zeeya said:

> Unfortunately, fortunately I haven't experienced Wisconsin's jails, laws, and stuff, but I'm learning. But I went through the state of Iowa's system. And the state of Iowa is kind of the same. You know, they let you out in the middle of the night with no money. You're walking on a cornfield country road with nowhere to go. So what do you do? You sleep outside. . . . So my thing is this, housing is needed everywhere, but I think it's desperately needed in the state of Wisconsin and the city of Madison. I travel on the bus through the city of Madison and I see all kind of homeless people. I've talked to some. Some are out of jail . . . some just getting out of prison. . . . You know, I lived in the streets of Chicago in Lower Wacker Drive, me and my children. You know, so being homeless is not a good thing. But here in Madison, I'm here to make a change in Madison for the homeless people. I'm going to see what I can do. You know, if I have to go out every day, and fill my purse up like I used to do every Wednesday and feed them I will because that's my passion about formerly incarcerated people living out on the streets of Madison when Madison

and the state of Wisconsin know they could do something. The money that they going to go over there and build that jail with, they need to give it to Na'Zeeya Bey so she can take it and build something for these homeless people. ("WISDOM 11x15 Blueprint," 2014)

The story of EXPO leader Rachel Shramek, who also represents WISDOM's chapter in Eau Claire, illustrates some of the reentry challenges facing people with substance abuse problems. Her experiences demonstrate the potential of Wisconsin's Treatment Alternatives and Diversion (TAD) program as well. Rachel has publicly shared her story.

Rachel said that she was *"born into a house with a lot of dysfunction and mental health problems"* ("WISDOM 11x15 Blueprint," 2014). She adds that, "I didn't really have parents growing up [.] . . . You know, I had parents, but they weren't mentally there and sometimes physically not there. I had been in and out of juvi as a child. It started with truancy. I got pregnant at 15, married at 16." ("Prison Alternatives Boosted," 2015). Rachel said:

> I became extremely addicted to drugs. At first, it was just pills. Then came opiates, then methadone. Eventually I was iving meth. The first day I did meth, I lost my son, and that was the most traumatic thing in my life. He was my everything and it was really traumatic for him. We were completely separat-ed[.] . . . I hated myself from that point. I was completely on the streets from there. I got 13 charges in 2013. I almost lost my whole life, but once I got to the point where I was sitting in that jail cell, and I had the opportunity to join my drug court, AIM court, my life was changed. I believe that God was with me through the entire process, and I believe that he is here now just walking into the buildings. Like I'm just in awe what has changed in the past year. I am a taxpayer[.] . . . I go to church really religiously. I'm a mom again. I have my son. ("WISDOM 11x15 Blueprint," 2014)

The drug court has helped Rachel overcome her addiction to drugs. Rachel explains the impact that the drug court has had on her life. She says,

> "[I]t's almost like a miracle. It's almost like you're a whole person, not like this jaded, angry drug-addicted person that is very unstable. You're a mother. You're a normal person." She adds that "when it works you save a life, and when you save one life, the ripple effect of that is saving my son's life" ("Prison Alternatives Boosted," 2015).

My own experience demonstrates some of the common reentry challenges facing people who suffer from mental illnesses. My case also illustrates some of the flaws of Wisconsin's penal system. I have suffered from paranoid schizophrenia since I was a teenager. I have committed several crimes that were associated with this disabling mental condition. I went to prison for the first time after I got convicted of armed burglary in 1999. The judge sentenced me to thirty months in prison and twelve years of probation. I was only nineteen-years-old at the time. The judge sentenced me shortly before Wisconsin began to implement truth-in-sentencing so I was eligible for parole after I served 25 percent of my sentence. I went in front of the parole board a couple of times. Although I had a nearly perfect record of behavior and participated in all of the programs I was required to, the parole board denied my early release both times. Many other individuals had similar experiences. It seemed as though Wisconsin was already beginning to treat people who were sentenced under the old law like they had been sentenced under truth-in-sentencing. Under the old law, people became eligible for parole after serving 25 percent of their sentences. Truth-in-sentencing abolished parole and forced people to serve their entire sentences as well as periods of extended supervision in the community. The Wisconsin Department of Corrections forced me to stay in prison until my mandatory release date. I served twenty months of the thirty-month sentence. I spent most of the time at Racine Youthful Offender Correctional (RYOC) Facility, and I spent the last month at Fox Lake Correctional Institution.

The DOC released me in July of 2000. Fortunately for me, my mother agreed to let me stay with her at her house in Madison so I did not have to worry about finding housing. However, I struggled to find employment. My probation officer let me know that I had to either get a job or attend school after I got released. I was not yet considered to be disabled at the time because I had never applied for Supplemental Security Income (SSI). Shortly after my release, I applied for the program and began to receive SSI, Food-Share benefits, and Medicaid. I applied for many jobs in the first few months after I got out, but I did not receive any offers. Nearly all of the employers required me to check the box which inquires about conviction and arrest history. I did not get interviewed for any of the jobs that required me to check the box. I have had opportunities to work since being released, but none of the employers who hired me asked about conviction and arrest history on the initial application.

I could not find a job when I first got out so the only option I had to avoid violating my probation was to enroll in college. I enrolled in the liberal studies program at Madison Area Technical College (MATC). I did well enough in the courses at MATC to get admitted to the University of Wisconsin–Madison. I completed courses at UW-Madison for a couple of years, and then I decided to transfer to Upper Iowa University (UIU) in Madison for my last year. Although I either attended part-time or dropped out at times when my mental health deteriorated, I eventually graduated with a BS in human services in 2006. For my senior project at UIU, I created a strategy for reducing overcrowding in the Dane County Jail. I became interested in this topic because just seven years earlier, I had slept on the floor in the jail for several weeks because of overcrowding. The support that I received from my family and the educational opportunities I received during the first six years after my release helped me to avoid returning to prison.

In 2003, I decided to move to a public housing building on S. Park St. in Madison. I became eligible to move into public housing after my disability determination. Low-income older people and poor individuals who suffered from disabling mental or physical conditions resided in the building. Several low-income single mothers lived in adjacent buildings. During the three years that I resided in this area, I got to know many residents and became familiar with challenges that marginalized groups in cities often face.

After I graduated in 2006, I chose to move to Milwaukee and enroll in the master's program in urban studies at the University of Wisconsin–Milwaukee (UWM). During the three years I resided in public housing and during my undergraduate coursework, I developed an interest in public housing, urban policy, and urban poverty. I had opportunities to learn more about these topics during my time in the urban studies program. I graduated in 2009, but before that I had another experience with Wisconsin's penal system.

One day shortly before the start of my second year of graduate school, a couple of Milwaukee police officers arrested me for disorderly conduct while I was experiencing symptoms of my mental illness. I was still on probation for the crime I committed eight years earlier so the police officers took me to jail. I went to court three days later. The prosecutor, the public defender, and the judge all agreed that my behavior did not fit with the definition of disorderly conduct. The judge dismissed the case, but my probation officer did not let me go home. My probation officer, who had no training in mental health issues, moved forward with the revocation process. My former probation officer, a mental health specialist in Madison, did not agree with the decision of my probation officer in Milwaukee. He believed that an alternative to revocation program would have been a better option. My probation officer forced me to stay in the Milwaukee Secure Detention Facility (MSDF) for nearly six months while I fought the revocation. Eventually, a Milwaukee administrative law judge revoked my probation. After spending a few more weeks in a county jail, I went to court again. I faced a maximum of twelve years in prison, but fortunately for me, the sentencing judge decided to let me go home.

This incident demonstrates the need for reform in a couple of important areas. All people with mental illnesses should be assigned only to probation officers who have completed specialized training in how to work with this population. Furthermore, individuals on probation, parole, or extended supervision should not be incarcerated while awaiting revocation decisions on rule violations that do not involve new crimes.

I spent all of my time at MSDF in its special needs unit. All of the people in this unit suffer from disabling mental or physical conditions. During my time there, I met hundreds of people who came and left while I fought my revocation. I only met one other individual who challenged a revocation decision in the nearly six months I stayed in the institution. The agents of some of the people who were there because of minor rule violations put them in alternative to revocation programs, but almost all of the people who faced revocation chose to not challenge their agents. However, when I told people in the facility about my case, nearly all of them agreed that I should not have been incarcerated after the judge dismissed my case.

The probation officer of a person I shared a cell with decided to revoke his probation because he drank alcohol and missed an appointment with a treatment provider. He faced three years in prison, but he did not challenge the revocation decision. When he went to court, he told the judge to give him the full three years in prison. The judge proceeded with the revocation and sentenced him to three years in prison. He thought that he would be better off doing three years in prison than continuing to be under the supervision of the DOC in the community. He believed that his probation officer would eventually revoke him anyway. He knew that he would not be given credit for any time served on probation. He chose to be revocated largely because he would then no longer be under the supervision of the DOC after he got released from prison.

Although nearly all of the individuals I met had not been charged with new felony crimes, many of them chose to revoke themselves so they could get out of MSDF as soon as possible. The living conditions in this facility are much worse than in most other state prisons in Wisconsin. One person I met in MSDF had previously done time at the Supermax Prison in Boscobel. He believed that MSDF was worse than the Supermax Prison. The inhumane conditions in MSDF often exacerbate the mental illnesses of people who stay there. During my stay in the institution, one person attempted to commit suicide, corrections officers had to put several other individuals under suicide watch, and a few people severely mutilated themselves. In addition, I witnessed a few fights in the facility.

People who are detained at MSDF have few opportunities to participate in rehabilitation programs and little freedom. Individuals who stay in the facility's special needs unit are locked in a cell that they share with one other person nearly all day. They only get out each day for three short dayroom periods. The entire special needs unit is in one small room on one floor. People only get to leave this room for court or medical emergencies. They never get to go outside, and they cannot see outside. MSDF provides few recreational opportunities to people. The recreation room is a small room that only has a ping pong table, one pull-up bar, and two cardio machines. Individuals occasionally get out for religious services in the recreation room. People detained in the special needs unit are not allowed to have headphones so they cannot relax by listening to music. The institution provides few reading materials, but people can get books sent in from the outside. MSDF offers inadequate services for individuals with mental illnesses. The special needs unit has a social worker, a psychiatrist, and a psychologist who infrequently meet with people. Individuals in this unit do not get any face-to-face visits with friends or family members. Many people serving time in MSDF do not fight their revocations because they want to quickly get to a prison where they will have more freedom, more recreational opportunities, and more opportunities to participate in rehabilitation and educational programs.

I have been able to stay in the community since 2007. During this time, I earned two master's degrees and worked for several nonprofit organizations. My case demonstrates the potential of rehabilitation programs. Several psychologists, psychiatrists, and counselors helped me to reach the level of functioning that I am at today.

I am currently a PhD candidate at the University of Wisconsin–Milwaukee. My research interest areas include penal policy, mass incarceration, social movements, community organizing, African American history, and prisoner reintegration. My experience in the Wisconsin state prison system played a central role in my decision to specialize in penal policy. During the time I spent in Racine Youthful Offender Correctional Facility, Fox Lake, and the Milwaukee Secure Detention Facility, I learned about several flaws in the penal system of Wisconsin. At MSDF, I met hundreds of people who got sent to prison for technical violations that did not involve new crimes. Unjust revocation policies are just one of many inadequacies in the state's carceral system.

My experience in the prison system of Wisconsin as well as my experience with the reentry process inspired me to become involved with WISDOM's 11x15 campaign, EXPO, and Project RETURN. My activities in recent years include serving as a member of MICAH's 11x15 campaign task force (Milwaukee Inner-City Congregations Allied for Hope is the Milwaukee chapter of WISDOM), chairing WISDOM's statewide revocations workgroup, serving as a board member of Project RETURN, and helping to lead EXPO. My participation in these groups has helped me develop a more prosocial identity and a purpose for my life. I believe that my work with these organizations played a central role in helping me desist from serious crime.

CONCLUSION

This chapter demonstrates that formerly incarcerated people can succeed if society gives them certain types of support when they reenter communities. People with records are often denied the types of support they need because of the assumption that they will continue to commit more crimes. However, consistent with previous research, the stories of EXPO leaders show that obtaining employment, housing, educational opportunities, drug treatment, mental health treatment, peer support, and family support can help previously imprisoned people desist from crime. These stories along with the aggregate data I provide illustrate the importance of providing support to people returning from incarceration. Moreover, the leadership opportunities that organizations like WISDOM, Project RETURN, and EXPO have provided to these individuals appear to have helped them turn their lives around. This provides support for LeBel's (2009) finding that participation in advocacy work can help formerly incarcerated persons desist from crime.

The organizing efforts that I examined in this chapter provide further evidence that a nationwide decarceration movement has emerged. Toney (2007) argued that a reentry movement led by previously imprisoned people had begun to emerge nearly a decade ago, but he did not examine any states in the Midwest. The efforts of WISDOM and EXPO show that a movement to end mass incarceration and structural discrimination against people with past convictions has also begun to emerge in Wisconsin.

The stories of EXPO leaders illustrate the importance of ending structural discrimination against formerly incarcerated persons. Maintaining this new system of exclusion, which Michelle Alexander calls the "New Jim Crow," will only weaken communities in Wisconsin. Previously imprisoned people who do not obtain employment, housing, educational opportunities, drug treatment, and mental health treatment are more likely to return to prison for new crimes. This system of exclusion can lead to increased levels of serious crime and increased spending on corrections. It can also increase poverty and weaken local economies. Dismantling structural discrimination against people with records will make communities safer, strengthen families, reduce child poverty, and strengthen local economies. The impact of ending this discrimination would be the greatest in communities most disproportionately affected by mass incarceration like Milwaukee's 53206 zip code.

The organizing efforts of EXPO members demonstrate that people who are the most directly impacted by problems can play central roles in changing unjust systems that cause these problems. EXPO leaders have helped to change conversations around penal policy in Wisconsin. Just months before WISDOM launched its 11x15 campaign, a group of Republican legislators led by State Senator Alberta Darling introduced State Senate Bill 207. This bill would have enabled employers to legally discriminate against people who have been convicted of felonies. Two years later, however, Alberta Darling and many other Republicans supported a bill which expanded funding for Wisconsin's transitional jobs program. This program provides opportunities for individuals with past convictions as well as others who have barriers to employment. Wisconsin legislators are now beginning to consider a wide range of other penal policy reforms.

My review of the literature on what works in helping formerly incarcerated people succeed as well as the stories of EXPO leaders suggest that the enactment and implementation of several new policies can help to make Wisconsin communities safer, strengthen families, and save taxpayers money that can be reinvested in other needed services. EXPO leaders have already had an impact on several policies in Wisconsin, but much greater changes are needed.

The cases of Jerome Dillard, William Harrell, and Charles Hampton provide examples of the harm that the war on drug has caused to Black men in Wisconsin. Jerome, William, and Charles spent many years of their lives in prison for nonviolent drug crimes. Numerous studies show that drug treatment programs can reduce recidivism and drug use. Wisconsin now imprisons Black men at a higher rate than any other state partly because judges send them to prison for drug crimes at a disproportionately high rate. Wisconsin public officials must do more in the future to end racial disparities in sentencing. In addition, they should increase funding for alternative to incarceration programs for those who suffer from addiction and end racial disparities in access to these programs.

Rachel Shramek's story demonstrates the potential of Wisconsin's TAD program. TAD funding enabled Rachel to participate in a drug court that has helped to turn her life around. The drug court helped Rachel overcome her drug addiction and desist from crime. Evaluations of the TAD program suggest that it reduces recidivism, reduces imprisonment, and saves taxpayers money. Right now, Wisconsin spends just $4 million dollars per year on TAD. One study found that increasing this amount to $75 million dollars per year would prevent more than 24,000 people from going to jail and prison each year ("Human Impact Partners," 2012). Wisconsin policymakers should increase funding for TAD.

My case and other cases of EXPO leaders illustrate the need for Wisconsin to reform its unjust revocation policies. No formerly incarcerated person should be sent back to prison for violating a rule of supervision that does not involve a new crime. Crimeless revocations play a central role in maintaining mass incarceration and racial disparities in imprisonment in Wisconsin ("Wisconsin Department of Corrections," 2015). Incarcerating individuals for rule violations that do not involve new crimes destroys lives, contributes to overcrowding in jails, and adds nothing to public safety.

Brian Osei's case shows the potential of Wisconsin's transitional jobs program. This program enabled Brian to obtain a full-time job which has allowed him to support his family. Although not all people who participate in the program will go on to find permanent, full-time jobs, evaluations suggest that it can increase the likelihood that people with past convictions will obtain employment and stay out of prison (Buck, 2000; Finn, 1998; Redcross et al. 2009; Rossman and Roman, 2003). One study in New York found that individuals who participated in a transitional jobs program returned to prison at a lower rate than a similar group who did not participate in the program (Redcross et al., 2009).

Although Wisconsin recently took a step in the right direction with its new solitary confinement policy, this policy still enables DOC administrators to engage in what is considered to be torture by international standards. EXPO leaders William Harell and Talib Akbar regularly share stories about the devastating impact solitary confinement can have on individuals. Both of them speak about the psychological toll that time spent in isolation took on them. Wisconsin should follow the lead of the international community and limit the amount of time someone can spend in solitary confinement to no more than fifteen consecutive days.

Rodney Evan's case provides an example of why Wisconsin should take seventeen-year-olds out of the adult system. Wisconsin officials sent Rodney to the adult prison system when he was seventeen and this contributed to his pattern of recidivism over the next two decades. Research demonstrates that Rodney's case is not uncommon. Youth who spend time in adult prison systems are more likely to recidivate than juveniles who get sent to the youth system ("Centers for Disease Control and Prevention," 2007). No teenager should be detained in an adult prison.

The educational opportunities I received played an important role in helping me succeed after my release from prison. The education I obtained has opened up opportunities for me that I would otherwise would not have been qualified to pursue. Numerous studies suggest that people who complete college programs in prisons recidivate at lower rates. Federal policymakers should restore Pell grant eligibility for all people who are incarcerated in state prisons.

Wisconsin should ban the box for private and public employers throughout the state. My own experience and the experiences of other EXPO members show that the box on job applications where employers inquire about an applicant's conviction and arrest history is a significant barrier to employment for people with records. Numerous studies demonstrate that previously imprisoned individuals who obtain employment return to prison for new crimes at lower rates, but less than 40 percent of formerly incarcerated people are employed one year after release. Many employers are reluctant to hire people with records, and most employers still include the box on the initial application. Pager (2007) completed a study which suggests that employers tend to call back applicants with past convictions at much lower rates, particularly if they are Black. Reducing employment obstacles for formerly incarcerated people can make communities safer, strengthen families, decrease child poverty and strengthen local economies. Evaluations of ban the box policies in places such as Durham, North Carolina, and Minneapolis show that these initiatives can help previously imprisoned individuals obtain employment. Furthermore, none of the people with records hired in Durham have engaged in illegal conduct at workplaces (Atkinson and Lockwood, n.d; "City of Minneapolis," 2009).

Wisconsin could safely cut its prison population in half by

- fully funding TAD,
- ending the practice of imprisoning people for crimeless rule violations,
- giving people a fair chance to be released on parole, and
- reducing recidivism for new crimes by banning the box, increasing funding for transitional jobs, and enacting other policies that reduce structural discrimination against previously imprisoned people.

If Wisconsin implemented these policies, it would be able to close down several prisons and save billions of dollars over time. The money saved could be reinvested in programs to help formerly incarcerated people find jobs and housing as well other needed services like public education, public transportation, and health care. Sentencing reforms would enable Wisconsin to reduce its prison population even more.

This chapter raises several questions for future research. More research is needed to determine how the 11x15 campaign emerged and evolved, the strengths and weaknesses of the organizing approach used during the campaign, and how social movement theories and research on organizing relate to the campaign. In addition, further research can help us gain a greater understanding of how and why EXPO members became involved with organizing, the roles they played in the 11x15 campaign, and how participation in the campaign affected their lives.

Few studies examine organizing efforts led by formerly incarcerated persons and how these efforts can help people with records turn their lives around. Individuals with past convictions are helping to lead a decarceration reform movement that is emerging and evolving in various ways in different locations. Further research is needed to help us gain a greater understanding of the evolution of this movement, the leaders of this movement, and how and why people with records became involved in the movement.

REFERENCES

Abrahamson, S. (2012, May 26). Wisconsin court system taking smarter approach to mental health issues. Retrieved from http://host.madison.com/news/opinion/column/shirley-s-abrahamson-wisconsin-court-system-taking-smarter-approach-to/article_4f8c84b2-e074-5e61-996c-95d9dac6083c.html.

Alexander, M. (2012). *The New Jim Crow: Mass Incarceration in the Age of Colorblindness*. New York: The New Press.

Almquist, L. & Dodd, E. (2009). *Mental Health Courts: A Guide to Research-Informed Policy and Practice*. Council of State Governments Justice Center.

Atkinson, D. V., & Lockwood, K. (n.d.). *The Benefits of Ban the Box: A Case Study of Durham, NC*. The Southern Coalition for Social Justice.

Annie E. Casey Foundation. (2011). Giving Former Prisoners Positive Returns. Retrieved from http://www.aecf.org/blog/giving-former-prisoners-positive-returns/.

Austin, J., & Irwin, J. (2000). *It's about Time: America's Imprisonment Binge, 3rd ed*. Belmont, CA: Wadsworth.

Bureau of Justice Statistics. (1990). Table 6.56 Rate (per 100,000 resident population) of sentenced prisoners in State and Federal Institutions on Dec. 31. By region and jurisdiction, 1971–89. *Sourcebook of Criminal Justice Statistics*.

Bureau of Justice Statistics. (2003). Table 6.29 Rate (per 100,000 resident population) of sentenced prisoners under jurisdiction of State and Federal correctional authorities on December 31. By region and jurisdiction, 1980, 1984–2003. *Sourcebook of Criminal Justice Statistics*.

Carson, E. A. (2014). Prisoners in 2014. Washington, DC: U.S. Department of Justice, Bureau of Justice Statistics.

Carson, E. A., & Golinelli, D. (2014). *Prisoners in 2012: Trends in Admissions and Releases, 1991–2012*. Washington, DC: U.S. Department of Justice, Bureau of Justice Statistics.

Caton, C. L. M., Dominguez, B., Schanzer, B., Hasin, D. S., Shrout, P. E., Felix, A., . . . Hsu, E. (2005). Risk factors for long-term homelessness: Findings from a longitudinal study of first-time homeless single adults. *American Journal of Public Health*, 95(10), 1753–1759.

Causey, J. (2014, May 13). The fear of driving while black. *Milwaukee Journal Sentinel*.

Centers for Disease Control and Prevention. (2007). Effects on Violence of Laws and Policies Facilitating the Transfer of Youth from the Juvenile to the Adult Justice System. Retrieved from http://www.cdc.gov/mmwr/preview/mmwrhtml/rr5609a1.htm.

Chattanooga, W.W. (2015, July 20). The moral failures of America's prison-industrial complex. *The Economist*.

City of Minneapolis. (2009). Retrieved from http://www.nelp.org/content/uploads/Glidden-Ltr-Minneapolis2004-2008.pdf?nocdn=1.

Civil Consequences of Conviction: The Impact of Criminal Records under Wisconsin Law (2012). Wisconsin State Public Defender.

Cleggett, C. C. (2008). NAACP Activist Helps Former Felons Re-gain Their Voting Rights and Dignity. *The Crisis*, 50–51.

Coursen, T. W. (2014). Reform Now: Solitary Confinement. Retrieved from https://vimeo.com/112913100.

Cuellar, A. E., Snowden, L. M., & Ewing, T. (2007). Criminal records of persons served in the public mental health system. *Psychiatric Services*, 58(1), 114–120.

Doedge, D. (2007, September 26). Drug sentences worse for blacks. *Milwaukee Journal Sentinel*.

Doing What Works to Keep Our Communities Safe. (n.d.). Minnesota's Community Corrections Act Counties.

Draine, J., Salzer, M., Culhane, D.P., & Hadley, T.R. (2002). Role of social disadvantage in crime, joblessness, and homelessness among persons with a serious mental illness. *Psychiatric Services*, 53(5), 565–573.

Durose, M. R., Cooper, A. D., & Snyder, H. N. *Recidivism of Prisoners Released in 30 States in 2005: Patterns from 2005 to 2010*. U.S. Department of Justice. Office of Justice Programs. Bureau of Justice Statistics.

Ex-Prisoners Organizing. (2015). Retrieved from https://www.facebook.com/expowisconsin.

Fishman, N. (2014). The Unvarnished Truth: 2014 Top Trends in Employment Background Checks. EmployeeScreenIQ.

For the Record: Reforming the criminal justice system. (2014). Retrieved from http://www.channel3000.com/news/opinion/For-the-Record-Reforming-the-criminal-justice-system/31867954.

Garland, D. (2001). *The Culture of Control: Crime and Social Order in Contemporary Society*. Chicago: University of Chicago Press.

Gerber, J., & Fritsch, E. J. (1993). *Prison Education and Offender Behavior: A Review of the Scientific Literature*. Texas Department of Criminal Justice: Institutional Division.

Gonnerman, J. (2004). *Life on the Outside: The Prison Odyssey of Elaine Bartlett*. New York: Farrar, Straus, & Giroux.

Hairston, C. F. (2003). Prisoners and Their Families: Parenting Issues During Incarceration. In J. Travis & M. Waul (Eds.), *Prisoners Once Removed: The Impact of Incarceration and Reentry on Children, Families, and Communities* (pp. 259–282). Washington, DC. The Urban Institute Press.

Hairston, C. F. (1988). Family Ties During Imprisonment: Do They Influence Future Criminal Activity?. *Federal Probation*, 52(1), 48–52.

Hall, D. (2015a, August 23). Wisconsin joins national push to curb solitary confinement. Retrieved from http://host.madison.com/news/local/crime-and-courts/wisconsin-joins-national-push-to-curb-solitary-confinement/article_0e64f216-46a7-11e5-a90c-230249690945.html.

Hall, D. (2015b, August 23). Making friends with a fly: One man's story of solitary confinement. *WisconsniWatch*. Retrieved from http://wisconsinwatch.org/2015/08/making-friends-with-a-fly-one-mans-story-of-solitary-confinement/.

Halsted, G. (2015, April 23). New State Parole Chief Faces Pressure From Justice Reform Advocates. *Wisconsin Public Radio*. Retrieved from http://www.wpr.org/new-state-parole-chief-faces-pressure-justice-reform-advocates.

Helping Men and Women Leaving Prison Make a Positive and Permanent Return to Milwaukee. (2015. OdysseyNetworks. Retrieved from https://www.youtube.com/watch?v=PFwVXfQcnmU.

Holzer, H.J., Raphael, S., & Stoll, M.A. (2004). How willing are employers to hire ex-offenders?.*Focus*, 23(2), 40-43.

Human Impact Partners. (2012). Healthier Lives, Stronger Families, Safer Communities: How Increasing Funding for Alternatives to Prison Will Save Lives and Money in Wisconsin.

Inciardi, J. A., Martin, S. S., & Butzin, C. A. (2004). Five Year Outcomes of Therapeutic Community Treatment of Drug-involved Offenders after Release from Prison. *Crime & Delinquency*, 50(1), 88–107.

James, D. J., & Glaze, L. E. (2006). *Special Report: Mental health problems of prison and jail inmates*. Washington, DC: U.S. Department of Justice.

JLUSA. (2015). About Us. Retrieved from https://www.justleadershipusa.org/about-us/.

Joint Committee on Finance Public Hearing. (2015, March 20). Retrieved from http://www.wiseye.org/Programming/VideoArchive/EventDetail.aspx?evhdid=9655.

Kelley, S. (2010, August 18). Mental Health Court keeping people out of jail, saving money. Retrieved from http://www.wqow.com/story/13004927/mental-health-court-keeping-people-out-of-jail-saving-money.

Kim, K., Becker-Cohen, M., & Serakos, M. (2015). *The Processing and Treatment of Mentally Ill Persons in the Criminal Justice System*. Washington, DC: The Urban Institute.

Langan, P.A., & Levin, D.J. (2002). *Recidivism of Prisoners Released in 1994*. Washington, DC: U.S. Department of Justice, Bureau of Justice Statistics.

Langemo, L. (2012). Community group hopes to slash number of state prison inmates. Retrieved from http://fox6now.com/2012/02/20/community-group-hopes-to-slash-number-of-state-prison-inmates/.

LaVigne, N. G., Shollenberger, T. L., & Debus, S. A. (2009). *One Year Out: Tracking the Experiences of Male Prisoners Returning to Houston, Texas*. Washington, DC: The Urban Institute.

LaVigne, N. G., Brooks, L. E., & Shollenberger, T. L. (2007). *Returning Home: Exploring the Challenges and Successes of Recently Released Texas Prisoners*. Washington, DC: The Urban Institute.

LaVigne, N. G., Visher, C., & Castro, J. (2004). *Chicago Prisoners' Experiences Returning Home*. Washington, DC: The Urban Institute.

LeBel, T. P. (2012). Invisible Stripes? Formerly Incarcerated Persons' Perceptions of Stigma. *Deviant Behavior*, 33, 89–107.

LeBel, T. P. (2009). Formerly incarcerated persons' use of advocacy/activism as a coping orientation in the reintegration process. In B. Veysey, J. Christian, & D.J. Martinez (Eds.), *How Offenders Transform Their Lives* (pp. 165–187). Portland: Willan Publishing.

Leichenger, A. (2014, March 20). How One Milwaukee Zip Code Explains America's Mass Incarceration Problem. *ThinkProgress*. Retrieved from http://thinkprogress.org/justice/2014/03/20/3401141/how-one-milwaukee-zip-code-explains-americas-mass-incarceration-problem/

Love, M.C., Roberts, J., & Klingele, C. (2013). *Collateral Consequences of Criminal Convictions: Law, Policy, and Practice*. Danvers, MA: Thomson Reuters.

Madison and Dane County Announce Annual Martin Luther King, Jr. Awards. (2008). Retrieved from http://www.cityofmadison.com/news/madison-and-dane-county-announce-annual-martin-luther-king-jr-awards-0

Maruna, S. (2001). *Making Good: How Ex-Convicts Reform And Rebuild Their Lives*. Washington, DC: American Psychological Association.

Mayer, G. (2015). *WISDOM Commissions EXPO Ex-Prisoners Organizers*. The Gamaliel Foundation. Retrieved from http://www.gamaliel.org/News/IntheNews/tabid/244/PostID/428/WISDOM-Commissions-EXPO-Ex-Prisoners-Organizers.aspx

Mayer, G. (2014). *WISDOM Wins Another $1.5 Million for Treatment Alternatives*. The Gamaliel Foundation.

Metraux, S., & Culhane, D. P. (2004). Homeless Shelter Use and Reincarceration Following Prison Release: Assessing the Risk. *Criminology and Public Policy*, 3, 201–222.

Mikkelson, M. (2015). Milwaukee Group Part of National Campaign to Ban the Box. *Milwaukee Public Radio*. http://wuwm.com/post/milwaukee-group-part-national-campaign-ban-box#stream/0.

Mitchell, M., & Leachman, M. (2014). *Changing Priorities: State Criminal Justice Reforms and Investments in Education*. Washington, DC: Center on Budget and Policy Priorities.

MOSES. (2015). Expanding our Voices, Expanding our Strength, 2014–2015.

NAMI Wisconsin. (2013). Mental Health Courts in Wisconsin. Retrieved from http://www.namiwisconsin.org/nami-wisconsin-on-the-issues-blog/2013/08/05/175.

National Center on Addiction and Substance Abuse. (2010). Behind Bars II: Substance Abuse and America's Prison Population.

Nelson, M., Deess, P., & Allen, C. (1999). *The First Month Out: Post-incarceration Experiences in New York City*. New York: Vera Institute of Justice.

Office of Justice Assistance. (2008). Racial Disparity Oversight Commission Report to the Governor.

Osher, F., D'Amora, D. A., Plotkin, M., Jarrett, N., & Eggleston, A. (2012). *Adults with Behavioral Health Needs under Correctional Supervision: A Shared Framework for Reducing Recidivism and Promoting Recovery*. Council of State Governments Justice Center.

Osher, F., Steadman, H. J., & Barr, H. (2003). A best practice approach to community reentry from jails for inmates with co-occurring disorders. The APIC model. *Crime & Delinquency*. 49(1), 79–96.

Oversight of the Bureau of Prisons: First-Hand Accounts of Challenges Facing the Federal Prison System. (2015). U.S. Senate Committee on Homeland Security & Governmental Affairs.

Owens, M. L. (2014). Ex-Felons' Organization-Based Political Work for Carceral Reforms. *The Annals of the American Academy of Political and Social Science*, 51, 256-265.

Pager, D. (2007). *Marked: Race, Crime, and Finding Work in an Era of Mass Incarceration*. Chicago: The University of Chicago Press.

Pawasarat, J., & Quinn, L.M. (2013). Wisconsin's Mass Incarceration of African American Males: Workforce Challenges for 2013. Employment and Training Institute, University of Wisconsin-Milwaukee. Retrieved from

Petersilia, J. (2003). *When Prisoners Come Home: Parole and Prisoner Reentry*. New York: Oxford University Press.

Prendergast, M. L., Hall, E. A., Wexler, H. K., Melnick, G., & Cao, Y. (2004). Amity Prison-based Therapeutic Community: 5-Year Outcomes. *The Prison Journal*, 84(1), 36–60.

Prison Alternatives Boosted by Health Impact Assessment. (2015). Retrieved from http://www.pewtrusts.org/en/multimedia/video/2015/prison-alternatives-boosted-by-health-impact-assessment.

Public Policy Institute. (2015). Milwaukee Transitional Jobs Project. Retrieved from http://ppi. communityadvocates.net/policy_projects/milwaukee_transitional_jobs_project/.

Quinn, L. M. (2007). New Indicators of Neighborhood Need in Zipcode 53206. Employment and Training Institute, University of Wisconsin-Milwaukee. Retrieved from

Project RETURN. (2015). Retrieved from http://www.projectreturnmilwaukee.org/.

Project RETURN Summer 2015 Newsletter. (2015). Retrieved from http://www. projectreturnmilwaukee.org/project_return_pg3_2014.html.

Project RETURN Spring 2015 Newsletter. (2015). Retrieved from http://www. projectreturnmilwaukee.org/project_return_pg3_2014.html.

RAND Corporation. (2014). How Effective Is Correctional Education, and Where Do We Go from Here?: The Results of a Comprehensive Evaluation.

Richards, S. C. (2013). The new school of convict criminology thrives and matures. *Critical Criminology: An International Journal*, 21(1), 257–271.

ROC Wisconsin. (2015a). About. Retrieved from http://www.rocwisconsin.org/about/.

ROC Wisconsin (2015b). EXPO (Ex-Prisoners Organizing). Retrieved from http://www. rocwisconsin.org/our-work/expo/.

Rodriguez, M. N., & Mehta, N. (2015). Ban The Box: U.S. Cities, Counties, and States Adopt Fair Hiring Policies. National Employment Law Center. Retrieved from http://www.nelp. org/publication/ban-the-box-fair-chance-hiring-state-and-local-guide/.

Rodriguez, M. N., & Emsellem, M. (2011). *65 Million "Need Not Apply": The Case for Reforming Criminal Background Checks for Employment*. The National Employment Law Project.

Roman, G. G., & Travis, J. (2004). *Taking Stock: Housing, Homelessness, and Prisoner Reentry*. Washington, DC: The Urban Institute.

Ross, J. I., & Richards, S.C. (2003). *Convict Criminology*. Belmont, CA: Wadsworth Publishing.

Rossman, S. B., & Roman, C. G. (2003). Case Managed Reentry and Employment: Lessons from the Opportunity to Succeed Program. *Justice Research and Policy* 5(2), 75–100.

Schwartzapfel, B. (2015, July 30). Obama Is Reinstating Pell Grants for Prisoners. *The Marshall Project*.

Seiter, R. P., & Kadela, K. R. (2003). Prisoner Reentry: What Works, What Does Not, and What is Promising. *Crime & Delinquency*, 49(3), 360–388.

Solomon, P., & Draine, J. (1995). Issues in serving the forensic client. *Social Work*. 40(1), 25–33.

State of Wisconsin Department of Corrections. (2015). Inmate Profile 2014.

Statement of Jerome Dillard. (2015). *Oversight of the Bureau of Prisons: First Hand Accounts of Challenges Facing the Federal Prison System*. U.S. Senate Committee on Homeland Security & Governmental Affairs.

Steurer, S. J., Smith, L. & Tracy, A. (2001). *Three State Recidivism Study*. The Correctional Education Association.

Sullivan, E., Mino, M., Nelson, K., & Pope, J. (2002). *Families as a Resource in Recovery from Drug Abuse: An Evaluation of La Bodega de la Familia*. Vera Institute of Justice Research Report. New York: Vera Institute of Justice.

Table of the Saints. (2015). Retrieved from http://www.tableofthesaints.org/.

Thacher, D. (2008). The Rise of Criminal Background Screening in Rental Housing. *Law & Social Inquiry*. 33, 5–30.

The Coalition for Public Safety. (2015). About The Coalition. Retrieved from http://www. coalitionforpublicsafety.org/about/.

The Cost of Corrections: Wisconsin and Minnesota. (2010). *The Wisconsin Taxpayer*.

The Sentencing Project. (2014). Unlocking Justice: Organizing to Address Mass Incarceration. Retrieved from http://www.sentencingproject.org/doc/ Organizing%20to%20Address%20Mass%20Incarceration%20-%20Slides%20FINAL.pdf.

The White House Office of the Press Secretary. (2015). FACT SHEET: President Obama Announces New Actions to Promote Rehabilitation and Reintegration for the Formerly-Incarcerated.

Thompson, A. C. (2008). *Releasing Prisoners, Redeeming Communities: Reentry, Race, and Politics.* New York: New York University Press.

Toney, M. W. (2007). *A Second Chance—For the First Time: Movement Formation Among Formerly Incarcerated People.* (Unpublished doctoral dissertation). University of California, Berkeley.

Travis, J. (2005). *But They All Come Back: Facing the Challenges of Prisoner Reentry.* Washington, DC: The Urban Institute Press.

United National General Assembly Sixty-sixth session. (2011). Retrieved from http://solitaryconfinement.org/uploads/SpecRapTortureAug2011.pdf.

U.S. Bureau of Labor Statistics. (2015). Earning and unemployment rates by educational attainment. Employment Projections.

Van Stelle, K. R., Goodrich, J., & Kroll, S. (2014). *Treatment Alternatives and Diversion (TAD) Program: Participant Outcome Evaluation and Cost-Benefit Report (2007–2013).* University of Wisconsin Population Health Institute.

Vielmetti, B. (2015, October 7). Support growing for bill to return most 17-year-olds to juvenile justice. *Milwaukee Journal Sentinel.*

Visher, C. A., Debus, S., & Yahner, J. (2008). *Employment after Prison: A Longitudinal Study of Releases in Three States.* Washington, DC: The Urban Institute.

Visher, C. A., & Courtney, S. M. E. (2007). *One Year Out: Experiences of Prisoners Returning to Cleveland.* Washington, DC: The Urban Institute.

Visher, C. A., Kachnowski, V., LaVigne, N., & Travis, J. (2004). *Baltimore Prisoners' Experience Returning Home.* Washington, DC: The Urban Institute.

Voice of the Ex-Offender. (2015). What We Do. Retrieved from http://www.vote-nola.org/what-we-do.html.

Wald, P. K. (2008). *Bringing Welfare State Theories to the States: How Ideas, Actors, and State Structures Affect Welfare Reform Trajectories in Minnesota and Wisconsin.* (Unpublished doctoral dissertation). University of Minnesota, Minneapolis.

Walsh, J., & Bricourt, J. (1997). Services for persons with mental illness in jail: Implications for family involvement. *Families in Society: The Journal of Contemporary Human Services,* 78(4), 420–428.

William Harrell Testimonial. (2015). Retrieved from http://tableofthesaints.org/testimonials

Winterfield, L., & Castro, J. (2005). *Returning Home Illinois Policy Brief: Treatment Matching.* Washington, DC: The Urban Institute.

Wisconsin Department of Corrections Presentation to the Criminal Justice Council: Data and Trends. (2015). Dane County Government Legislative Information Center.

WISDOM. (2015). Retrieved from http://prayforjusticeinwi.org/about-us/.

WISDOM 11x15 Blueprint for Ending Mass Incarceration. (2014). *WisconsinEye.* Retrieved from http://www.wiseye.org/Programming/VideoArchive/EventDetail.aspx?evhdid=9387.

Yahner, J., & Visher, C. (2008). *Illinois Prisoners' Reentry Success Three Years after Release.* Washington, DC: The Urban Institute.

Chapter Five

From Retribution to Health

*How Communities Are Changing the
Conversation about Incarceration*

David Liners

It is time to stop talking about what people deserve, and to start focusing on what they need.

The concept of "deserving" is, in almost all circumstances, not helpful. It is a concept that excuses the abandonment of large segments of our society to poverty—dividing the "undeserving" from the "deserving" poor. The phrase implies that we should help only those who are poor "through no fault of their own." On the flip side, the idea of "deserving," mashed with the faux morality of unfettered free market capitalism, leads to the bizarre concept that multi-millionaires "deserve" their wealth. Nowhere is the concept of "deserving" more pervasive than in the criminal justice system. It lies at the root of a system that has done irreparable damage to individuals, families and communities. It is the irrational rationalization for a system that is inordinately harsh—especially for people of color and low socioeconomic class.

The American system of criminal justice is tremendously flawed and has led to unprecedented levels of incarceration. The United States leads the world in per capita incarceration, by a large margin. We incarcerate far too many people, the majority of whom are ill, with addiction and/or mental health issues. We incarcerate people for far too long a time and we make it nearly impossible for people returning from prison to live healthy, "normal" lives.

As the state coordinator for WISDOM, the network of faith-based organizations working for social justice in Wisconsin, I can attest that many of us have worked for years to reform the criminal justice system. In recent years,

WISDOM's broadest and deepest efforts have gone toward ending mass incarceration in Wisconsin. We have fought for many different kinds of changes, including increasing access to alternatives to incarceration, reducing the use of torture in the form of solitary confinement, and reducing barriers to employment and housing for people being released into society. The efforts thus far to end this state and national shame are good and noble, but inadequate.

Mass incarceration is built on a system that needs to be torn down and rebuilt from the ground up. It will not really be fixed with a few reforms around the edges. Until we stop seeing the criminal justice system as a mechanism for punishing people according to what they "deserve," the problem will remain. Our judgements about the worthiness of our fellow human beings are inextricably linked to racial attitudes and other biases, both conscious and unconscious. Until we find another lens, we cannot build a just system.

In this chapter, I will argue for a different basis upon which to build a new, more rational, more compassionate criminal justice system. I do not pretend to be a sociologist or criminologist, and this chapter is not based on academic research. Rather it is based on the insights I have gained through many years of experience as a community organizer, listening to public officials, formerly-incarcerated people, family members of people in prison, faith leaders, and many other "non-experts" who have come to gatherings all around Wisconsin to try to understand our criminal justice system and how we might make it more humane. I have come to believe that instead of starting with a conversation about worthiness or deserving, we need to start with a conversation about the health of our society. Our goal should not be to punish appropriately, but to do those things that will restore individuals, families and communities to health and wholeness. To have health as a goal is not simply to work to cure disease (e.g. addiction or mental illness), but to create the conditions where people and entire communities can be in balance and thrive. The goal of restoration to health is not only a better moral foundation for a criminal justice system, but it is also rational, measurable and achievable.

A health frame for our system of justice needs to extend beyond "second chances." Many people born into a world of poverty, racism, scarce opportunity, and an educational system that restores order through exclusion and punishment, are still looking for their *first* chance. Others who are trapped in the criminal justice system have chronic diseases, and need four, five or ten chances.

The current paradigm of worthiness and punishment treats relapse as a grave moral failure, deserving of increasingly severe punishment. If we were to look through a lens of health, we would see things differently. I remember visiting a member of the legislature along with an older member of WIS-

DOM some years ago. The lawmaker protested that it was senseless to invest in treatment, since "most of them relapse." My friend responded by saying, "I've had open heart surgery four times. Are you telling me the first three were a waste of money?"

Before proposing a framework upon which to rebuild the criminal justice system, I will look at some of the most common reasons given for our current state-sponsored system of punishment, and where those break down. Then, I will look at some laudable ways in which some people have tried to initiate a discussion of the system. Finally, I offer at least a glimpse of what it might look to have a justice system based on the goals of health and restoration.

OUR CURRENT CRIMINAL JUSTICE SYSTEM

While some might argue the point, I would like to believe that no one set out to create a system of mass incarceration, much less to create the sort of inordinate suffering faced by communities of color in our country. Before going further, let's take a moment to look at some of the supposed goals of our jails and prisons.

Particular Deterrence

The idea of particular deterrence is the first goal of imprisonment, based on the belief that by getting a criminal off the street we can ensure that he or she will do no more harm to innocent people. This goal is clearly met in some cases, as there are some people who, for whatever reason, are out of control and cannot be trusted to go about freely and unsupervised.

The first problem with this goal is that it applies to a relatively small group of people. The vast majority of the people in our jails and prisons are *not* out-of-control sociopaths. Many of the people in prison are much more of a danger to themselves than they are to others, and most are not a danger to anyone.

The second problem is that there is no sense of proportion in the system. Even the few who constitute a threat to us are often kept in prison far too long. The fastest-growing percentage of the US prison population is of people sixty years old or older. (They are also, by far, the most costly inmates.) Many inmates who were once dangerous have not been for a very long time. Prisons themselves know this—many long-term prisoners have jobs outside of the institutions where they have no special supervision, and they return every day on the honor system. Some drive prison-owned vehicles thousands of miles per year unsupervised. It stands to reason that if prisoners are at such low risk of harming others that they are allowed to travel alone, then there is clearly no need to *deter* such inmates from anything. Others are simply too old or too sick to be a threat. For example, in Wisconsin, WISDOM members have tried to advocate for a prisoner who was in prison for nineteen years before he died. He had parole denied him four times, even though he was blind and quadriplegic.

Most prisoners will not grow old in prison (at least not all in one sentence). If the goal was specifically deterrence, one would imagine that we would be making great efforts to rehabilitate people while they were behind bars, to reduce the chances that they will commit a new crime upon release. In reality, the first place that prison budgets are cut is programming. We have cut back on educational opportunities for prisoners around the country. Whenever someone tries to introduce or increase rehabilitation programs, there is no lack of politicians decrying the programs as a waste of money on people who are hopeless, or who "don't deserve special treatment."

If the goal is deterrence, the first thing to be done is to vastly increase the resources devoted to alternatives to incarceration, especially for people with addictions, mental health issues, or who have been chronically unemployed. There has been a move towards increased resources for alternatives (in part because they are much cheaper), but the resources available do not nearly match the potential demand for the services. Alternative programs are not only cheaper, they actually reduce the recidivism rate. Whether the goal is deterrence or fiscal prudence, it would make sense to divert every possible person from jail or prison, saving the few places in secure facilities for serious treatment programs for the very few who legitimately need to be feared.

General Deterrence

Another rationale for incarceration is "general deterrence." The theory is that when an example is made by punishing someone who has broken the law, others will think twice and decide not to do the same thing.

The main problem with this concept of "general deterrence" is that it simply does not work. Most people who commit crimes do not sit down to do a thorough cost analysis ahead of time. (I sometimes wonder if legislators imagine a desperate young man planning to rob a convenience store. Perhaps they think he will consult the statutes—if armed robbery carries a fifteen-year sentence, he will go through with it, but not if it is twenty-five!) Most people do not consider the severity of the punishment they might receive when or before committing the crime. If they calculate anything, it is the likelihood of getting caught. Furthermore, with the vast majority of people in our jails and prisons having substance addictions or mental illness, it is likely that the crimes committed are a result of one of these two conditions, rather than due to lack of deterrence. Neither addiction nor mental illness is something people can calculate their way out of.

Rehabilitation

A third stated goal of the criminal justice system is to "reform" individuals who have been convicted of a crime. The language used in the titles of our prisons reflects a bygone era when we believed that our institutions were really "correctional facilities" or "reformatories." There was once a belief that prisons could receive criminals and help turn them into productive, law-abiding citizens. From the late 1970s until fairly recently, there was a belief among some criminologists and most policy-makers that nothing we did in prison really worked to meet this goal. There was a general assumption that rehabilitation was not achievable. It is interesting to note that, precisely in the era when nearly everyone gave up on rehabilitation as a goal for the system, the size of the prison population grew exponentially. The explosion of jail and prison populations was NOT an attempt to help people reform and get healthy.

The "nothing works" ideology has slowly been eroding among academics. Evidence-based studies of things like drug treatment courts have shown that there are plenty of alternative interventions that do work. Other evidence can be found in prisoners themselves. The human spirit is remarkably resilient. Despite having been given up on, and despite incredible odds and barriers, people in prison find the strength in themselves, their religious faith, their families and each other to rehabilitate themselves. Prisons may not be the best place for people to reform. People manage to reorient their lives, many times in spite of the criminal justice system.

Punishment

The final major reason traditionally given for incarceration is that we need to punish people who do bad things. They deserve to be punished. Punishment seems to be, after all is said and done, the only explanation that jibes with the reality of mass incarceration. It is the motif that dominates the public discussion of crime and punishment.

In WISDOM's work, we often hear about the decisions given by the Parole Commission for denying a prisoner's petition to be released. A common reason given to a person who has been in prison for decades, who has completed every program offered, and has had an exemplary record of behavior for many years is that, "to grant parole would be to diminish the seriousness of the crime." There is never any explanation of the kind of calculation that leads to such a conclusion. It just seems to be a very subjective sense that punishment will somehow rebalance the scales and the commissioner believes more weight still needs to be added to the punishment side.

The concept of punishment as an appropriate response to improper behavior is deeply ingrained in us. It is not just limited to "law and order" conservatives. Among many of my fellow opponents of mass incarceration, the first reaction to news that another white police officer has killed another unarmed African American youth is, "he should go to prison for the rest of his life!" Progressives can be heard to bemoan the fact that nobody went to prison for causing the financial crisis that led to the Great Recession. The targets might be different, but the worldview remains the same: we need to respond to bad acts by causing the offender to suffer, and the way to do that is to lock him/her in a cage.

A huge problem with the idea of punishment is that we seldom hold serious discussions about it. It is a concept that is tied to emotion and to a certain kind of morality, with little regard for proportionality. Sometimes, we seem to give certain victims of crime the moral authority to decide how much punishment is sufficient. (It is not uncommon for some people to become very angry with crime victims if they are not demanding "sufficient" punishment.) Other times, the calculus seems to be that the offender should suffer as much as the victim. Sometimes, it seems that no punishment is sufficient.

The concept of punishment is a very interesting one for people of faith, like many of the members of WISDOM. Punishment is a theme throughout most religious traditions and is presented either as God's responsibility (not ours), or as something that must be meted out with moderation and restraint, always tempered by mercy. A preponderance of faith traditions have clear stances that oppose capital punishment, for example, and Pope Francis has clearly stated that life sentences without possibility of parole and extended solitary confinement are both immoral. It is troubling that these issues do not seem to rank as "hot button" issues that people of faith care about. Like greed, an intemperate desire for vengeance is so common in our American culture that the faith community often fails to recognize it as counter to its most basic teachings.

SOME CURRENT CONVERSATIONS ABOUT ENDING MASS INCARCERATION

The Financial Cost of Incarceration

Many people have been hopeful that we might reach a bipartisan consensus to end mass incarceration when the price tag finally got so big that people would no longer stand for it. It seems, on the face of it, to be the perfect place for different political ideologies to converge.

Libertarians think we have categorized too much human behavior as criminal, and that too many people are in prison for things that shouldn't be any of the government's business in the first place. Conservatives don't like spending a lot of taxpayer money—and prisons are very, very expensive, especially when compared with alternative programs. Libertarians and conservatives tend to believe the government is generally incompetent, wasteful and counter-productive, and that prisons are no exception. Liberals view prison spending as money that is being taken away from more worthy uses—like healthcare, education, and housing. Either way, all agree we are spending too much on incarceration.

In Wisconsin, many reformers thought the tipping point might have been reached a few years ago when the amount of tax money spent on prisons overtook the taxpayer contribution to the University of Wisconsin system. It caused quite a stir for a few weeks. Then, everyone got used to the idea. Now, it is just one more fact of life that most everyone accepts as a sad reality. In Wisconsin, cost has not proven to be compelling enough to actually catalyze real change.

Many in the progressive movement see prison spending as a means by which public money is being transferred to the wealthy and to large corporations. In this view, prisoners are just the commodity. They believe that through ideas cultivated by groups like ALEC (the American Legislative Exchange Council), a huge system has been created that effectively transfers tax dollars to the coffers of wealthy corporations who reseed the fields each year through generous campaign contributions and high-priced lobbyists. The resulting mass incarceration is one more form of corporate welfare.

Unfortunately, the conversation about money has not created the kind of consensus for reform that many of us had hoped for. On the one hand, the discussion about profiteering and the financial incentive to maintain the "prison industrial complex" can become circular. It is clear that there are some who are making a lot of money from jails and prisons and prisoners. What is not clear is whether that was the original intent of the creators of the system, or if it is opportunism.

No matter what the system is, there are those who will seek to make a profit from it. If there are prisons and prisoners, clever people will learn how to position themselves to make money from them. It may well be true that corporations with an interest in incarceration have helped to write and promote laws like "three strikes and you're out" or very harsh immigration policies in order to create more business for themselves. It may also be true that those same corporations, seeing the movement toward treatment alternatives for certain drug offenders, have begun to look into changing their business model to include running AODA treatment centers.

In the end, it doesn't much matter. The fact is that far too many people are languishing in our jails and prisons. Incarcerated people themselves mostly come from very poor families, who are made even poorer in the process. And, the fact is that there are companies, individuals and units of government that are cashing in.

Whether it is the motive or the excuse, the reason that the cost of prisons has not pushed us to stop incarcerating so many people comes back to the even more fundamental issue of punishment and merit. When I have spoken to groups and have mentioned the high costs of incarceration for taxpayers, people often treat it as though it is not a discretionary expense. Most Americans assume that the first and most important function of government is to maintain order, and to punish those who threaten that order. If we need to save money, we need to cut it from other, less essential functions, like education and health. To save money in the prison system itself, legislators in Wisconsin occasionally propose things like cutting down to two meals per day in the prisons, or further cutting rehabilitation or education programs in the prisons. I long ago learned to be careful when speaking to judges or prosecutors about the cost of prisons. They are apparently deeply offended by the idea that they should consider the cost of incarceration when making decisions about charges or sentences. They seem to view indifference about the cost of jails and prisons as a virtue. They would much rather talk about what lawbreakers deserve.

When giving presentations to various religious and civic groups, I sometimes talk about the tremendous costs borne by the family members of those incarcerated. Not only have they lost an income, but they pay high prices for things like phone calls, "amenities" (like a radio, or a pair of shoes or pants other than those issued to inmates), and travel to and from distant prison facilities. Though the groups I speak to are usually somewhat sympathetic, it is not unusual for someone to respond by saying something like, "they should have thought about that before they decided to commit a crime." The culture of punishment apparently extends to children, spouses and parents. Somehow, the sense that those in prison are bad people excuses harsh treatment of those who would seek to maintain a loving relationship with them.

Racial Disparities

Another current discussion pertains to the immense racial inequities manifest in our current state of mass incarceration. Racial imbalance exists at every stage of the system: African Americans are more likely to come into contact with the police in the first place (often due to racial profiling, or to high-intensity policing in African American neighborhoods), more likely to be charged and convicted, and more likely to be given a lengthy sentence. When released, African Americans are more likely to have parole or supervision revoked. The inequality at each step in the process serves to compound the overall imbalance.

There can be no doubt that the criminal justice in the United States skews heavily against people of color, especially African American men. The racism is systemic and includes implicit bias. The numbers are so overwhelming and so well-documented that they cannot be argued. As with the extravagant price tag on our prison system, one would think that would be enough reason to be alarmed—to cause immediate, urgent calls for an overhaul of the whole system. After all, ours is a country in which a large majority of people would agree that racial injustice should be relegated to the past.

It seems as though Americans have a very hard time sustaining a serious conversation about race. I believe that, in part at least, it is because people have tended to equate racism with moral failure. I have been involved in many conversations over the years with public officials in our state, in which the subject of racial inequities was broached. On several occasions, the response of the official was to say, indignantly, "I am not a racist!" There was no personal accusation made in the conversation, just a presentation of facts. We live in a world where any statement about race immediately devolves into a no-win discussion of who is to blame. It is very hard to get my fellow white people to understand that discussion of white privilege is not an indictment of them—an implication that somehow they do not *deserve* the lives they have. Even more so, it is not to imply that they are frauds who *deserve* to be miserable. As long as we are all about blame and merit, we are in a futile conversation. "If it's not my fault, it must be yours. I'm not bad, so you must be."

Even among those who are not in denial about the devastation that has been wrought by racism, there is a problem when the focus is on blame. I hear too many progressives who understand that racism is systemic, who might even understand and claim that their own privilege is directly related to the injustices faced by people of color, yet cannot seem to get about the work of healing. As long as we are talking about "deserving" and blame, there are some who will rightly identify some of the causes (even naming themselves sometimes) but who will stop short of trying to fix the system.

A DIFFERENT PERCEPTION OF THE
OBJECTIVES OF THE CRIMINAL JUSTICE SYSTEM

Viewing "Justice" through a Lens of Health and Healing

Through the ROC (*Restore Our Communities*) Wisconsin Campaign, WISDOM is attempting to take on a variety of short-term and longer term issues. One goal is to reduce the number of people going into jail and prison by increasing our state's commitment to Treatment Alternatives and Diversions for people with addiction or mental health issues. WISDOM is putting pressure on the state to stop using solitary confinement for longer than fifteen days—a practice most of the world's governments regard as torture. We want to see greater use of "compassionate release," and increased opportunity for longer-term prisoners to demonstrate that they can be returned to their families and communities. We are working for the reduction of revocations back to prison for "technical violations" of supervision. We'd like to "Ban the Box"—to take the "have you ever been convicted of a crime?" question off of the front page—for every job and housing rental application in the state.

As gravely important as those issues can be in the lives of thousands of people, none of them is the ultimate aim of the ROC campaign. Dozens of WISDOM members, more than half of them formerly-incarcerated, met over the course of several months in 2015 to design the ROC Wisconsin Campaign. We discussed, over and over, what we were really trying to accomplish. If our campaign to reform the criminal justice system was successful, what would it look like? The results were these four principal aims:

For Wisconsin to invest in the programs and strategies that will end the racial and economic disparities that fuel mass incarceration.

We recognize that the criminal justice system is connected to our educational, housing, healthcare, transportation and economic systems. The criminal justice system is both a result and a contributor to systemic racism and economic inequities that attacked most convicted people long before their first arrest. Reform of the criminal justice system is an important part of the broader goal of ending systemic injustice in our state and nation.

For Wisconsin to reduce it prison population to 11,000, and to reduce the number of people on extended supervision.

We have challenged Wisconsin to reduce its prison population by half—to eleven thousand. That goal is achievable, it is in line with the best practices of other states, and it can be accomplished if the people of our state demand that our leaders be smart on crime and strong on justice. At the same time, the number of people on extended supervision must be reduced to reasonable levels.

For Wisconsinites to view people who have been convicted of a crime as human beings, members of families, and assets to the community.

Those convicted of a crime are people—not statistics. Every human being is capable of growth and change. Even as we debate the most appropriate way to keep our communities safe and to rehabilitate those who have committed crimes, the ROC Wisconsin campaign is dedicated to lifting up the irrevocable humanity of every person in our state, with no exceptions.

For formerly incarcerated people to be restored to full participation in our communities, our economy and our civic life.

ROC Wisconsin seeks policies and laws that provide those who have spent time in jail or prison opportunities to work, to continue their education, to live in decent housing, to regain their full citizenship, and to be free of fear of being sent back to prison if they do not commit a new crime.

The aims of ROC Wisconsin are, in the end, about changing the questions we ask ourselves about people who live in poverty and people who have conviction histories. They seek to push us toward curbing the conversation about what people deserve and replacing it with a conversation about what people need. What does everyone need in order to be able to actualize their potential as unique, gifted children of God? What must be done to restore and repair what has been damaged?

What If "Health" (What People Need) Replaced "Punishment" (What People Deserve)?

The discussion of restoration and potential is ultimately a discussion about health. If we were to see health as the goal of a completely re-envisioned criminal justice system, here are some of the things that would be different.

We would stop using the criminal justice system for health problems (like addiction and mental illness).

Things like drug treatment courts and mental health courts are a step in this direction. At their best, they use evidence-based best practices to guide people through treatment programs that help them to deal with the root issues that got them into trouble in the first place. I have seen wonderful things happen to people in these alternative programs, guided by wise and compassionate judges whose goal is to give both an opportunity and the means for a person to recover.

The eventual goal of WISDOM is to move these treatment programs out of the "criminal justice" system completely. While it is admirable that people in the criminal justice system seek to use the tools of public health and health care to achieve more rational ends, it would make even more sense for such programs to be the province of public health. Treating a health problem with a health solution is the first important step. The next step is to remove it completely from the realm of courts and jails and criminal records. There are those who fear that treatment alternatives detract from responsibility. They are concerned that defining the issue as a disease is to "give a free pass" to the person who has transgressed society's norms. Of the many unfounded fears surrounding criminal justice policy, this may be the easiest to allay.

Anyone who has ever been in a serious alcohol and other drug addiction (AODA) treatment program can tell you that it is not an abdication of responsibility. The individual needs to become responsible for his or her own sobriety, and it is very difficult. I once had a drug court treatment judge tell me that the people who typically left the program unsuccessfully were the ones who came to her and said, "Please, just send me to prison—it's a lot easier."

We would focus on making victims whole again.

If we can focus on health rather than punishment as a goal, it will change the way we deal with the victims of crime. The status quo is not primarily designed to make victims whole again. There is some concept of restitution, but in too many cases it turns out to be symbolic. As a matter of fact, we tell the offender that they have a debt to the victim at the same time that we severely limit her/his ability to ever pay that debt. There are certainly cases where the victim of the crime needs to be protected from further harm at the hands of the offender—and those situations need to be handled well. Such offenders are not the majority of people in our jails and prisons. For everyone else, we operate under the odd notion that it is somehow "justice" for the victim to know that the perpetrator of the crime will suffer. There may be some temporary satisfaction, but it does not really heal or restore the victim to wholeness.

If we make a real commitment to the restoration of victims, we will put significant resources of the state toward things like counseling, financial reparations, and other measures that will really help crime victims to regain as high a quality of life as possible. We do this, and appropriately so, after very high-profile crimes like the September 11th attacks, or Sandy Hook. Unfortunately, we do not have that same kind of commitment to people who are victimized by the kinds of crimes that do not make the headlines. So many of our children, especially those living in poverty, are victims or witnesses to violence, yet there are few resources dedicated to their healing. The line between victims and perpetrators is a thin one. Most people in prison were victims of crime long before they ever committed a crime. If ours was a health response, we would spend as much or more of our money and energy providing the help that is needed in that first instance.

Prisons and jails would be places of healing and restoration.

If we are to look at our justice system through a health lens, prisons and jails need to be seen in the way that we see hospitals. For good reasons, we do not want people to spend more time in the hospital than is necessary. We try to avoid sending people there unnecessarily, and we move them out as quickly as possible. We reserve hospital beds for people with acute health issues and a specific need to be there. For most people, hospitals are not the best place to be rehabilitated, and we have learned that concentrating too many sick people in the same environment for a long time can have negative effects. In the same way, we need to use jails and prisons sparingly, and only for as much time as is absolutely necessary.

If we look at prisons as a place to heal and be restored, we would use solitary confinement only in rare cases where safety concerns are present. Then, it would be used only for a few days, until better arrangements could be made. In a health-based system, the length of sentences will be figured by the amount of time needed to restore the person to wholeness. That is something that can be estimated with real evidence and science, which is quite different than the confused, inexplicable moral judgement that goes into deciding how much time a person *deserves* to be incarcerated for.

Prison personnel (and post-prison parole officers) need to be trained to act as teachers, mentors and healers. Our goal for those who have broken the law and have proven themselves unable to function productively in society should be similar to our goal for the person with any other health problem. We need to put our energy into doing everything possible to get them back on their feet and making a positive contribution.

There are a very few people who can never be rehabilitated and allowed back on the street. These are the extremely rare people whose mental and/or emotional state is untreatable. These people (who, I would stress again, are very few in number) simply need to be treated with compassion and kept safe and as comfortable as possible. Perhaps the healthcare parallel would be hospice care.

We would focus on the health of our neighborhoods and our society.

We have learned from the public health sector that health is not just about the individual. Though some of our health outcomes are the result of genetics and lifestyle choices, the more certain predictors of health are social and environmental. It is bad for your health to be poor. It is bad for your health to be a person of color in a racist society. Again, this is not a matter of opinion or ideology; it is a fact. If we really want people to be healthy, we will repair some of the social structures that pull large numbers of people in the direction of poor health outcomes. The same is true in the realm of criminal justice. The tremendous increase in jail and prison populations is not the result of millions of individuals simultaneously losing their moral compass. Human nature has not changed very much in recent decades. And, only the most vicious racist would claim that African Americans are somehow more evil than white people. The victims of our society's systemic racism and great economic inequity are individuals and families, but they are not the cause. In an atmosphere where opportunity slips further from the grasp of the marginalized, and where most of the available minimum wage jobs are worth less and less, a lot of things go wrong.

Where would we start? We have a lot of options. There are so many problems in our punishment-based system that there are many entry points to begin to repair it. Here are just three good potential starting places if we really want to start changing the conditions that underlie mass incarceration:

- So many issues related to incarceration can be traced to unresolved childhood trauma that we could begin with a huge commitment to a healing outreach to children;
- We could also start by raising the minimum wage and guaranteeing a job for everyone who wants to work;
- And, it would help if we had drug and alcohol treatment available immediately for anyone who seeks it.

This are just three examples. There are plenty of other entry points. We need not to see them in competition with each other. (We should ban people from saying, "Yes, that would be good, but you know the *real* problem is . . .") We eventually need to do them all, and we need to get started wherever we can.

CHANGING THE QUESTION

Everyone Means Everyone

The shift of paradigm needs to be for everyone in the system, not just a few. In Wisconsin, it has been very striking to see how we have reacted to the "heroin epidemic" in comparison to the way we have dealt with crack, or even methamphetamine addictions. We have been much more compassionate in our response to heroin. It is wonderful to see legislators, public health officials and even law enforcement pushing to provide treatment for people caught up in the latest wave of opioid addiction. One might question why we see heroin addiction as a health problem, requiring a health solution, while we have treated crack and meth as problems best tackled by law enforcement and punishment. Could it be that the typical heroin abuser is a middle-class white person, while the typical crack addict is African American and the typical meth user is poor?

We ought not to begrudge heroin users of the public health solution. We are doing the right thing by seeking compassionate, evidence-based health solutions for their affliction. The trick is to see everyone else with the same eyes with which we see the heroin addicts. Everyone needs a chance to get healthy, and not to be kicked while they are down.

There are some ways in which the tides are turning in the criminal justice system. Over the past couple of years, there has been increased sympathy for "nonviolent drug offenders," and there is a consensus that we have been too harsh with them. While that is a wonderful step in the right direction, we need to extend that same sympathy to other justice-involved people as well. We can reform our system when we treat everyone as a human being in need of healing and capable of being a valued member of their family and community. While that sounds good in theory, it is a challenge to include violent criminals, even sex offenders and drunk drivers, in that category. This does not mean that there is no accountability or personal responsibility, it does mean that we ask ourselves what they need, not what they deserve.

If everyone means everyone, it also includes police officers who abuse their authority and take the lives of unarmed people. We cannot say that prisons are counterproductive and still advocate for rogue police officers and perpetrators of corporate and financial crimes to be sent there for a long time. How would the conversation change if we were to ask what those offenders need in order to be transformed into healthy, productive contributors to the common good?

We Need a Mass Movement

Our criminal justice system is not just in need of a few technical tweaks. A few common sense steps in the right direction would not be a bad thing, and there are simple things that could greatly reduce human suffering in the criminal justice system right now. But, we cannot stop there. Our nation needs to have a massive conversation about values, where we talk about the real-world implications of concepts like "health," "forgiveness," and "healing." This is why I am so glad to work for a faith-based organization like WISDOM, and our national umbrella, Gamaliel. In the end, the conversations we need to have are rooted in theology. That is not to say the conversation can be joined only by "religious" people, but it will be productive only when we are willing to put our deepest beliefs and convictions on the table. In most faith traditions, "justice" has to do with things being in proper order—it is not particularly about punishment and vengeance. In that sense, to promote justice and to promote health are very much related endeavors.

It is curious that in modern America, we have relegated things like "forgiveness" to the private realm. It is a virtue for a person to learn to forgive, but it has not been promoted as a collective virtue. We need our faith leaders and other opinion leaders to begin to call for a public morality that includes forgiveness and second chances—not as something exceptional for a few deserving people, but as the norm.

The depth of change required to make our system of justice more balanced and more promoting of equity and second chances is far beyond what we can expect from our political leaders. It is a mistake to look to them for that level of leadership. We need to transform our communities from the bottom up, and from the inside out. We need to build a mass movement that demands serious change and that refuses to tolerate the "business as usual" of mass incarceration.

The Criminal Justice System Will Not Be Fixed by the "Experts"

Because we need a paradigm shift, not a technical fix, we need some unlikely people to lead the change we seek. First and foremost, we need formerly-incarcerated people to lead the way. They are the ones who know what works and what does not work. They know what interventions might have helped them early in life, and they know what they need today. They understand what it means to spend months and years behind bars. It is wasteful for us not to include them in the solutions; they are the leading authorities. One of WISDOM's accomplishments I am most proud of has been the organization of a statewide group called EXPO (EX-Prisoners Organizing). Their motto is "You have the right to NOT remain silent." EXPO members want more than just to survive. They want to turn their experience into the energy, wisdom, and power that is needed to make it better for those they left behind in prison, and for generations yet to come.

It is easy to feel overwhelmed by the complicated criminal justice system. The rules, the terminology and the history are almost impenetrable for all but the most dogged and studious activists. We cannot allow that to slow us down. It is not our responsibility to make a new paradigm fit into old structures, bureaucracies and rules. If the system can only accommodate a discussion of punishment and has no place for healing and reconciliation, it is the system which must adjust, not the advocates.

Mass incarceration is the logical outcome of a society that tolerates huge racial and economic disparities, and that allows its policies to grow out of fear and anger rather than out of hope and reason. Mass incarceration is not only the end product of all our nation's injustices, but also puts a magnifying glass on them. This is why it is such an appropriate place to begin the important work of dismantling structural racism and economic inequity. If we can deal with this deepest, darkest manifestation of our collective turpitude we can dare to believe we might be able to create a more just society. It all begins when we learn to ask the right questions.

Chapter Six

Passion and Freedom in Human Services

Alfred T. Kisubi

This chapter discusses the constraints as well as the opportunities of passion as the earnestness, the inwardness or commitment to seeking meaning in our individual lives, as client empowerers in human services. The argument is that without passion, it is impossible to make human services education and practice meaningful to oneself as a human services professional, and subsequently it will be a challenge to work for the liberation of the lives of the oppressed clients. The chapter contributes some philosophical insights into the need to search for meaning of life, the "I-Them" dilemma, emotivism v. empiricism, and individualism v. passion debate in human services. It also stipulates that the human service professional's realization and application of such realization to helping paves the path to the oppressed client's freedom.

INTRODUCTION

Although we may reject transcendent absolutes in human services, we still need guidance, support and inspiration. The solution to this dilemma has been to push each individual, group and society to develop the same capacities that human beings have had for at least fifty thousand years (Owen, 2007) and to further develop techniques for bettering the world that former generations did not know. These capacities and techniques are humanity's ultimate means of transformation. However, this thinking assumes that each person is going to accept the challenge to develop these capacities. In real life this has been shown to be impossible. Some societies, just like individuals, have lagged behind the rat race. Hopelessness, poverty, exploitation, and meaninglessness in life have characterized people of different races, gender,

handicaps, and age as a result of their being discriminated against and exploited. One prisoner makes this need to be rescued abundantly clear in *A
Heart Turned Inside Out*:

> I pain, I ache. I've lost my way. I need some guidance.
> What has happened to me? The way I used to be?!
> I scream to be loving—again I want to love; But wait!
> This tossing and turning, it feels so good
> Is it true, can it be?! Is this me—Anew again?!
>
> Babies screaming;
> Mothers yelling for their children to come in and eat
> Kids hanging out in large groups, drinking and smoking
> Police sirens raring loud as a police car speeds past
> Someone selling drugs; cages and bars on the windows!
> Man do I have a headache!
>
> Broken Windows; rundown buildings; another World!
> But not far from this one—
> Gang graffiti and empty beer cans
> Unkempt lawns—boarded windows
> Poor people—Violence—Gun Fight—Drugs!.
> Noise and loud people yelling; kids running around
> People buying drugs; cars pulling in and out
>
> People look lost as one beats his wife
> Security walking around
>
> Drugs, alcohol, fighting
> Cockroaches
> Cats of all nature
> Graffiti on the walls
> Children crying and running naked
> Beat up cars, a certain smell in the air!

"THE CRACK!"

> That crack in the wall
> Don't look good at all
> The presence of it cause's me pain,
> If I don't fix it I'll go insane.
> It is a crack even a nail can't fix.
> I mean, I can't even use a cement mix.
> You see, this is a crack of destruction,
> One that always cause's corruption.
> So this is my advice. . . .

We need to come together and be carpenters of life.
I mean, it's time for us to go to work
Day and night,
To stand strong in this crack fight!
Getting rid of the smack
Before our children of tomorrow get wacked
I mean crack is not just that Blemish we came to know.
You see, it's a new high tec. form of that drug they call Blow!
So to stop that killer of our Race
I think we need to work hard to get rid of that crack
Give society a whole brand new face!
Clap your hands and sing this "Serenity Rap":

We all chilling out on a natural high,
Reading N.A. Books trying to stay dry,
Serenity Prayer from the man above,
No Longer Drink! No Longer a Drug!

Thought for the day, "Keep an Open Mind"
Thank Act I for being so kind.
So when you're feeling low and there's nowhere to go,
Get on your knees and pray.
If I don't fix it—I'll go insane.
(Mark Larse, 2016).

Human Services are supposed to rescue such people. However, the professional must be cautious with the client who might be suspicious of the professional's intervention. Once I had a weekly seminar at a Midwestern US Drug Alcohol Corrections Center (DACC) with inmates and asked them to write poems. Several of them expressed both friendliness to me and suspicion of my intentions. "This person seems friendly," one wrote. "It looks like we're going to see a movie. I wish I could be free like the rain coming down hitting the ground" ended his cordiality. Then he added, "Why are you asking us to write these things down—to be used against us? I hope what we watch on the video is interesting." He also questioned my preparedness, "Why didn't you come prepared with something to write with?" Others also wrote

What will tonight bring in this group? I'm excited about tomorrow. I want today to get over. Am I really ready to get married? I like the rain. I wonder if we will have a tornado drill tonight! I'm glad Alfred came tonight—glad to see him. I'm really full right now—I ate too much. I feel really sad for the people in Somalia who have nothing to eat and who are dying. I wonder what we will do tonight and what your poetry is like! Sometime I wish I was not here. I was wondering how my father is—I am so self-centered that I forgot him. I was looking at the assignment as punishment again. I was only thinking of myself. I would like to go to sleep—why does every one want my thought—people tell

me things but I would not tell them. I will stuff my feeling because who I give
them to is not here. Happy—satisfied—I like coming here to meet together
like this and Dr. Kisubi is uplifting! He's pretty funny. Scared—thunder scares
me. Sad—haven't heard from Ms. Rose. Worried—How she thinks of my new
decision. Content—with how I am doing on my program – treatment.

This chapter therefore argues that there must be a golden mean between the
emphasis of the capacities of the individual and passion on the side of the
helper and the human services educator, who by the nature of the phenomena
they work with must be eclectic relativists.

The second part of the chapter argues that through passion motivated
praxis the human service professional will pave the way to freedom for the
person(s) under care. It defines praxis as used by Paulo Freire (1970), and
explains the relationship between praxis, humanization, and oppression.
Also, the two parts of praxis and how they are (diametrically) related are
described and explained together with how the "problem posing" education
described in chapter two of Freire's *Pedagogy of the Oppressed* facilitates
praxis. "Freedom" ranks among the least understood words in the American
(World) political and educational vocabulary, and accepting the view that
Americans treat freedom as if its meaning is self-evident, the chapter attempts to illustrate how hotly its meaning is usually contested.

Many philosophers and social theorists have grappled with the question
of freedom. "What makes it possible?" they ask, and "What is the difference
between civil liberty, and freedom of the individual?" As Freire would point
out, it is not enough for the church to champion freedom of faith at the
expense of individual freedom from oppression. It is when human services
professionals passionately work for the freedom of the oppressed that they
can stop their pain.

What then is freedom? Freedom, like Shakespearean beauty is in the eyes
of the beholder. It is relative and dynamic. It changes from group to group
and from time to time. Conservatives, such as Montesquieu, and Burke or
even Ronald Reagan, in their account of freedom and how it is to be secured
make a false beginning. Like Montesquieu (1748, 1914) does in the *Spirit of
the Laws*, most conservatives have the following definitions of freedom:

(1) it consist only in the power to do what one ought to will and not to be
constrained to do what one ought not will . . . (2) it is the right to do all that
the civil laws, custom, mores or folkways permit. (Bk. XI, Ch. 1, 3).

These conservatives overlook the fact that we ought to be constrained by
just or unjust laws to do what we ought not to will or be prevented from
doing what we ought to will. This chapter deliberately leaves out conservative views on what freedom ought to be and will stick to liberation theology
per the frameworks espoused by Freire and the various shades of pragmatism
by Rousseau and Dewey.

One only has to look at the current conflicts between Christian fundamentalists, and secular definitions of freedom or at the controversy over whether the Nicaraguan Contras were "freedom fighters" to see the lack of consensus regarding what constitutes freedom. Instead of pitching philosophers against their adversaries in an everlasting debate about freedom, the second part of the chapter starts with Freire's theory of education as the practice of freedom, and then proceeds to Rousseau's Emile and Dewey's democratic education as a key to freedom.

PART I

PASSIONATE HUMAN SERVICES ROLE MODELS

First we look at passion as a perquisite for liberating human services. As a multidisciplinary profession, human services professionals draw upon the values and experiences of many passionate people who have made important contributions in related fields, including Daniel Hale Williams (pioneer in heart surgery), Charles Richard Drew (pioneer in preserving blood), Percy Lavon Julian (industrial chemist), Booker T. Washington (educator and founder of the Tuskegee Institute), Mary McLeod Bethune (educator), Carter Godwin Woodson (historian), Frederick Douglass (abolitionist), Robert Sengstacke Abbott (newspaper publisher), W. E. B. DuBois (a man of many professions, but above all, a spokesman for civil rights), Jack Roosevelt Robinson (athlete and civil leader), Martin Luther King Jr. (crusader for social justice) (Stratton, 1965), Carl Rogers (counseling), Jane Adams (social work), Marie Montessori (education), and Erik Erickson (development psychology).

These ancestors are role models to those in training, before they can become role models to those they set out to serve. Therefore, in search of ourselves as a prerequisite to helping those in need, we must unite our scientific efforts and the concrete revolutionary action to end suffering and marginalization of individuals and groups (Freire, 1973). We emulate role models because we each grapple with the following muse, which is found in Soren Kierkegaard's journal:

> What I really lack is to be clear in my mind what I am to do, not what I am to know, except in so far as a certain understanding precedes every action. The thing is to understand myself, to find the idea for which I can live and die. What would be the use of discovering so called objective truth, of working through all the systems of philosophy and of being able, if required, to review them all and show up the inconsistencies within each system; what good would it do to be able to develop a theory of the state and combine all the

details into a single whole, and so construct a world in which I did not live, but only held up to the view of others? (Bergman, 1991, p.1).

Kierkegaard was twenty-two years old when he raised this fundamental question about his life (Bergman, 1991). However, he did not find the answer in his pleasure-seeking adventures nor did he discover it in the depth of scholarly understanding for he learned that without "subjectivity" knowledge becomes a chance semblance, a heap of information, and a succession of details without focus and significance. The principles of life he discovered were not only rationalism, mysticism, or empiricism, but also inwardness and passion. To Kierkegaard, like to humanists and human service professionals, passion means the same as the earnestness, the inwardness, or the commitment with which martyrs act. It is quite impossible to make education or human services meaningful to one's life without being passionate.

To humanists and human services professionals the adage "Education makes life more meaningful" changes to "Being passionate makes life more meaningful." In short, we must go beyond intellectualizing about what we have learned. It is imperative that we focus our attention on the objects or contents of knowledge as well as our relationship with it. More specifically, what does it mean to say that "being passionate makes education more meaningful to one's life?"

Students who are in the process of becoming humanistic helpers, especially those just about to set out to empower their clients, must themselves be treated as individuals. What is needed in making knowledge and the educative process more meaningful to each person is inwardness, that is, *passion*. We must go beyond intellectual reflection and critical analysis of our beliefs. What we have learned and accepted must be taken into our action for only then shall knowledge take on a meaning for our lives and those of our helpees, including individuals with a criminal record, who are most likely to have been denied passionate treatment at some point in their lives.

Most of the inmates I worked with at a Midwestern US DACC craved not only for freedom, but also for love and passion. Here is *My Dream is You*, a composite poem composed by the author based on thoughts from a dozen prisoners craving for love and human understanding:

Once, I was afraid I'd never find someone to really care about.
I wanted someone perfect, at least for me.
A special kind of talking, an honest way of listening;
Not being afraid to laugh or cry; Kindness and understanding;
Fun and Excitement; someone who would fill my heart with joy
I guess I expected a lot, but I'm a believer!
And I believed that someday, someone's particular magic
Would transform my life—
So, in spite of all the waiting, all the loneliness,
All the Almost-Giving-Up; it's been worth it:

It's all been worthwhile and wishes really do come true.
Because what I always wanted isn't a dream—It's you!.

You will Always Have My Love
Sometimes I wonder what it is that I did to deserve you. . . .
The love and happiness I am feeling
The countless smiles you have brought to my face.
The sheer joy you have given my life, since you have entered it.
My days are brightened just by hearing your voice.

My nights, by having you next to me; and every minute in between
By knowing that you are there, even when you are miles away
I will hold you in my heart—Cradle you in the depths of my soul—
For as long as you wish to be there you have shown me your friendship,
You're live, your understanding, and your trust.
And sometimes I wonder what I could ever do to repay you.
Then I realize that all you really want from me is my love. . . .
And that, you know you already have.

The Poem you old in your hand
The poem you hold in your hand is a very special Poem.
Not because it's from me . . . . But because it says something
I want you to know today and that I want you to remember forever
Within the words of this poem I want to say that you are incredibly special to me.
You are so important to my day—and so essential to the smile within me.
That certain space where our lives overlap is the place that brings me the most understanding,
The most peace and the nicest memories, and a joy that some of my heart so constantly
When you hold this in your hands, I want you to think of me smiling softly at you,
and thanking you for all that you are . . . . To me!

As Time Goes by, Our Love Will Only Grow Deeper
I love you; I can't say it enough to show how happy I've become
There is a strong feeling in my heart that gives me self-confidence.
I am a better person because I not only have faith in myself,
But also the faith you have given me from your love, and your trust.

I love you; there is a certain bond between us.
Expressed by Touch and by the part of life we have experienced together.
This is serious love, not infatuation; A love I hope will last forever,
So that as time continues, we can only be drawn closer.
I love you; I have finally learned what it means.
It's a feeling that only comes with experience, and I can't say it enough but I love you.

"I Think She Love" While being locked up, she said she loved
I think she loved to see me mad. My head is held-low, I walk very slow.
The love she gave, has kept me sad. May mood is perceived to be very depressed
I think she loved to hear, I love. But I don't think she knows that I have reached my goal

I think I love myself.

I have a wish. I have a wish and only one when my day of freedom soon will come. A day when I can watch the birds sing; a day I can watch winter change to spring. I have a wish holding each other so; dancing and singing on the sun. One day shortly we would become one.

But all of this is just a wish, and thought swimming very hard like fish.
So now all I fell is hurt and hate and wait impatiently for just a date

After five years in Jail, I still sit here on a ten year bit alone in the cold lonely cell
The love letters stopped, my self-esteem has dropped.
This is why, every night I pray to my creator above, in hopes he'll send me someone to show me love.
I guess what I'm saying is, my time shouldn't be hard only if I had that someone to call or to send me a love card.
Now don't get me wrong, I came from a loving home. It's just that all my mistakes in life cost me that home and my future wife. So I now sit and write my poem, which is the way I choose to mourn. Also, it's a way to share my views because, deep in my soul I have the sickness of . . . Prison love Blues! My life is quite trivial. . . . So I'm not going to go into the past scenario.
The window in my cell is covered and smeared, not allowing me the sight of outside fears
But through the windows of my soul, I behold a monster deep within my soul.

I closed the windows to this place, turning the fear, to hate for the soul
So I consume self-knowledge and with very low self-esteem I swallow my pride.
I open my eyes to see the monster has died.
Its in my heart you'll always be, when I close my eyes, you're all that I see
I look to the sky and the Lord above I scream to him, it's you I love. It's in your heart
I hope to be when you close your eyes, do you think of me?

I remember the night when we first met how you looked so beautiful!
I'll never forget how you looked so innocent in the dark of night
How your eyes were like diamonds in the full moon light
I could see it in your eyes when you looked at me that we would be together
In love for eternity
This night I'll always remember in my heart I'll never forget the greatest night of all
Is the night when we first met, when I think of better days all I see is you
Then I think of our future and all the things we'll do
Our better days are yet to come although we've had quite a few when I thing of better days
I think of being with you, you are my special angel
From heaven you were sent on a cold moonlit night
For me, you are only meant to watch over me and guild me through the times
My one and only angel I thank God that you are mine

A special kind of love is a love that comes from the heart
I know our love grows stronger each day that we're apart

Your special kind of love is the only love for me
It's the love that we share, a love that will always be, although I cannot see you
You're always on my mind, a very special person, so sweet and oh so kind
You've captured my heart forever, only you have got the key
So hold me tight my lover and never let go of me.
I saw you last night, you were in my dream
So I held out my hand and you came to me when our hands touched I said "hold on tight"
And you gripped my hand hard as we flew through the night I said "Where shall we go?"
And "What shall we see?"
You said it didn't matter you were glad to be with me
So I took you even higher to the moon we shall go, the stars were on fire
And they made your face glow I thought it would last forever or so it seemed
Then I awoke with a jerk. It was only a dream! So I turned my head to one side
And wished you were near. Then I felt something cold and wiped away the tear.

Oh Lonely Child, you stare through those sad eyes into a world full of despise
You open your mouth—your words over the hills rise
No one hears you cry
In unexpected birth you are formed to remain innocent until you are born
Before you breathe your first worldly breath you face problems of addiction and death
Your risks are high, your chances mild, and Oh lonely child!

I wish I could have comforted you through those lonely months as you grew
I cry tears you may never shed over the lonely road that lies ahead
Oh what you could've been, if they only waited to see you could've been important, if they only believed what now of the world you leave, for the air you may never breathe
Your lips that may never smile, sorry you had to die.

I hear you calling I wish I could come but I still have work, left undone
This world that you've left behind has taken its toll destroying my youth, now I am old
I wish you would have stayed to help me along
Troubles have me weary and weak, I'm no longer strong
My eyes are heavy with sleep, my wounds run deep Where your grave site rests, my tears have dried along with my spirit when you died
Somehow I can't let go; again I hear you calling maybe this time I follow.

My head hurts,
I wish I didn't have a cold
I wonder what Shelly's doing!
This seems weird
I feel like hell
I wish I had a small vacuum tube to drain my sinuses
I remember it raining and I was with my Girlfriend at the Park.
I wonder what it will be like when I go off ground tomorrow
Damn, I wish I could chop off my head—it hurts. Damn cold!
I think this is weird! (Compiled by Alfred Kisubi, 2016)

Alfred T. Kisubi

COMMITMENT TO HUMANISM:
THE I-THEY PROBLEM

To put it differently, committing ourselves to a set of beliefs implies that we are voluntarily surrendering ourselves to live by these beliefs and to accept the consequences of our action stemming from our commitment. And when we act according to our personal commitment which happens to deviate from the norm or the prevailing views, we become non-conformists. But non-conformity by itself is no virtue at all, for non-conformity is nothing more than a consequence of ones acting out of sense of duty to personal commitment. On the other hand, our personal commitments, convictions, may also be in agreement with the dominant views of the time. The philosophical question that arises is, "Which proscriptions and prescriptions should we regard first and vital: the Herbert Spenserian *generalized other* (Freudian *super-ego* or Horton Coolie's *looking-glass other*) or our own Freudian *id* or the Spenserian *I*?

In human services, where we are (or should be) committed to assisting the individual in achieving optimum human potential (Harris et al., 2004) we ought to resolve this I-They problem before we can enable our clients to do the same. Existentially, each person should act according to one's own personal beliefs regardless of the consequences because actions motivated by anticipated consequences are necessitated or compelled by either fear or greed, that is, fear of danger or greed for rewards. All this is not to encourage irrational and /or capricious behavior. Rather, this is a challenge for everyone to become infinitely interested in one's own life and to go beyond mere intellectualizing and abstract thinking about what is real, true or worthwhile.

If we are to become infinitely interested in our own existence we must ask not only about whether or not our beliefs are true or false. We must also inquire about how we are related to the beliefs which we have accepted, or to which we have committed ourselves. The primary motivation for acting should not be either the fear of punishment or of loss of property or life nor should it be the desire for rewards, wealth or fame. Only the sense of duty one has toward ones commitment should determine ones decision to act or not to act. This ability to act inwardly with passion or to reveal ones beliefs in action in spite of threats, dangers and rewards constitute moral or authentic freedom. It is a resounding victory for the "I" over the sometimes stifling "They." A necessary solution to the I-They problem, a personal empowerment.

ABSTRACT THINKING AND MEANING IN LIFE:
COMICAL FIGURES AND HYPOCRITES

In view of what has been said, what shall we say about a person who is primarily concerned with the acquisition, evaluation and critical analysis of objective knowledge and abstract thoughts? While there are many things we can say about such a person, we mention the following two: comical figures and hypocrites.

Comical Figures

At best, such a person becomes a comical figure because he/she attempts to find a meaning for his/her existence by neglecting those particularities, unique qualities, which make what he/she is, a unique human being. Since such a person does not ask "What does it mean to my life that something is true for me?" the answer is not forthcoming. Further, regardless of the person's intellectual competence or the amount of knowledge the individual possesses, his/her attempts to find the personal existential meaning from objective knowledge and abstract thoughts is doomed to failure because they are generalizations based on those common elements which belong to all members of a particular class or group of "things." Such a person is comical because he/she annihilates oneself as a concrete individual in order to understand oneself.

As Kierkegaard once described, this individual is like a doctor who, in his/her preoccupation with dispelling the patient's fever, finally dispels the fever but also kills the patient with a prescription overdose. Especially, in the present age wherein the social and natural sciences are growing rapidly as empirical sciences and their keepers are providing us with more and more generalizations about people and society, it is not too difficult for many to attempt to know themselves or carve their self-image by classifying themselves into certain objective categories, for example, personality types, and other ideal-type paradigms and ascriptive stereotypes created in the name of science.

This approach too is limited in celebrating *muntu* (human), because empirical data may say much about *muntu* in general, as homo sapiens, perhaps, but very little, if any at all, about *muntu* as a unique and concrete individual. This is not to belittle the behavioral and social or physical science, because I have a masters in sociology.

Besides, before I took fancy to the social sciences and education I had advanced study of chemistry and biology that led me to a veterinary institute where I studied animal husbandry. But it does not mean that the search for the meaning of life should not be directed toward ourselves as objects of empirical investigation or abstract speculation, as benefactors, not victims of our own quest for knowledge and discovery. As Kierkegaard pointed out,

> An abstract thinker, one who neglects to take into account the relationship between his abstract thought and his own existence as an individual, not careful to clarify this relationship to himself, makes comical impression upon the mind even if he is ever so distinguished, because he is in the process of ceasing to be a human being (Bergman, 1991, p. 1).

Hypocrites

The intellectual who attempts to find the meaning for his/her existence only from objective knowledge and abstract thoughts thus becomes not only a comical figure but also a hypocrite. Consider a person who intellectually accepts the principle that it is good to be truthful thus everyone ought to be honest. Because this person does not go beyond intellectual acceptance, he/she may frequently act contrary to the principle he/she has accepted. A person who has the word "truthful" constantly in one's mouth, epistemology and research methodology, but acts contra-wise is nothing more than a hypocrite, perhaps the worst kind of hypocrite for he/she will intellectualize about why he/she does not, or need not, or cannot act according to one's own principle. This kind of hypocrisy breeds what Karl Jaspers calls the Sophist(s) and described thus:

> He/she finds his/her truth home in intellectualism. There he/she feels comfortable, for there only can he/she readily fulfill his task of persistently conceiving the steam of thought as something other than it is. He/she has a passion for discussion. He/she uses grave and decisive words, adopts radical attitudes, but never stands his or her ground. Outwardly he/she sees eye to eye with the others and then proceeds to act after his/ her own fashion as if nothing whatever had been said. It is a vital matter for him/her that everything should be treated rationally. He/she accepts modes of thought, categories, and methods without exception, but only as a form of speech, not as embodying the substantial movement of cognition. His/her thoughts have a syllogistic consistency, so that, by the use of the logical instrument of which every thinker is familiar, he can achieve a momentary success. But the emotionalism of his/her rhetorical professions of resoluteness enables him her to slip away like an eel from any resolver which it might trouble him her to fulfill.

Karl Jaspers tells us to have a life, together with our science. According to Jaspers, even scientific knowledge, if there is anything to it, is not a random observation of random objects; for the critical objectivity of significant knowledge is attained as a practice only philosophically in inner action (Wautischer et al., 2012). It is not enough to intellectualize in Human Services. Research to update our knowledge and technologies should go hand-in-hand with our individual search for the meaning of life. It is when we have blended our knowledge, technology and the meaning of life that we can either teach the young to help others or even do it ourselves. We must not succumb to the gravitational pull of cultural lag and generational gap, yet at the same time we should never part with the elements that make society possible. We need science in human services to understand reality, which is seen as fleeting. Change is the essence of helping. To change people through helping is to empower them to grow. In the helping interaction the helper and the helpee should mutually treat each other as unique individuals who have idiosyncratic needs and values. Neither dogma nor blue-print suits all individuals all the time. As the sophists would teach us, there is no such thing as universal morality, your truth is as good as mine, and that is the most important tenet of the humanism in human services. However, according to Socrates, every society needs a code of morality to glue it together, and this makes the issue of individual free will v. society determinism even more challenging in humanism and most of all in human services.

PART II

PAULO FREIRE, JEAN JACQUES ROUSSEAU, AND JOHN DEWEY ON EDUCATION AS THE PRACTICE OF FREEDOM: IDEAS FOR SECOND CHANCES TO THE OPPRESSED

Paulo Freire, a Brazilian, lived through the depression of the 1930s and so did Ronald Reagan. It was interesting that while Freire was a populist interested in giving a second chance to the poor, disadvantaged, illiterate, and the oppressed in society and became concerned with adult illiterates, Ronald Reagan became a reactionary conservative, who demeaned the poor for being on welfare and together with Margaret Thatcher championed a neoconservative neoliberal "free-market" economy around the world that has created a large gap between the poor and the rich in between and within countries.

After University, Freire, as professor, chose to teach reading and critical thinking. Though his work is grounded in Catholicism, he is not an orthodox Catholic, because he thinks conservative Catholicism condones oppression and condemns dissent. Freire attacked the arrogance of the rich oppressors and because the church encouraged the poor parishioners to passively accept the oppressive status-quo, Freire quit the church. He turned to Marxism as a way of constructing a new liberation theology. Freire argued that class struggle is essential for the removal of oppression. Reasoning with oppressors is futile, he contended.

Taking Marxist theory very seriously Freire believed in dialectical materialism, which believes that history is divided into stages (thesis) and during each stage, classes struggle (Antithesis) to change the status quo. Freire changed the names of the Marxist social classes. He replaced "bourgeoisie" with "oppressors," and the "oppressed" replaced the "proletariat." He did this because Marxist theory was not meant for agrarian society in Brazil but for industrialized societies such as Germany and England (Marx, 2009). For Freire, the oppressors were the ruling military elite and the rich business people, while the oppressed were the peasants. Frantz Fanon whose revolutionary theory is similar to Freire's divided the oppressed peripheral capitalist society in the Third World into the following classes: the petty bourgeoisie, the petty proletariat, the lumpen proletariat and the peasantry. Like Marxists, and Fanon, Freire believed that the oppressors use their power to control and oppress people. They control mass media, schools and the economic system. They instill fatalism and develop a false consciousness among the people. They make the little guys believe that the bourgeoisie class is the only one that works. They develop a culture of servants by a process Fanon calls "lactification" (Fanon, 1963, 2004). Servile culture is characterized by a dependency syndrome—perpetrated by handouts from the oppressors to the oppressed. These handouts could be threats, sanctions, coercion, or indoctrination through church and school.

Marxism as a revolutionary theory argues that whenever some people are privileged and others deprived, some are exploited and others exploit. Protests and eventually, revolutions will occur when the underprivileged become aware of these objective conditions—and organize to eliminate them. According to the "Objectivist" perspective, subjective class consciousness reflects objective and undesirable social realities. Leaders only act as "Midwives" leading the oppressed to understand the objective state of his or her affairs (Unseem, 1975).

Freire follows the same trend of thought. In his view, genuine theory can only be derived from some praxis rooted in historical struggles. He also knew that action without critical reflection and even without gratuitous contemplation is disastrous activism. Praxis therefore is the uniting of scientific efforts to understand political economy and the concrete revolutionary action to end oppression, which makes the oppressed people unable to meet their own basic needs (Ryan, 1976). In some cases oppression manifests itself in the form of the oppressed being doped, boozed, underpaid, violated, and incarcerated in large numbers by the oppressor.

Uniting theory and practice is what Freire calls praxis. He has a point as far as revolutionaries are concerned. History has shown us that the philosophers such as Voltaire and Rousseau influenced the French and American revolutions; Thomas Hobbes and John Locke influenced the Jeffersonian Declaration of American Independence for liberty and property and the pursuit of happiness. Marxist ideas encouraged the peoples of Asia, Africa, and Latin America to throw off colonial shackles.

Like Frantz Fanon, who learned about revolution by experiencing it in the French-Algerian War, Freire argues that one will understand revolution in action. Freire adds that the combination of the theory and practice of a revolution (praxis) must be done by the oppressed themselves who know where the shoes pinch. For Fanon it was the lumpen proletariat, who after failing to make ends meets in the capitalist city, would return to the peasants, incite them and lead a revolution. Freire argues that all the oppressed needs is to be educated in order to be humanized. He believes that since the human being is created in God's image s/he needs to go through the process of realizing complete humanization. This must be accomplished by the struggle against oppression by the people through praxis or as for Fanon, violence. In *Pedagogy of the Oppressed*, we find in "Education as the Practice of Freedom" the basic components of Freire's literacy method. These elements are: Participant observation of educators "tuning in" to the vocabulary universe of the people; their arduous search for generative words at two levels—syllabic richness and a high charge of experiential involvement; a first codification of these words into visual images which stimulate people "submerged" in the culture of silence to "emerge" as conscious makers of their own "culture"; the decodification by a "culture circle" under the self-effacing stimulus of a coordinator who is no "teacher" in the conventional sense, but who has become an educator-educatee—in dialogue with educatee-educators too often treated by formal educators as passive recipients of knowledge; creative new codification, this one explicitly critical and aimed at action, wherein those who were formerly illiterate now begin to reject their role as mere "objects" in nature and social history and undertake to become "subjects" of their own destiny (Freire, 1973, viii).

This literacy educational blueprint summaries the kind of education Freire would recommend for humanizing the oppressed. In this type of education an educator is a coordinator who facilitates social inquiry. Through this education as a humanizing process, the oppressed come to perceive their own illiteracy as the cultural artifact of those who oppress them. This is a first release from those written words which their oppressors had kept imprisoned in the magic tool box . . . of the stewards of the culture of silence (p. viii). Education in the Freire mode is the practice of liberty because it frees the educator less than the educatees from the twin thralldom of silence and monologue. Both partners are liberated as they begin to learn, the one to know self as a being of worth, despite the stigma of illiteracy, poverty, or technological ignorance—and the other as capable of dialogue in spite of the straitjacket imposed by the role of educator as one who knows. I argue in agreement with Frere in this commensurate view of teacher and student as mutual beneficiaries in the learning-teaching process. I have experienced it myself as teacher-student.

Paulo Freire's central message is that one can know only to the extent that one "problematizes the natural, cultural and historical reality in which s/he is immersed. Problematizing is the antithesis of the technocrat's "problem-solving" stance. In the latter approach an expert takes some distance from reality, analyzes it into component parts, devises means for resolving difficulties in the most efficient way, and then dictates a strategy for policy. Such problem-solving, according to Freire, distorts the totality of human experience by reducing it to those dimensions that are amenable to treatment as mere difficulties to be solved.

On the other hand through "problematizing" an individual and an entire populace carries out the task of codifying total reality into symbols and doing so can generate critical consciousness and empower them to alter their relations with nature and social forces. This group consciousness leads to group reflection and organizing. This reflective group exercise should thrust all participants into dialogue with others whose historical "vocation" is to become transforming agents of their social reality. According to Freire only an education that "problematizes" things, a "problem-posing" education, as described in chapter two of *Pedagogy of the Oppressed* will facilitate praxis by making people subjects, instead of objects of their own history.

Freire, Rousseau, and Dewey

Now we turn to describing the understandings of individual and social freedom that underlie the works of Freire, Rousseau and Dewey. Freire's notion of freedom has always been dynamic and rooted in the historical process by which the oppressed struggle to "extroject" (the term is his), the slave consciousness which oppressors have "introjected" into the deepest recesses of their being. He also pays attention to the special oppression asked by the forces of democratic "freedom" or civil "liberty." Accordingly, he sees liberation as being both a dynamic activity and the partial conquest of those engaged in dialogical education (p. viii).

Paulo Freire, just like Thomas Hobbes, John Locke, and Jean Jacques Rousseau, believes that the tragedy of humans is their domination by the force of myths which turn against them; destroy and annihilate them converting them into mere spectators. Following Enrich Fromm's words in *Escape from Freedom*, Freire laments the demise of freedom by believing that wo/man "has become free from the external bonds that would prevent him from doing and thinking as he sees fit . . . the more s/he does this the more powerless /she feels, the more is s/he forced to conform . . ." (Fromm, 1960, pp. 255–256). In order to overcome helplessness, Freire advises society to be able to develop a flexible critical spirit, through education as practice of freedom. Equipped with such a spirit, humans will "perceive the contradictions in their society as emerging values in search of affirmation and fulfillment clash with earlier values seeking self-preservation" (Freire, 1973, p. 7).

According to Rousseau's idiom, human is by nature free, and the political order which promotes that freedom is the more solid for doing so (Plamenatz et al., 1972, p. 81). Rousseau believes that a human is "true to nature" when her/his passions are not insatiable, when they can all be satisfied, and when the attempt to satisfy them brings her/him, not enemies but friends. S/he is then at peace with self and neighbors. S/he is vigorous, free, and happy. Her/his freedom is not independence or license from social control, though, for we all need our neighbors as much as they need us. It is mutual dependence, cheerfully accepted (p. 382).

Rousseau loved freedom, unlike Plato who cared for it so little. Like Plato though, Rousseau thought evil a kind of anarchy. However, Rousseau was more anxious to prevent than to restrain it. For him the good man is not the strong man armed with virtue on guard over his soul. He did not want government of the foolish (full of appetite) by the wise (philosopher kings). He wanted a society "where the passions need little or no restraint, where humans need few defenses against themselves and each other because they live together under such conditions that is comes easily to them to love and help one another; a society where no human is dependent on a superior but only on friends and neighbors, on an entire community, on a society of equals in whose life he takes a full part." (pp. 390–391).

In his book on education, Rousseau makes Emile's tutor his friend just like Freire argues for a good relationship between educator and educatees. Emile's tutor is a companion, not a master. The tutor does not punish or scold, does not impose discipline. The tutor merely creates the environment enabling Emile to discipline himself/herself. The tutor teaches the pupil to be self-reliant and cannot succeed unless the tutor's lessons are so discreet that the pupil scarcely feels them to be lessons. The tutor does for the pupil, in a corrupt society, what the social environment would do for the human being in a properly constituted state. The tutor makes the pupil a person of good will, who freely accepts the legitimate rules which must be accepted for the public good, but question those that are draconian and illegitimate. Though there is an illiberal part to Rousseau's philosophy, it is his love of freedom, and of equality conceived as a means to freedom, which is more often to the fore. This love he tried to reconcile with the need for order through his doctrine of the general will. General will means the will of the sovereign that aims at the common good. Each individual has her or his own particular will that expresses what is best for her/him. The general will expresses what is best for the state as a whole. For Rousseau, however, the general will is not an abstract ideal. It is instead the will actually held by the people in their quality as citizens. It is laws that are accepted as just and those who don't follow the general will are breaking the law.

Rousseau comes close to order through his doctrine of Montaigne, who in his *Essays* tells us to let nature take her course, to deal gently with our neighbors and ourselves, not stifling our passions when they hurt us by finding harmless outlets for them. There is a place in nature for everything, let us follow her example and find a place for everything in ourselves. Rousseau, like Montaigne, when he learns human beings try to impose their preferences on their neighbors (such as the Reagan administration supporting the contras or the Bush administration invading Afghanistan and Iraq), he is moved to ask them by what authority they do so. Freire would quickly point to the oppressor and the oppressed.

John Dewey's work can be seen as a reaction to the mechanization of education and work that had accompanied industrialization in the United States. His theories called for a humanization of the classroom. The schools, at least could treat people as human beings rather than as machines and they could be used to overcome the alienation that seemed to be an inevitable concomitant of urban industrial life. Like Rousseau's Emile and Piaget's psychology, Dewey's Philosophy of the open classroom led to the progressive education movement he championed in the 1920s and 1930s in the United States. Committed to pragmatism he charged that the schools of his day were too rigid and constraining and that they taught students to be passive and docile. He advocated more freedom and democracy in the classroom.

In the second half of the nineteenth century, a period of rapid growth and change saw the growth of pragmatism. For the first time education theorists suggested that schools should be direct agents of social change. Dewey and others suggested that schools should, and could, solve the problems of society by changing or reconstructing it. Schools were to be initiators of change. As mentioned earlier, Dewey and all pragmatists were committed to a democratic form of government and in the process of government, backed by an education for democracy. For a leading pragmatist, John Dewey, education should release in individuals their intelligence so as to make democracy work. His aim was to enable individuals to cooperate intelligently in problem-solving situations. Education should be, for all individuals for as long as possible. The content of such education cannot remain fixed. It must constantly be in a process of change; selection being based on the information young people and adults need in order to solve intelligently the problems they face. John Dewey believed that children learn what they do rather than learn by sitting still and memorizing facts. He said that in educating kids, we are making the world of tomorrow since today's kids are tomorrow's citizens. For him, the task of democracy is forever the creation of a freer and more humane experience in which all share and participate.

Discussion

In focusing on praxis at the grassroots, let us address the question whether welfare or the private sector or nonprofit organizations or NGO's give second chances to those who deserve it. We have come a long way, haven't we? One African American lady spoke about the second chances that African Americans had gained through the liberation struggle and pointed out the remaining bottlenecks. As she pointed out, "During my lifetime, I saw the black/white signs removed from the Southern Railroad station. I saw the signs of segregation come down at the doctor's office. I saw young black women getting jobs at the banks. I saw young black men hired to the police department but only deployed to arrest fellow blacks. I was instrumental in getting a black woman a job in the tax assessor's office. So when I'm gone, you can just say, I tried to feed the hungry, to clothe the naked, to shelter the homeless. That was my calling, to help the helpless, till I lost the Maiden Black Storefront Nursing Home to the thump of the gavel at pitiful City Hall" (Arwilla Huff Davison, 1921–1994)

I think about her words every Black History Month, a celebration not to be taken with the usual beer and ribs. The celebration must compliment the spirit of the movement that brought the celebration into being. We must not allow the separation of Dr. Martin Luther King Jr., and other gallant leaders like him from the movement. We are challenged today to resurrect the message and let it stand beside all our great messengers, past and present.

Once, during Black history month I asked a group of inmates to write an essay about Martin Luther King Jr. and one of them wrote what Martin Luther King Jr. meant to him. He said King signifies freedom, equality, and *hope*. Here is the full essay:

> History has displayed the triumphs and victories of many men. One who I think stands out amongst most is Doctor Reverend Martin Luther King Junior, A man who has fought the battles of racism and segregation for many years. Dr. King's efforts have paved the way for not just one set of individuals - but any group of individuals who were discriminated against. His struggles go deeper than protests and ideas. It was a manner in which he did so, a peaceful manner, a nonviolent manner. The name Dr. Martin Luther King Jr. means numerous things to me. It means freedom, freedom in which one had to fight for faith. With that things will get better and we as people will overcome victory. The Victory of overcoming the obstacles that stood in the way, along our journey. It means celebration, a celebration that marks the end of a successful journey. It was these four components in which Dr. King's combined to give a glimmer of light, that shines and helps guide people through segregation and racial tension. His effort brought a lot of meaning to the word equality.

It is evident that many years ago this Country assess many Great Black Leaders, but there's one in particular I'm pertaining to now—Dr. Martin Luther King Jr. Unlike most Great Black Leaders who stood up and spoke to the Nation of Blacks. Mr. King spoke up for everyone in general as a whole course. His main goal was for us to have equal rights. As a matter of fact one of his famous sentences consisted of—"I had a dream that one day man would be judged not by the color of their skin, but by the contents of their character." She was considered a role model not only by blacks, but of people all over the world because of his belief in peace, love, and equality.

He was awarded with the Nobel Peace Prize which is the world's most respected award, but that award in his mind was no accomplishment at all, due to the fact that society didn't consist of being equal.

But if you look back in the past there was several other Martin Luther King's only difference were the names such as Malcom X, Abraham Lincoln and also when you take a look at it Jesus Christ, due to the fact that they all realized that we share the same biology regardless of ideology which we come to accept by encountering knowledge by accepting knowledge we learn to share and gather wisdom. I can sum up what Dr. Martin Luther King Jr. meant to us in one work, "HOPE,"—Hope that society will continue to strive timelessly every day to bring Peace to the world so that we all may be able to live in Peace and Harmony. From my understanding of Dr. King instead of him wishing the people to give him a National Holiday, he would have instead preferred a National World Wide day of togetherness—so could in one day succeed worldwide everyman and every man in one of his most famous sayings "Free at last, Free at last—thank God we are free at Last" (Antonio Franklin, 2016)

Washington may be where the rhetoric is pumped out, and a bill becomes law, but our local communities must be where the action takes place for passionate human services professional work to encourage the individual freedom of the client. We had better be prepared, especially given the counter-revolution now going on in the country. All eyes are on Washington these days, where the great debate begins between an administration committed to a proactive government role in solving the nation's critical social problems and a congressional majority skeptical of government's ability to do much of anything domestically right, except fight crime by incarcerating individuals and foster economic growth.

Our orders are already out in the context and text of the crime bill: "Don't attempt to get out of line; just shut up and obey; because we're going to use you up; and, then we're going to throw you away. It takes three strikes; and you're out! Don't think you can ever make us accountable for our white-collar misdeeds. Remember that it isn't wise to bite the hand that feeds you. And there's just not enough for everyone to live in luxury. So, someone has got to go; and it's not going to be the socially-registered billionaires!"

THE BATTLE OF THE BUDGET

The Battle of the Budget is the first test of strength as the adversaries press different conceptions of how government can best use its resources. Don't look for new programs to create jobs or to expand training and education opportunities for the poor, whose education and skills deficits keep them in poorly paid jobs or worse still unemployed.

Neither the resources nor the will are currently available in Washington and state capitals to pass such initiatives. Do look for proposals that sharply cut government programs aimed at sustaining poor people and creating opportunities for them to enter the mainstream, besides giving second chances to former convicts. Is this not Reaganomics revisited, and is it not nice, especially for those who fancy to say, "Well, we really hate to do it; but we are accustomed to the good life; and, someone's got to pay the bills; someone has got to get the knife?" "You've done nothing wrong; you've been quite dependable; but, you've got neither wealth nor power; so, you're the one who's expendable. What's that you say about justice? What is all that silly talk? Don't you know that justice is just a commodity on the auction block? And while you're making our profits; we'll be lounging by the pool. We've got to be well rested to be in shape to rule." Sounds like the Orwellian pigs on *Animal Farm*, doesn't it? Expect a welfare debate that centers not on creating jobs and providing necessary services, but on moving women and children off the welfare rolls and curtailing benefits. And expect increasing state and local responsibility in designing, financing and implementing social programs.

The congressional majority plans to cut and cap social spending entitlements and turn them over to the states. Even if that fails to win approval, still there will be much more state control of such programs. So our eyes should also be vigilant on the state capital and on the city halls, because that is where much of the action will be in the coming months and years. As responsibility and resources are shoved down to local level, it is important to have robust, activist citizens and organizations with the know-how and the clout to influence the way local governments use the funds Washington sends to them. That means an important new role for community human service organizations and for both opinion and action human service leaders especially in disadvantaged communities.

Grassroots praxis requires the combined efforts of human service workers and of many leaders of opinion and action who must try the best they can under duress to nurse the wounds and redress the dignity of every one suffering with the scars of oppression. Passion and freedom must be taught to all children in America, who will become citizens in their communities, where they will need skills to advocate for others and themselves. We can use a passion-freedom perspective to educate people on such critical issues as crime, welfare, education reform, and others.

As human service workers we must use passion to mobilize all people in our communities to become actively involved in solving these issues. We hope in the debates of reform, always going on in Washington, DC, well-meaning people will not lose their "storefront nursing homes" as Mrs. Arwilla Huff Davison, whose auto-eulogy was given above.

Right now, the infirm, the lanky, the frail, the thirsty, the handicapped, the hand-cuffed, the tender and vulnerable, the bereaved, the beleaguered, the widowed, the recovering, the hungry and convalescing are all in unison loudly crying out their *Song of Tears* to all legislators, but particularly to human service workers:

I know you know the value of life;
Your progeny and ontogeny
Determine what my posterity and I are worth
Reserving for yourself, ivy-league wealth
The highest living standard on Earth!

My life is in your hands
You take away my pride
Take away my self-esteem
Everything in the ghetto is yours
The barrio is also yours!

Everything I've got is yours
You take away my dreams
You're my lord and master
You control our destiny
I'm just human sacrifice;
To you that is always nice?!
I pay the price;
You don't think about it twice,
You just roll the dice

I stomp in the rain storm
With a thump I tramp
Do you hear the thump?!
The thunderous thud!?
As you stoop the gavel
Of human sacrifice,
To the gravitational pull of politics!?

There's a crack in our liberty
Does that ring a bell?
Does the ghetto chime and knell?
Hear it in the house and senate?!

Yes, there's a crack in our liberty!
Thud, down the Newt Gingrich gavel
As we slip through the cracks of heated debate
Yoked, and yanked out of mainstream;

Our sinews spiked, and spent.
Chimes of a contrived contract toll
Death of our time looms over the knoll
There's a crack in our welfare
But, please spare my civil rights
Save my human rights!
As I think about the future,
Make strategic plans,
Resist any Evil Eye!
Though soul gobblers pounce
As they dance atop our dreams.
(Alfred Kisubi, 2016)

In conclusion and from assessing the extent to which the ideas analyzed in the foregoing paragraphs, I consider it important for us as a society to promote freedom and give all individuals a chance and/or a second chance. We must uphold and abide by the noble principle of human services which stipulates that every individual in society is entitled to services which will prevent individual pain, maintain integrity, enable the individual to deal with realities, stimulate personal growth, and promote a satisfying life for the individual and family. The fleeting nature of the individual, which calls for changing strategies and a multifarious epistemology in human services, is expressed clearly in the following passage:

The whole person should be served by human services. People should not be known by their labels. No one is only a toothache, a neurosis, or a learning disability. The provision of human services needs to be undertaken in an atmosphere of respect and understanding of every individual's uniqueness, with full recognition that people are dynamic, constantly changing in an ongoing process of "becoming" (Ericksen, 1981, 9).

REFERENCES

Bergman, Samuel, H. (1991). *Dialogical Philosophy from Kierkegaard to Buber*. Albany, NY: State University of New York Press.

Derathe, Robert. "Jean Jacques Rousseau," *Encyclopedia of Social Sciences*. pp. 563–670.

Dewey, John. (1897). My Pedagogic Creed. New York.

Dewey, John. (1900). The School and Society. Chicago.

Dewey, John. (1902). The Child and Curriculum. Chicago/New York: The Seabury Press.

Fanon, Frantz. (1963, 2004). The Wretched of the Earth. Translated from French to English by Franklin, A. (2016). *Essay on What Dr. Reverend Martin Luther, Jr. Means to Me*. Unpublished essay for Black History Month.

Freire, Paulo. Education for Critical Consciousness. New York, The Seabury Press, 1973.

Harris, Howard S., Maloney, David C., Rother, Franklyn M. (2004). *Human Services: Contemporary Issues and Trends.* (3rd Ed.). Boston, MA: Pearson Education.

Kisubi, A. T. (2016). *Song of Tears.* Unpublished poem.

Kisubi, A. T. (2016). *My Dream is you.* Unpublished poem.

Marx, Karl. (2009). *Das Kapital.* Washington, DC: Regnery Publishing.

Montesquieu, Charles (1748, 1914). *The Spirit of the Laws.* Translated by Thomas Nugent, revised by J. V. Prichard. London: G. Bell & Sons Ltd.

Owen, J. (July 18, 2007). "Modern Humans Came Out of Africa, "Definitive" Study says". *National Geographic News.* Retrieved October 18, 2016 from http://news.nationalgeographic.com/news/2007/07/070718-african-origin_2.html.

Plamenatz, "Burke," and "Rousseau," *Man and Society: A critical examination of some important social and political theories from Machiavelli to Marx.* London: Lowe and Brydon Printers Ltd., 1972, Ch 9, pp. 332–363, and Ch 10, pp. 364–442.

Wautischer, H., Olson, Alan M., Walters, Gregory J. (2012). Philosophical Faith and the Future of Humanity. New York: Springer Science + Business Media at www.springer.com. Also read more at: http://www.brainyquote.com/quotes/quotes/k/karljasper310613.html

Chapter Seven

Crime, Justice, Drugs, and Deviance

A Human Services Perspective

Derek Dich

Crime, drugs, and deviance have unfortunately become very serious issues within the United States. It seems that almost every breaking news story has to do with some criminal activity related to drugs and deviance. The sad part here is that American society appears to have become warped in the sense that its members are drawn to these stories of murder and drug abuse. This chapter focuses on questions regarding the social factors that have contributed to both an increase in crime along with inequality in terms of punishment and how the relationship between drugs and crime has become so tightknit from a human services perspective, especially considering how the issues of drugs and crimes affect people all through their lives.

Some members of our society believe that crime has gotten bigger, "better," and far more widespread within the country. Violence is also everywhere: on the internet, on television, in books, and in films. We are constantly being bombarded by it even we try our best to avoid it. We soak in violence constantly, so is it truly a surprise that there are so many violent acts and crimes committed? "And though levels of violent crime are not as high as they were at their peak in the early 1990s, they remain higher than they were before the dramatic increases in imprisonment of the past 40 years" (Skolnick & Currie, 2011, p. 323). The very same can be said about drugs. Drugs are also seen throughout all media sources in our country. It seems as if drug abuse has even oddly become glorified at times, such as the stories about celebrities in rehab. Instead of shaming drug abuse and advocating for drug avoidance, our society now pokes fun at "crackhead" celebrities and bumbling alcoholics. This strange shift has created a seemingly lackadaisical view of crime and drugs. The reality is that crime and drugs have become a huge issue for all types of people within the country. Many minorities and people who live in low-income areas are often times the ones who get disciplined and imprisoned for criminal activities. It makes little sense that a celebrity is glorified and allowed to walk free after successful rehabilitation, while other people, especially the poor, are simply locked away for years if they are found to have abused drugs.

As a society we have witnessed very unfair trends with regard to imprisonment. "Two trends are responsible for the increase in imprisonment. First, the courts are imposing longer sentences for such nonviolent felonies as larceny, theft, and motor vehicle theft. . . . Second, drugs have become the driving force of crime. More than half of all violent offenders are under the influence of alcohol or drugs when they commit their crimes" (Skolnick, 2011, p. 339). This situation is a sad testimony to the state of American society. Crime and drugs have become the "best of friends." With that, such bigtime white-criminals are able to evade any type of criminal justice punishment. "The three strikes laws, like our criminal justice system generally, most often sweep up people from the lower end of the social and economic spectrum—especially the minority poor and minorities. At the other end of the scale is another kind of criminal—the affluent offenders, often corporate executives, who commit so-called white-collar crimes" (Skolnick & Currie, 2011, p. 324). There exists a mass-inequality in regards to criminal justice consistency and fairness. Should these white-collar criminals not face the same discipline as those living in poverty? Are all people not equal in America?

Compared to other advanced countries, it unfortunately appears that the United States may have the highest rates of violent crimes and drug abuse. "International comparisons of crime date, while inexact, do provide rough approximations of how crime is patterned geographically. What is known is that among the industrialized nations there is not much difference in burglaries, bicycle thefts, and other property crimes. What is striking, however, is that among these nations, the United States has much higher rates of violent crimes (robberies, assaults, murders, and rapes)" (Eitzen, 2010, p. 193). This is most likely due to the countries wide economic gap. People living in poverty are more desperate than those with financial security. Because of this yawning gap between the rich and the poor, more crimes are being committed and thus more people are becoming imprisoned. "The United States has the highest rates of serious violent crime of any advanced industrial nation, and at the same time it confines a greater proportion of its people in jails and prisons—six times the proportion in the United Kingdom, nine times that in Sweden, twelve times that of Japan" (Skolnick & Currie, 2011, p. 323). In my view, the violent crimes in the United States are the unfortunate result of our societal system. In a democratic country with as many freedoms as America has, it is no surprise that gaps are created across the board. Is it completely fair? No, but that is the nature of this country. With inequality, we see the outbreak of violence and frustration. That being said, we claim to love our freedoms, and yet we call for equality in all areas of our society. In that case, the United States would seem to subscribe to socialist ideals. We cannot have equality when we do not have equality in work-ethic and opportunities for everyone. We could give two different people the exact same task and receive two vastly different responses. Calling for complete equality in America makes the assumption that everyone wants the same and that everyone is willing to put in the same amount of work. I would love to have a completely optimistic view and state that everyone deserves exactly the same, but I cannot fully subscribe to that. I wish that people could get the help that they need to diffuse violent crimes.

This is where the importance of Human Services comes into play. The field needs to work hard on expanding its advocacy and preventive aspects. From the perspective of this field, we can certainly improve upon the issue of crime and drug abuse in America. To achieve this goal, we must first start with peeling back the layers of these issues and looking at why people commit violent crimes and abuse drugs in the first place. Locking up drug abusers in prison does not solve their problem. By addressing the preexisting issues, we can then bring about change. As Homan (2011) pointed out, "[I]ssues bring an undesirable situation into focus in a way that leads to action" (p. 331). By dissecting the issues that exist beneath crime and drug abuse, we can identify what actually needs to be addressed and changed. Once we identify the actual causes, we can then go public and advocate for positive change using any number of approaches, including "press conferences, public demonstrations, and other acts as forceful coming-out events" (Homan, 2011, p. 343). In my own community, we have a major issue concerning heroine abuse. Recently, we started to see more public dialogue and the formation of panels to bring the issue to light. This may be exactly what we need to do through Human Services policies.

Regarding drugs, other advanced countries that have legalized drugs that are still illegal in the United States have experienced better results. The Netherlands, for example, has legalized marijuana and "The Dutch experience with decriminalization provides support for those who want to lift U.S. criminal penalties for marijuana possession. It is hard to identify differences between the United States and the Netherlands that would make marijuana decriminalization more dangerous here than there" (MacCoun & Reuter, 1999, p. 214). In my view, the US government would be wise to legalize marijuana and other drugs and privatize them. Think of all of the tax dollars that the government could collect on marijuana purchases. It could simply become another taxable item for Americans to consume. Alcohol, which is legal, is a far worse drug with many more problems for Americans. I also do not think that everyone would suddenly start smoking marijuana just because the drug was legalized. After all, alcohol is a legalized drug that many people do not use and have no interest in ever using. The reality is that even though marijuana and other drugs are illegal within the United States, they are still widely used. I honestly feel that we should be able to move past the conversation about marijuana legalization and focus the country's time and resources to some more pressing social issues. It does not seem reasonable that an often times recreational drug becomes a more debated topic than, for example, poverty, the education system, racism, sexism, and so forth. It almost feels as if the US government keeps these seemingly unimportant issues alive so as to distract the nation from other more pressure ones.

Violent crimes and drug abuse are often hush-hush issues within our society, but Homan (2011, p. 347) informs us that "[L]eadership involves some degree of risk taking." Shedding light upon such leaders and bringing them to the forefront is absolutely necessary to create future change. Nothing that lies in the shadows will ever get enough attention or support. We can also find leaders in our communities who have had personal experiences with the issues of crime and drug abuse. If we can find someone who is willing to take the risk and put their name and face on these issues, we stand a good chance of getting people's attention. We can go out and find personal stories from individuals who have faced these issues. Bringing them into our cause can help create a personalized and genuine purpose. It is that much more powerful to hear advocacy from individuals that have come out at the other end of these issues. With all of this, we can then call for action. We can advocate for more drug-awareness programs and the formation of new facilities to help people and hopefully deter them from feeling the need to commit crimes. Simply spreading word of existing resources could perhaps be beneficial. Many people are completely unaware of the drug-treatment facilities that already exist within their communities. As with any other social issue, creating a strong, community effort is the key to improvements.

I can relate to the issues of crime and drugs very easily. As I mentioned above, heroine has become a major issue in the city where I live. Our community has lost far too many young individuals to heroin and other drug overdosing. Many students that I have graduated from high school with have passed away over just the past five years. I have also heard stories about how these drug habits have led to so many crimes. When someone is abusing a drug and becomes addicted, he/she does whatever he/she can to get that next fix. This situation oftentimes involves other crimes to get more money to purchase more drugs. In these cases, I feel that their conscious and sense of judgment has left them and they become consumed by their habit. Also, my mother actually has taught at the local jail for many years. I have known her to have come into contact with "criminals" who are simply individuals facing hardships. Our society often assumes the worst of people who commit crimes and go to jail. Many times these individuals are under the influence of something and are in a terrible place. I still do not condone stealing or any crimes, but I do understand where a lot of these people are coming from. When you have nothing, you often feel as if you have nothing to lose. As a small community, West Bend never seemed to have many crimes happening in it, and this has changed in more recent times. I think this change has a lot to do with the change in our economy and an overall downward drift of our society. I also feel that it has a lot to do with the increase in drug abuse. On a personal note, I have thankfully never been addicted to drugs and never felt the need to commit any crimes. However, in some ways, I just feel sorry for those who do, and as I think of a future Human Services practice, I plan to do the best I can to never pass any quick judgments on those who get themselves involved in these acts.

The issues of crime and drugs can be easily linked to many other social issues in our society. First, crime and drugs can be linked to the power of corporations in the sense that bigtime corporations are often able to evade punishment for the crimes that they commit. Those not at the helm of big corporations do not share this luxury. Regarding racism, minorities are often times unfairly viewed as criminals. This is why we see such a high rate of incarceration for African Americans and Hispanics within the country. This is sad and wrong, especially because people of all colors and backgrounds commit crimes. White corporate CEOs seem to be exempt from these stereotypes, while African Americans have to live with it on a daily basis. Schools and family issues are also closely related to crime and drug abuse. When individuals are uneducated and have problems at home, they become much more likely to commit crimes or abuse drugs. The same can be said about those who do not have jobs and equal work opportunities and are put into desperate situations. From the foregoing, one can conclude that the problem of crimes and drugs in our society is much more complex than we usually realize. To adequately address the problems of crime and drugs, we must, as a society, be willing to address the problems in our communities comprehensively. Limiting any remedies to only crime and drug issues will not provide the transformation we desire.

REFERENCES

Eitzen, D. S. (2010). *Solutions to Social Problems: Lessons from Other Societies.* (5th ed., pp. 193–194) Boston, MA: Allyn & Bacon.

Homan, M. (2011). *Promoting Community Change: Making It Happen in the Real World.* (5th ed., pp. 329–376). Belmont, CA: Brooks/Cole Publication.

MacCoun, R. J., & Reuter, P. (1999). Does Europe Do It Better? Lessons from Holland, Britain, and Switzerland. In D. Stanley Eitzen (Ed.) *Solutions to Social Problems: Lessons from Other Societies.* (5th Ed.) Boston, MA: Allyn & Bacon.

Skolnick, J. (2011). Wild Pitch: "Three Strikes, You're Out" and Other Bad Calls on Crime. In Skolnick, J., & Currie, E. (Eds.) *Crisis in American Institutions*. (14th ed., p. 335–352). Boston, MA: Allyn & Bacon.

Skolnick, J., & Currie, E. (2011). *Crisis in American Institutions*. Boston, MA: Allyn & Bacon.

Chapter Eight

STEP Industries and Its Origins

Anonymous

I was born in 1933 in Milwaukee, Wisconsin. My sister, Sally, came along two years later. My father, an electrical engineering graduate from Marquette, lost his job in 1936 and we started a long series of moves to various locations as Dad sought to support the family with employment at many different companies. In 1949–1950 we were living in Toledo, Ohio. In my junior year at DeVilbiss High School, Dad announced that we were moving to Atlanta, Georgia, and in my mind, life had ended. I finished high school at North Fulton in Atlanta in the spring of 1951 and was accepted for entrance to The Georgia Institute of Technology starting in the fall of 1951. At this point in life, I had not had alcoholic drinks away from home and only sips and tastes there. At the Georgia Institute of Technology, I joined a fraternity and my membership of that fraternity started my drinking education. When I graduated from Georgia Tech in 1955, I received two degrees, a 'Bachelor's of chemical engineering and a PhD in drinking. I had excelled in the drinking education. It is likely that I was drinking alcoholically by 1955. Indeed, I was drunk essentially every weekend and had already started the practice of drinking to get drunk.

Since I was in the Air Force ROTC at Georgia Tech, I had an obligation to serve on active duty. Originally, I had been scheduled to become a pilot, but an eye examination ended that ambition and I was ordered to report to Francis E. Warren Air Force Base in Cheyenne, Wyoming, in the fall of 1955 for supply officer training. I had already accepted employment with the Kimberly-Clark Corporation and was working at the Corporation's Memphis mill as a manufacturing understudy.

I met my future wife, Hilde Kraus, at the Officer's Club in Cheyenne shortly after arriving in Wyoming and we were married on February 9, 1956, in Douglas, Wyoming. I was later ordered to report to Patrick Air Force Base at Cape Canaveral, Florida. We rented a very small apartment that was right on the Atlantic ocean in Cocoa Beach, Florida. Our first son arrived in nine months and after a total of twenty-one months on active duty I was released and returned to Memphis where I continued to work at Kimberly-Clark. I was not in Memphis very long and was asked to go to New Milford, Connecticut, as a process engineer for a new mill that was under construction there. The posting to New Milford, Connecticut, started a long series of moves with Kimberly-Clark Corporation. From New Milford, Connecticut, back to Memphis, Tennessee, and later onto Beach Island, South Carolina. From South Carolina, I was sent to Conway, Arkansas, and finally also sent to Neenah, Wisconsin. When we lived in South Carolina, God put a man across the street from us who would eventually carry to me the message of recovery. Meanwhile, my drinking was progressing and was becoming much more of a problem with the passage of time. When I finally stopped drinking I was drunk every night and every morning I would resolve to not do that again and by noon I was planning the evening drunk.

Somehow at Kimberly-Clark Corporation, I had been promoted to vice president of manufacturing for the Consumer Products Division. My superiors were starting to wonder about my performance, but they had no idea that my work performance was greatly affected by my drinking. At that point in 1979, my former neighbor from my days in South Carolina again appeared in my life. He had been sober for two years and for the first time in my life I listened to what he had to say about alcoholism. For a lot of years I had been in "denial" that my drinking was a problem and my friend destroyed that idea. He also told me that if I concluded that I was an alcoholic, I would need help to recover. He suggested Alcoholics Anonymous and in my mind I rejected that option. Instead, I decided to go to Kimberly-Clark's employee assistance program.

On August 19, 1979, I met with Dr. Dedmon, the head of the program and after a long discussion I finally convinced him that I was an alcoholic. He said that I could never drink again from that moment on. I immediately felt some relief as if the weight of the world had been lifted off of me. What a simple thing. Why had I never thought of it? Just don't drink. I had not told him about my marijuana use or the occasional valium I took and it was therefore a piece of cake to stop drinking. When the urge to drink struck, I would either smoke a joint or pop a valium.

I had been traveling to the mills to set the following year's budgets and when I returned I again met Dr. Dedmon. He said I needed to go to treatment and sent me to Oshkosh to a new outpatient program called "HALT." My primary counselor in the program was Dave Lambert. Mr. Lambert was assisted by Cheryl Wondra. HALT was a great program and I learned that treatment involved a crash course in the Alcoholic Anonymous program. Since I had very little patience, this kind of treatment was wonderful for me and I learned a great deal in the program about alcoholism and about myself. I could not believe the damage I had caused to my family and those around me. We worked through the fifth step in treatment and fairly soon after completing the five first steps of the HALT Program I went on to complete the sixth, seventh, and eighth steps. I started working on the ninth step. About the time of my second meeting with Dr. Dedmon, I started to work with Shirley Webster who was a counselor in the Employee Assistance Program. Shirley was hired by Kimberly-Clark Corporation after she had worked at Hazelden as an alcohol or other drug addiction (AODA) counselor. Shirley was a great help to me and actually found the man that eventually became my sponsor, namely, Jim Patterson. Between Shirley and Jim I received lots of loving guidance and suggestions. Jim would listen to my litany of problems and then say, "well that doesn't sound too bad and if you don't drink, read the big book and go to meetings everything will work out." I hated that response as I wanted Jim to solve my problems and I could not see that he had actually given me the answer. My first year in recovery was spent fighting pretty much all suggestions and then slowly improving as I gave up and worked the steps to the best of my ability.

After I had approximately a year of sobriety I had an intense desire to help others. I think I first went to Dr. Dedmon and said something like I was ready to help Kimberly-Clark Corporation with the folks there who were drinking that I could see needed help. Naturally this approach was rejected, but they did get me on the board of directors for the Mooring House [a halfway house] and there I first learned that many alcoholics in recovery had a very hard time obtaining employment as their work records were so bad that no one would hire them. I also learned that many alcoholics seemed to have a low self-esteem and lots of other issues that prevented them from becoming useful members of society. In addition, I was going to five or six meetings a week and I often heard newcomers complaining that sobriety "sucked as they couldn't find work." One day, as a part of my job, I was touring the corporation's Lakeview Diaper Manufacturing Facility in Neenah, Wisconsin, and I observed what happened when the operator of a machine pressed the reject button to remove a small portion of the machine's output that had some sort of defect. The machine produced about a thousand diapers per minute. Occasionally there would a small number of defective diapers. As an example, each time they changed a roll of material, there would be a small number of defective diapers that had to be rejected. When he pressed the reject button, and given the speed of the machine, a huge number of diapers were rejected and most of these rejected diapers were good diapers. Kimberly-Clark Corporation could not sort these rejects as the wage rates were too high to affordably do so and the Corporation also did not have the staff to sort the rejects that were generated intermittently in the production process. One day, God put the idea in my head that a company could be established to sort the diapers and such a company could employ recovering drug or alcoholic folks or members of their families. The idea was that employing the drunks could help them establish a good work record, improve their self-esteem, and help them learn how to work again so that they would be employable, and after a period of time, move on to other employment or even return to school if they so wished.

I secured the permission and approval of Darwin Smith, CEO and chairman of the board of Kimberly-Clark Corporation to proceed with the setting up of such a company with only one restriction. The lone restriction was that I would receive no income from the new company as long as I was employed by Kimberly-Clark Corporation.

So we started to form a company and select key people. It was our desire to operate under the general traditions of Alcoholics Anonymous. Andy Anderson, a member of the community who seemed to have the leadership and needy skills, was asked to be the president of the company and he willingly accepted, but essentially before we were operational, he resigned and did what he had wanted to do all along. His desire had always been to establish a treatment center for the Fox Valley. He excelled in this effort and helped many people to break the bonds of alcohol and drug addiction.

Jim Patterson was then approached and asked if he would be the president and he agreed. Jim had a wonderful way of working with others and he strived to make the company operate under the general traditions of Alcoholics Anonymous.

We asked Hugh Holly, another member of the community whom I had known along the way, if he would accept the position of operations manager and he accepted. At the time, Hugh was working as AODA counselor in Oshkosh. I had met him at Alcoholic Anonymous meetings in Waupaca and saw him as a very bright strong leader. Dave Lambert also recommended Jim Hanseder for the Financial Manager position. It was a great recommendation.

When the basic group was in place other issues were addressed. We needed money and towards this end, a group of us went to the First Nation Bank of Neenah and asked for a loan of $300,000 to start the company. The money was quickly granted and latter we found out that the bank assumed that we were a part of Kimberly-Clark Corporation and that Kimberly-Clark would secure the loan. This never became an issue as the loan was repaid within a couple of years once the company was operational.

We established a board of directors. John H., Hugh Holly, Jim Patterson, Jim Hanseder, Dick Auchter, Shirley Webster, Pricilla Catlin, Jerry Schaffer, Dean Grant, and Wayne Summer comprised the initial board. There was a story about each of these people and a reason they were selected. Many of them are now long gone. Andy Anderson was on the board for a very short time before he resigned and Jim Patterson was thus hired to replace Andy.

We needed a name and I think Pricilla Catlin suggested STEP and it was selected as the name and the company became STEP Industries.

Thus the company was established and we began to hire recovering people to sort diapers. I think the most important thing that happened however was the establishment of a loving and caring atmosphere that was significant in helping many people recover their self-esteem, establish a good work record and again become employable and useful members of society. Hugh Holly set the proper and winning operational tone.

Chapter Nine

STEP Industries and Me

Michelle Devine Giese

I was born the youngest of eight with siblings ranging from six- to nineteen-years-old, being the sixth girl. My childhood was filled with many caregivers and surrogate parents, most of whom were my siblings and their significant others. My first nephew was born when I was three. This was devastating to me, and maybe my first memory, as I was no longer the baby of the family.

I began going to preschool when I was three and kindergarten at age four. I always had at least one relative in my classes as my father had a large family, and the town was filled with many cousins.

During the summer when I was seven, we moved from Owen-Withee, Wisconsin, to Stevens Point. We moved away from some of my siblings, which was a huge change in my life. Shortly after the move, an addition niece and nephew were born. I think this is where and when I became more independent but also felt a bit of a loss. I began taking dance classes and was given opportunities that small town living did not afford.

Two years later, my parents, sister, and I moved to Appleton. Moving was very difficult for me this time. Not only did we move away from more siblings, but we moved in the day school begun. I had no friends and did not know a soul in Appleton. Friendships grew quickly, and school became more of a social activity that I enjoyed.

In junior high and high school, I was on the pom-pon squad and became captain my senior year. School came pretty easy to me with little effort. I did not study hard or stress over homework as some of friends did, but I did enough to get Bs.

During this time, I also experimented with alcohol. I would drink here and there, but it never had a huge pull for me. The first time I got drunk was at a house party when I was senior in high school. I remember not being able to think real clearly feeling really good. At that point, I saw the appeal and understood why people got drunk.

I grew up in a house where alcohol was available but not abused. There was drinking at some family events, but it was usually not the focus of the event. The family was filled with siblings who either liked to drink or only drank once or twice a year. I had not seen much abuse of alcohol in my life until I became the abuser.

I went to college at UW Stout when I was just seventeen years old. Within my first month of college, I got an underage drinking fine for drinking in the dorms. I think I was lonely, trying to make a new life at college, and trying to figure out where I fit in. Many of the males in our dorm were older and had friends with houses, so most weekends were spent going to house parties if I wasn't visiting home. I found that parties were much more fun if I was drunk. I began to look forward to parties and not go home as often. In a short amount of time, I found I was drinking once a week or so, usually drinking to excess and not realizing I drank too much until it was too late.

I joined a sorority, thinking there would be more opportunity to drink and more parties to attend. I was right. The drinking became a Thursday–Sunday binge, often staying in bed well into the afternoon, only to get up and do it all over again. I experimented with speed and marijuana during this time, but alcohol was really my drug of choice. My drinking was out of control at this point. I was missing classes because I could not get up for them even if they were in the afternoon, skipping them to go to the bar, or going to the bar for lunch and not leaving until close. I was always either the person who did not want the party to end or the one passed out in the corner. In 1991, I got my first OWI. I lied during the assessment, was given minimal alcohol education, and sent on my way. In 1993, I managed to graduate with a BS in business administration and a concentration in human resource management with a 3.6 GPA in my core classes.

I got a job in Minneapolis, Minnesota. I tried to get my drinking under control. I would only drink more than a six-pack if I did not have to work the next day. I would drink only at home alone if I had to work the next day, but this was short lived. Soon, I could not stop at just six. My job kept me moving around the Twin Cities to different stores: opening them, hiring and training staff, fixing issues like low sales or cleanliness, and then move to a different store. In 1994, I got my second OWI with a blood alcohol content of .27. I did not feel drunk that night. I remember it all very clearly. I spent ten days in jail, ten days on home arrest, and had to go to alcohol education again. The corrections officials at the jail called the judge to see if I could do all my time at home and not in jail (they did this without my knowing), as they did not think I should be with the population at the jail. The judge said no, so I had to spend my time in jail.

My drinking continued to escalate. I began drinking in the morning to get rid of the hangover and shaking. I could not function without that first drink in the morning. At this point, I had been drinking daily for about two years. I was drinking pretty much all waking hours until I passed out every night. One day, I went in to work hungover, and on my way back to getting drunk, my bossed called. I got irritated and quit my job. At this point, things were unraveling as I was barely paying my bills, barely functioning, and not happy with my life. I remember thinking some nights it would be ok if I just did not wake up in the morning.

I asked my parents if I could move home in April of 1995. They had suspected that my drinking was out of control but did not know what to do. They tried talking to me about it, but my denial and wrath were strong. I job-hopped a lot and never kept employment very long. I started keeping a bottle under my bed so if I awoke in the night, I could drink to go back to sleep. I often had a hard time standing up straight. I was always lightheaded. My vision was like looking down a tunnel; I could not see what was on either side of me. I knew I was in bad shape, but it was just too overwhelming for me to think about my life without alcohol. My whole life had revolved around alcohol for so long I could not envision a life without it, and I knew enough about alcoholism that I could never touch it again if I stopped. I was not ready for that.

On October 15, 1995, my whole life changed. I was in a major car accident on Highway 10. I walked away with whiplash, and the other people with bruises, but we all could have died because of me. I could have killed four innocent people. My family filled the emergency room soon after the accident. I told the officer at the scene that I needed help for my alcoholism and asked him to tell my parents.

The next day, which was the day before my twenty-fifth birthday, with the help of my sister's EAP program, I was in Theda Clark's residential treatment facility. My sister and father dropped me off. My sister describes it as dreary and drab, and my memories of it were of a safe place. During the assessment, the counselor asked me what I thought about out-patient treatment, and I told her I would drink that night if she sent me home. Being in a safe place where I could not access alcohol, I was grateful as I knew I could not stop myself from drinking.

Treatment was scary, emotionally draining, but uplifting also. I was filled with embarrassment, shame, and guilt, and they helped me work through it. They helped me see that decisions I made were not good, and it did not mean that I was not good. They helped me identify what I needed and how to express it to myself and others. They taught my parents that it was not their fault nor was it my fault; it is disease, and once diagnosed properly and treated, I could recover. They told me what I needed to do if I wanted to recover. They told me I had to change my whole life, not just stop drinking.

They told me I had to change my friends, my hobbies, and the places I liked to go. I listened, and life changed.

After fifteen days, my insurance would no longer cover my stay, so I moved back home. My parents had gotten rid of all the alcohol in the house and gotten coaching from my counselor about changes in our new lives together, as their lives with me where changing too. I began intensive outpatient treatment four nights a week for three to four hours plus one-on-one time with my counselor. When the six weeks were up, I told her I was not ready to be discharged and kept going for two more weeks. Treatment taught me to identify risks and ask for help, so I did. Many people in the group thought I was crazy for wanting to stay longer, but I knew I needed it. I then went to three months of relapse prevention, one night a week. During this time, I met great new friends with whom I went to meetings, ate pizza, drank coffee, watched the Packers, and laughed. Life was getting better.

During these months, I was also going to court for the car accident I caused. I was looking at up to eight years in prison. I had a public defender that helped me through the process along with the support of family and new friends. In February of 1996, I was sentenced to four months in jail, five years of probation, and the loss of my driver's license for five years. I was scared, grateful, and relieved.

I had been working part-time at JC Penny's since November. I did not have a driver's license, so my parents, sister, or friends would drive me. My coworkers did not know I was an alcoholic. About once a week, someone would ask about going out for drinks or going to Chi Chi's for margaritas. I would just say that I could not go, too embarrassed and ashamed. I thought about going and ordering a non-alcoholic drink, but I remembered the counselor warning me of going to bars to "fit in;" after a while, it could lead to ordering a real drink, and that could lead to me picking up right where I left off. I did not want to risk it, so I never went. Pretty soon they stopped asking and treated me differently. One day, I told one of my coworkers why I didn't want to go out with them. Soon many coworkers knew, and I was embarrassed. I tended to work better with the older, more mature crowd and just focused my job.

One day at relapse prevention, someone mentioned they got job at STEP Industries. I asked what it was, and they said it was a place where everyone was in recovery. I remember thinking "no way" (yes, that is the exact thing I thought). I had never heard of such place, where everyone was in recovery. I called the next day. I had an interview and almost was not hired as Fritz (who did the interview) thought I would be able to get a job elsewhere because I had a bachelor degree. I told him I was going to jail, and I needed to work in a safe place. I told him about the people at JC Penney, and the next day he called and offered me a job. I was thrilled. In March of 1996, I started working at STEP Industries and entered jail.

STEP Industries is a social enterprise offering hope to men and women recovering from alcohol or drug addiction through personal growth and transitional employment. STEP offers a safe place where the past does not matter; only what is happening today and what people are doing in their recoveries matters.

On my first day at STEP, there was a group of us waiting for orientation. The team leader doing the orientation introduced herself as Kelly. She said she was in recovery and started out working on the same line we were going to work on. I was thrilled; she just said it. She was not afraid or embarrassed. It put me at ease. Everyone shared a little bit about themselves, how long they had been clean, and how they ended up coming to STEP. Nobody mentioned past jobs or education, just talked about their recovery. We were all the same! I could tell people I was an alcoholic, and it did not even faze them. I finally felt like I belonged. She talked about improving our work records from the past and what it meant to be a good worker. She taught us how to punch a time clock, what was expected of us, and what we could expect from STEP.

Kelly introduced us to the team, gave us each a buddy to help train us, and we started working. The buddy was more than a trainer; they shared their story too about how they got to STEP and where they were now in life. It helped me feel like I was in exactly the right place. The work was boring and sometimes hard, but the people were fabulous. When I was scared about going to jail, someone who had been to jail told me to hang in there and that it would get better. People asked me to go to meetings or out for dinner. I asked someone about a ride to and from work when I found out she lived by me, and we became very good friends.

Each morning, we started out with "huddle." It was kind of weird at first, but after a couple days, I thought it was great. In huddle, we talked about how we did the day before with our production and if there were any issues. During huddle, we would talk about struggles we may be having and celebrated sixty, ninety, or however many clean days someone had. We would read from a recovery related book, exercise, say the serenity prayer, and then go to work. It was a great way to start each day. I thought "I can do this until I get out of jail, and then I will get a 'real job' in about four to five months." Little did I know how STEP would become part of me and my future.

Jail was awful, as it is supposed to be. The food is horrible. There is no privacy. People are very negative, but I have always been grateful for the experience. In AA Big Book, it states that if we do not stay sober the outcome is "jails, institutions, or death." I knew jail and did not what to know the other two. The time in jail affirmed with me that I did not want that life anymore. I wanted a different life and a different direction than where I was going six months before.

After I got out of jail in July of 1996, my dad suggested I stay at STEP until I had a year clean. He thought it would be good for me to focus on my recovery and not worry about my career for a while. We had been told that if I stayed clean the first year my chances of long term recovery were better, so I felt like staying was the best thing for me to do. After a few months, I became a bagger on the diaper line and then a key person. I kept production counts, did quality checks, and filled in for the team leader when she would be on vacation. I really liked working with new employees and helping them learn the tricks I used to keep me on course throughout a day- breaking down my goals by the hour and playing little games and challenges with myself. I made a lot of great friends. We had camaraderie and supported each other. I continued to live with my parents and work weekends at JC Penney as I had many bills, fines, and restitution to pay.

I was coming up on my year of clean time when my team leader told me she was moving on to a different job and thought I should apply to take her place. I talked to my parents, and they thought it was a good idea to stay in the environment I felt comfortable in. They knew I liked the people I was working with, so they were supportive. I became a team leader in training November of 1996. I loved it. I really enjoyed the new people, leading huddle, and getting to know the employees while working alongside them. We all took breaks together, talked about recovery, and shared what was going on in our lives. A few months later, the diaper line was being closed. I thought I may be out of job but instead was training to work in the research and development department as a team leader. I now had a room with twenty to twenty-five people who were working on studies for Kimberly Clark. We had people from twenty-six to seventy-five years old working together, teaching, sharing, and supporting each other. I enjoyed pulling up a stool at a table, gabbing, and working with the crew. We had contests, quizzes, and sharing sessions. During the time as team leader, I had the responsibility of evaluating and providing consequences for workers. These were some of the hardest times. When the people I had grown so close to and loved relapsed, missed work because of relapse, or died, the lack of control and helplessness I felt was a tough lesson. I learned quickly that I could not control the actions of others, but I could and needed to support, validate, and hold people accountable.

After I had been a team leader for a few months, I had the opportunity to apply for a new job paying about $6.00 more per hour. It was for a place I had worked one summer when I was home, so they knew me and I knew them. I was really tempted because it would have meant getting out of debt sooner and starting on a road to quick financial stability. The more I thought about it and talked to people though, the less the money meant, the more my long-term health and sobriety meant, and the more I knew STEP was the right place for me to stay.

During my time as team leader, Fritz, who had hired, trained, and supported me, became very ill. He was diagnosed with small cell lung cancer. I was devastated. Fritz was one of those guys a lot like my dad; he did not talk a lot, but when he did, it was something he had thought about and was probably worth listening to. Fritz taught me how to deal with delicate personal matters with the crew in way that left them with dignity. He taught me that being upfront and truthful is always the best policy even when ignoring is easier. Fritz was a mentor gone too soon. Within a few months, I had inhaled my last cigarette never to pick one up again, not that it does call to me every so often.

About a year later, I became plant manager and then operations manager over two facilities in Neenah. In this new role, I interviewed all the potential employees, scheduled projects for the Neenah location, managed our Good Manufacturing Practices (GMP) compliance, hired and supervised team leaders, and helped with employee issues. I feel my most important job was helping provide a safe and supportive environment. When I say "safe," I don't mean trip hazards; we want to be safe from those as well but, more importantly, as drug and alcohol free place. I dealt with testing for the crew. Some of these situations were very difficult and heartbreaking.

Jamie was the vice president of STEP. He too had started folding diapers, and had been a team leader, as well as a plant manager so he had a lot of experience and was always there to help with difficult or sensitive situations. During my time as plant manager I hired three team leaders from within the STEP organization. They had been forklift drivers and key people in the STEP operation. STEP has always had a philosophy of helping and supporting the next person, and we have stayed true to our philosophy by promoting staff members from within. The best way for us to relate to our crew's struggles is to have shared in common struggles.

In 2003, Jamie had the idea of creating a human resource department for all the transitional employees. Prior to this all the team leaders had overseen their crew and this created some inconsistencies when people were working for multiple departments at the same time. Together we created the position, determined the roles and responsibilities, and communicated the change. Although it was challenging at first, it was best plan and idea for STEP in the long run. The changes and new positions brought consistence to the employee pathways and evaluation process. I was able to update the employee handbook so that it could be a better tool for the employees and staff members alike. The handbook gave the employees a place they could always go to talk or have their questions answered. It provided support to the other staff members when presented with a difficult situation. For me, it provided a great resource when working with the employees from the interview process, so that they could have their questions answered during the orientation process, and helps the new employees move on to their next endeavor. I have learned so much from the people I have met along the way and I feel a great sense of pride when I see someone who used to work here, and see that they are doing well and are happy in their newly found life. Those are stories that kept me going here at STEP through difficult times.

There are other stories of death and denial. I have learned a ton from these people as well. Jamie told me if I stayed here long enough I would attend a lot of funerals, which is a sad but true message. One of the most heartbreaking was Mike. Mike a transitional employee who became a team leader and was a very active Narcotics Anonymous (NA) leader in the area. Mike had tattoos, long hair, a great personality, and gave great hugs. He inspired so many young adults that were new to recovery and he was a great role model for many years but then Mike relapsed, but we did not know at the time. He continued to use for an extended period of time, while keeping it a secret. This secret soon led to Mike taking his own life. Everyone was devastated, including the staff, crew, as well as the entire recovering community. We all came together during this difficult time by talking, sharing, and supporting one another. Mike was a gift in life and the lesson in his death is that we don't always get to come back from a relapse.

In 2006, the company wanted to become ISO 9001 certified. We thought that having this credential would help us gain new customers, along with providing us with assurance to potential customers that we do quality work and would tighten up our processes internally to assure that exceptional work was done. Together with an assistant, we wrote down all the procedures to bring us to ISO compliance in early 2007. Our certification was a huge accomplishment as a large part of the ISO is training. Since the average length of stay at STEP is five to six months, we are constantly training and verifying. We have remained ISO Certified ever since, and thus being one of only a few nonprofits in Wisconsin.

During my time, STEP has evolved and changed many times. We have had to close plants in Stevens Point, Green Bay, as well as Fond du Lac, and have opened a location in Milwaukee. We have folded millions and millions of diapers to now doing no diapers at all. We have moved into different facilities and been hit by the recession, as well as the overseas competition. Until 2006 STEP had been 100 percent self-supporting. STEP even used to make contributions to other nonprofits, but that has long since changed. In 2006 we began writing grants and accepting donations. We need support to make it possible to do what we do for the recovering community and its members. We previously had over nine thousand people come to STEP since opening in 1982. We have offered second and third chances to many people in need of a fresh start and some compassion. STEP is still 95 percent self-supporting through the sale of its services to for-profit businesses. We currently do not get any state or county funding to provide our service to the community.

In mid-2007, Jamie took a job as executive director of Mooring Programs after being here for twenty years. We had worked closely together for many years so his moving on resulted in very mixed emotions. I would miss him as a great boss and mentor but I would be taking his place as vice president of STEP. I like learning new parts of the business and being more involved in the community as a whole while sharing what STEP does, but I found that I missed the day-in day-out interaction with the transitional employees.

In November of 2009, Hugh Holly who had been with STEP since it was just an idea left to be executive director of Nova Treatment. This was a very exciting and scary time for me. The outlook for STEP was shaky, as our future was unsure but I knew I had to do whatever I could to keep STEP around for the next person who accepted the position. I have gotten so much from STEP and have been given so many opportunities that I feel it is very important that STEP be here for anyone in recovery who wants the opportunity to start over. Since I have been here I have seen over six thousand recovering people come through these doors and I would like to see another six thousand.

Today we have a staff of sixteen people, fourteen of those who are in recovery, while thirteen of those staff members were once participants in the STEP program. These people are now the office manager, customer services representative, team leaders, operations manager, recovery coach, human resources manager, and maintenance manager. Some members are celebrating over twenty-seven years on staff, while others are celebrating their short time of two years as staff members. Together we have over 150 years of recovery combined. We have between 70–120 employees at any given time depending of project opportunities. Our biggest struggles relate to finding enough projects to be able to provide opportunities for those who need a second chance as well as donations to subsidize additional training and opportunities that we currently offer, or want to offer. A vocational training center opened in 2015 to help our employees gain much-needed computer skills and help with their job search. In 2014 STEP opened a women's sober living home. STEP also opened two men's sober living homes in 2015 all within walking distance to STEP Industries

In June 2017, the board of directions of Mooring Programs and STEP Industries began serious discussions of merging the two programs. Mooring provided gender-specific residential treatment for those with substance use disorder (SUD) as well as transitional residential treatment in Appleton. Nearly half the staff of Mooring had come STEP Industries and about 40 percent of the transitional employees in Neenah came from Mooring Programs.

In July 2017, it was decided that in the best interests of clients the two programs would merge. The merge took place January 1, 2018, and Apricity was formed. Apricity, meaning the warmth of the sun in the winter, is the only one of its kind to have residential treatment, transitional residential, sober living, a vocational learning center, and transitional jobs for those recovering from SUD in the United States.

Chapter Ten

STEP Industries and the Minimum Wage Debate

Kendra Green

When people hear the terms *nonprofit organization* or *human services agency*, they typically think of people or organizations that help out families, children, the elderly or even animals. They think of people who are in need. One group of people they may not generally think of is drug and alcohol addicts and individuals with a criminal record. Many people express the "blame the victim" mentality when they think about those who are struggling with addiction and those individuals with a criminal record. At STEP Industries in Neenah, however, this is not the case. The workers and volunteers at STEP Industries are dedicated to helping addicts and others with a criminal record find work. Since the unemployment rate amongst recovering addicts is so high due to the stigma of a poor work ethic amongst this population and a negative work record, this organization is extremely beneficial to those struggling with or recovering from addiction. While STEP Industries is not a rehabilitation industry, it does help recovering and struggling addicts to find work with partnering companies. While it is great that STEP Industries helps find and offer work to addicts to help provide them with a second chance and the ability to gain a better work record, living off a minimum wage paycheck is still problematic. Living off a low-wage job makes it hard to achieve a decent standard of living and it allows no room for savings, and minimum-wage jobs do very little to help stimulate the economy.

No matter who you are, addict or not, living off a minimum wage job is close to impossible if you are trying to support yourself, let alone keep up with today's standard of living. To just provide food, clothes, and a place to live is expensive today anywhere you are in the United States. I am referring here only to the basic needs of survival. If you have a family it becomes even more expensive. Then there is the expense of transportation, utility bills, medical bills, cell phone payments, along with countless other amenities. All these things add up, and a minimum wage job of $7.25 an hour is grossly inadequate in terms of covering living expenses. There is no living comfortably off this wage. As the years have gone by the minimum wage has basically stayed the same while the cost of living has risen dramatically. Like Jerome Skolnick and Elliott Currie point out in their book *Crisis in American Institutions*, "thirty-seven million Americans live below the official poverty line, and millions more struggle each month to pay for basic necessities" (2011, p. 91).

The employees of STEP Industries face this struggle as they try to make ends meet, living paycheck to paycheck. One could argue that it is better than nothing since addicts find it hard to obtain jobs in the first place considering that they are stereotyped for being lazy, or considering that their work history may not always be the best. At least STEP Industries helps them to get their foot in the door of the work place. STEP Industries can also give them the chance to build on their job experience, which could, maybe, lead them to another job down the road that might pay better. However, this is a bit unrealistic since there are college graduates today that are looking for better work and are stuck working minimum wage jobs as well. In order to give these people a better second chance at regaining their normal life back, I believe STEP Industries should pay a little more than the minimum wage. This doesn't just go for STEP Industries either, but for all minimum wage jobs and the individuals that rely on their employment. The wages should be raised to a higher pay as well for many reasons, two of which I will further discuss.

Another reason why STEP Industries should pay their employees more than minimum wage is because living off the minimum wage does not allow for anyone to save at all for anything. Accidents happen when you least expect them and they can happen to anyone. Being able to save money and have a safety net to fall back on in case you or a loved one gets sick, is in a car accident, or you need a new refrigerator because the one you had broke down is important. Life is full of surprises and no one wants the surprise of having to pay for a new car when they cannot afford it. The employees working at STEP Industries, as well as everyone else who works should be able to have the peace of mind that if something should happen or go wrong they are able to pay for it and not go bankrupt. One could argue that that is what having insurance and an insurance company is for. However, insurance, good insurance anyways, is expensive. Here in the United States we pay top dollar for our insurance and medical expenses and if you cannot afford it, you may just be out of luck. Many people are struggling to live off the minimum wage, STEP employees included, and they cannot afford to have really good insurance. Many businesses face their own challenges and do not have the money to provide coverage for their employees either. So therefore employees, along with other minimum wage earners, have to make the decision to either go without good insurance or have to choose to go without something else.

Another area that is problematic when trying to save while earning only the minimum wage is the lack of ability to save for retirement. At some point retirement will be unavoidable and everyone at some point in his or her life will become unable to work. When that day comes all individuals are supposed to be able to rely on their retirement funds and savings to get by. If they don't have these types of saving though, how are they supposed to get by? There is an increasing amount of people in the elderly community, and those age sixty-five and older are becoming homeless and have nowhere to turn. There are more elderly individuals in the United States than ever before and with this increase comes the growing need to take care of them. If they cannot afford this care though they are stuck relying on the government. Many may face this same challenge one day when they are no longer able to work and have to rely on assisted care or a nursing home to take care of them. While STEP Industries is only an organization that helps addicts get a second chance in getting back on their feet and is not meant to provide employment for long periods of time, it would still help those who do go through the program to earn more. It would help to build up not only their work history, but their financial safety net as well, for today savings is crucial with the decreasing hope and stability of Social Security. No longer can we rely on Social Security to take care of us when we get older, as retirement experts point out, "the three-legged stool has only two legs for the next generation" (Skolnick & Currie, 2011, p. 78).

The final issue that comes along with minimum wage employment is the fact that these jobs are not helping to stimulate the economy at all. Right now we are still in an economic crisis and having people with jobs that do not pay enough to keep up with today's standard of living, help them build a financial safety net, or save up for retirement is not helping. If people do not have the money, they cannot spend it. It is as simple as that. If people living off the minimum wage are worried about where their next meal is going to come from or how they are going to afford next month's utility bill, how are they going to be able to go out into the community and spend money on the movies, or new clothes, or go out for dinner? People or employees cannot afford to go out and celebrate six months of sobriety because if they do that is taking away from what little amount of money they have to pay for things like food and their home. In order to help out the communities we live in, we need to be able to put money into them. Unfortunately, today you cannot expect to fix something or get very far without money. Volunteering and nonprofit organizations can only go so far. By paying employees like those at STEP Industries who only receive the minimal amount of payment more money it will allow those who are struggling not only to save and live a decent life, but allow them to do the extra little things like go get ice cream or take a day trip to the zoo or a museum. There is so much that could be done to help those at the bottom like those going through STEP to rise above poverty and get closer to a better, more secure future. However, it will take the right attitude of the American people and the financial help from the government to make this possible.

America is one of the richest countries in the world, yet there are so many who suffer and struggle through life. We should be able to afford to help those in need like those working at STEP Industries. I agree with Skolnick and Currie's statement "one of the most troubling and enduring aspects of America's economic crisis is the inability of our economy to ensure a decent standard of living to everyone who works in it" (2011, p. 47). Being an addict is not a flaw in character or people being lazy or not wanting to change. Addiction is a disease that requires help and treatment to overcome it. While STEP does not play a part in the treatment of its employees, they see to it that they get a second chance at life and a new start. However, this fresh start would be more productive though if they were able to pay their employees more than the minimum wage. That way they could hope for better savings, a more secure future, and knowledge that they are able to help out their communities.

REFERENCE

Skolnick, J. H., & Currie, E. (2011). *Crisis in American institutions* (14th ed.). Boston: Little, Brown.

Chapter Eleven

Drug Use, Abuse, and Addiction

A Personal Experience

Pearl Wright

I have not been shy in my representation of my experience in dealing with drug use and abuse and addiction. I walked into a relationship with an alcoholic completely blind to the disease and its effects on people. The lifestyle of a user changes to fit a certain circular pattern, but there are also psychological and lifestyle changes in the users' entire sphere of friends and family due to dealing with the user. When I left that first relationship with an addict, I walked right into another one just as bad. This pattern is called codependency. The brain becomes accustomed to the emotional roller coaster of dealing with an addict, and seeks out the same kind of stimulus. Most of the people I knew drank or smoked a little weed. Some did cocaine recreationally. I was young and most of the serious cases of addiction among my group of friends had not yet set in. I thought the first guy was just a really bad drunk, and that it was a choice. I didn't know why someone would chose to be like that, but there were some behaviors I began to think were common to "really bad" users of a variety of substances. So my next relationship was an addict but I didn't see it going in. He had always been a really good friend, and I knew he drank pretty hard, but everybody partied and that would go away once we settled down—wouldn't it? Well no, it does not. After thirty years of relationships with addicts, some romantic, some friendships, and some my own children, I have come to know the world of an addict fairly well.

As Eitzen (2010) points out, the United States has made drug usage a crime. By doing so, it stigmatizes users. I run into many people who still think that a heroin addict has a choice of not using on any given day, who do not understand the pain and torment they are in if they try to make that choice to not use. By thinking addiction is a crime it stops people from considering the truth of the disease. Just throw them in jail is the American way. But without treatment, the user comes out of jail unprepared for functioning without the drugs. With stigmatization, they also have a hard time finding a job, finding a place to live, and many people now see them as an element they do not want to associate with. We all have a picture of what a criminal from prison is like in our heads, and we all have a picture of what we think a drug user looks like.

Part of the problem with making drug use a crime, is it actually does make criminals out of users in many ways. Eitzen's (2010) work on drugs point out that when the United States made use a crime, it raised the price of drugs. Theoretically this sounded like a good idea. What was not taken into account is the user reaches a point where use is not a choice but is necessary to their lives. Their entire life becomes centered around getting a drug that is expensive and dangerous to have in your possession. People have to spend large amounts of time putting together the finances to obtain the drugs, then sneak around dealing with people who are willing to commit a crime by selling drugs. Personal relationships are damaged because the drug comes first. Parenting is affected because the drug comes first. An addict will lie to cover their movements, and steal to pay for them. Many do not want to live like this but have little choice. If treatment were more readily available and affordable, my experience has shown that most addicts would reach a personal low and turn to treatment rather than crime.

As I mentioned before, use becomes a circular cycle. The only time an addict is willing to do anything to get off the cycle is when they are at the bottom of it. Once they have lost everything—maybe they are thrown out of their homes, or the court has taken their children, or they are facing legal battles. An addict must feel a sense of desperation to want to change. Usually all of our lives are somewhat circular. We hit bumpy times and then something happens to help us head back upward again. An addict begins to exhaust the sources of those something good happenings. They screw over enough people enough times, they have no friends left to use. They screw up enough jobs, they have no way to pay bills. Eventually all addicts hit bottom. Sometimes, multiple times. But if they are lucky, they will find treatment. Then starts a long process of retraining themselves to live in society successfully without drugs.

In Europe, as we have learned in class, there are different ways of dealing with drug users. First, soft "drugs" such as marijuana are almost legal in some countries. For harder drugs, many countries stress treatment, not incarceration. England had a program of heroin maintenance for its addicts, which provided supervised dosing in clean, safe environments. By not turning users into criminals, the user generally chooses at some point to leave the drugs behind and seek out treatment (Eitzen 2010). In the United States there are many policies which criminalizes the victims. Most Europeans countries try to help the addict break their habits or at least stay functioning in society at some level of positivity, Americans stigmatize the addict and turn them into outcasts. The most supportive help an addict in America can find is the 12 step groups; groups of addicts, for addicts. In meetings all over America every day there are hundreds of meetings where addicts try, with the help of the "Blue Book"—the bible of Alcoholics Anonymous, to help each other stay straight and sober. It is a volume full of behaviors common to addicts, and exercises to help teach someone how to recognize and face the behaviors. This is the basis of the 12 steps of the Alcoholics Anonymous (AA), Narcotics Anonymous (NA) and other stepped programs. It is with this spirit of addicts helping each other that the STEP program is founded.

From Eitzen's (2010) work, we do understand that a person is criminalized and stigmatized. By understanding the disease of addiction we see that addicts learn to live as addicts and criminals. When they choose to fight their addictions, many come out of treatment with criminal records, bad job histories, and broken relationships. They can't find jobs, no one wants a criminal drug user working for them. They can't find a place to live, no one wants a criminal drug user in their rental unit. A recovering addict can find themselves in a situation that non-addicted people would find difficult to deal with, but for an addict, there is the added pressure of that little voice in their head that repeats "you don't have to think about this, you don't have to hurt, you have friends in low places," and that voice can pull them right back into the world they fought so hard to leave very easily. Many have lost their ability to get around; cars are expensive and driver's licenses get revoked if you are caught using. Whether or not you were in a car, you lose your license if convicted of a high enough level of drug crimes, it is just one of the punishments the US courts put on a victim of addiction. There are also visits with probation officers who prod into every aspect of your lives, and some of them are difficult people to deal with. I have known many decent and fair probation officers, but also some to be very nasty hateful people who try to cause as much pain in their charges lives as they can, believing all crimes are crime and therefore the person is unworthy to be included in, and even dangerous to, our society. There are also usually ongoing court appearances for outstanding charges. This all makes it very difficult for a newly recovering person to function in society. Plus because they have learned how to live as an addict, they need to now learn how to live without the games and lies necessary for an addict to get along, and start being honest with themselves and others. For some, leaving the games and lies behind is the hardest thing. Even a simple question as "where are you going" sparks the urge to lie. You get so used to covering your tracks, you want to kick sand even when there are no tracks to cover.

Where does someone go to start rebuilding their lives? STEP industries is one place that a recovering addict can go where they are understood and supported in their long path back to functioning as a clean and sober member of society. Founded by addicts, run by addicts, this unique program is something I wish I had known about when I was trying to get my son back from addiction. I believe he would have not returned to using so quickly if he had been able to find a job to keep him busy and make himself feel good about himself again. I took this weak young man to every temporary employment agency I could find, and everyone said to him "It is going to be hard to get anyone to take you". The calls for work never came. He sat at home afraid to go out for fear he would "hook up" with his using friends, until the voice in his head got so loud he could not fight it anymore and off he went right back to using.

I wish that I would have known about STEP Industries then. What STEP does is gives a recovering a place to work, a paycheck, and a feeling of self-worth. When they see an addict engaging in behaviors that are more than obvious to the trained eye, especially one who taught themselves about how an addict acts with their own addictions, they can intervene. Addicts do what is called "stinking thinking" where they talk themselves into behaviors with bad reasoning. One good example of this pattern was presented to us by the director of the program when we visited. She talked about a worker who called in and said his ride didn't show up that morning so he could not come to work. She saw his thinking pattern and pointed out to him that the price of the bus to come to work late was less than missing a full day's pay. The worker/addict had found a way to avoid doing what he was supposed to be doing, which opens up a time frame to do what else? With an addict, that time frame is free usage time. "I got away with this now I can use and everyone will think I am at work." is an example of stinking thinking. "I blew this responsibility; I am unworthy, so why not use?" is another thought process an addict might use.

Another thing STEP helps their workers with is their required legal obligations. It is very difficult for a newly recovering person who has legal obligations to say to a new employer that they have to go to yet another court appearance or probation appointment and miss work again. An hour here, and hour there, it all adds up to not having a job quickly. I have also seen probation officers tour a client's workplace, which frustrates some employers and further stigmatizes the addict to their coworkers. At STEP, the agent can stop by without stigmatizing the client, and as a matter of fact, the agent may have more than one client at the site working. The management of the program understand the worker has to be at court or other ordered requirements. They will let the worker have the time off from the job necessary to comply with legal obligations.

Something that I think is very helpful at STEP is the group support. Addiction shatters relationships, or turns them into enabling situations. Significant others become trained to react in a fashion which helps the addict continue using. That is why addicts are told in treatment not to start any new relationships for at least a year (so the addict can learn not to manipulate people for their own purposes), and some counselors would even suggest married couples remain apart, especially if the partner is still using or refusing codependency counseling. Hanging out with your user friends is also taboo as familiar places and people that your brain recognizes as friendly to usage trigger chemical spikes that make an addict suffer cravings. Even your own brain is out to get you to use, to ease its pain. But with a group of recovering individuals all trying to straighten out their own lives, the addict is immersed in one big "12 step" meeting. Recovering addicts, as mentioned before, know the behavior and thinking patterns and can spot someone falling off right away. They need to constantly remind themselves of who they were as users, the mistakes they made, and the people they hurt. Telling others is part of many treatment plans. Being at STEP allows recovering addicts to tell their stories to those who understand how their lives got so crazy. Still, as the assistant manager and I discussed, you don't want to send a whole car load of recovering addicts out alone together often, as if one goes, the entire group could return to using.

A person might think of a program that takes recovering alcohol and drug addicts and form a negative view in their mind's eye of what the factory must look like. This view might be expected from what we know of what drugs and alcohol can do to a person's life. But we canot blame the victim and we should look not at what a person has done in the past, but what they are trying to do for a future. A tour of STEP will dispel any negative thoughts. The plant is food grade certified, not an easy certification to receive. This means the level of sanitation in the plant is very high. STEP is also ISO certified (STEP 2014). In manufacturing, this ranking is coveted and respected worldwide. It means that when STEP establishes a procedural outline with their customer, they have been found to follow that procedure consistently. I have a long work history in manufacturing and quality control, and have experienced the certification process first hand. It is a rigorous process where all facets of manufacture technique, quality control measures, and record keeping are painstakingly reviewed to assure consistency in procedure. The plant is clean and set up well, and the employees are proud of what they have accomplished. The workers were quick to welcome our tour group and ask us what brought us to them that day.

The STEP program keeps an addict busy, keeps them earning some money so they can start rebuilding their lives, gives them a safe place to be where changes in behaviors are quickly recognized, and helps them meet their responsibilities (a *huge* part of addiction therapy is about living up to responsibility). I was honestly impressed with the concept and the conditions I witnessed in the plant. I will definitely keep them in mind as I go on to make my way in the area of chemical addiction therapies as a resource and as an example of what an agency can do to treat and rehabilitate an addict rather than the usual American response of incarceration and stigmatization.

REFERENCES

Eitzen, D. S. (2010). *Solutions to social problems: Lessons from other societies.* 5th Ed. Boston: Pearson Education, Inc.

STEP Industries. (2014). Mission and History. *Mission: STEP Industries.* Retrieved from http://www.stepindustries.com/about-step/mission.

Chapter Twelve

Getting a Second Chance and Giving Second Chances to Others

A Personal Journey

Patricia McCourt

Looking back now, I am able to realize the hell I endured is part of my healing process. Mine is not a story of anger or rage, violence, or physical abuse. Rather, a story about secrets, silence, abusive mind games, revenge, and control. It is a story of how abandonment can lead to unhealthy relationships and how the acceptance of mental and emotional abuse lead to depression and self-destruction. A story of how, if given power, secrets and mind games have the ability to destroy inner beauty, self-image, and self-esteem. This is a story of a journey through deep pain and sorrow and the steps I took to overcome the effects that mental and emotional abuse left behind and finally, how I was able to find love again—not only in others, but more importantly . . . in myself.

One of my earliest memories of my father is when he spanked me for throwing a book at my sister. I was probably five at the time and had been acting up all morning. My mama threatened that if I did not behave, my father would deal with me when he got home from work. I do not remember if I was scared or not, but I do remember that it was nothing new—I was always in trouble. Being the middle child might have had something to do with my acting out, but nevertheless—I waited for my father to return home and administer my punishment. When he spanked me, he did not use his hand; rather, he used the wooden paddle he made. My name was printed on one side and my sister's name on the other. It was no surprise that my name was faded, due to the number of times it had been used. I do not recall what the paddling hurt most—my bottom or my pride—but I do know that it was generally the only attention I got from my father and I was willing to take what I could get.

For as long as I can remember, my father worked construction. His amazing talent and skills allowed him to excel in his craft. As a child I enjoyed playing in his workshop, digging in the sawdust, stacking blocks of wood, nailing pieces together to create my own design, anything, just to be near him. I wanted his attention. I wanted his love. I wanted him to want me; I am not sure that he ever did. It seemed as if I was more of a nuisance, in his way and underfoot. He kept himself very busy and most of the time I felt he was too busy for me.

I was in elementary school when I realized my father had a wandering eye. It appeared that he no longer saw my mama as the beautiful woman she was: kind hearted, gifted, loving and faithful. Instead, he focused on the physical changes that childbearing had left on her small stature. Her days of modeling had passed and were replaced with the beauty of motherhood, cooking, cleaning, sewing, playing, and making sure that her girls knew Jesus. He no longer wanted my mama. When I was eight years old, my father moved on to other things.

As a single woman, my mama took good care of my sisters and me. She made sure we had a roof over our head and a safe place to call home. In the beginning, we visited my father every other weekend. Spending time with him at his tiny apartment was difficult, and it was not long before he tried to get us girls to persuade mama to take him back. He talked about his pain and how much he missed all of us. He gave us flowers to pass on to mama, but she was not interested. She had experienced too many lies, too much hurt. Eventually, he gave up and before long, his visits extended to monthly and then we saw him a few times a year. He did not call much and we did not call him either. He was busy with his new life and we were busy trying to live ours. Abandonment, guilt, and shame began to build inside me as I attempted to understand my father as a person. I struggled as I fought to hide the hurt and pain I felt. I did not want to like him, let alone love him, but I did and it left me feeling empty and confused.

It was during this time that my role in life changed. I was no longer a happy and secure child. My life had become scripted, as if I was a puppet in a play, responding to the actions of others rather than trusting my own instinct and allowing my own feelings to be important. I acted out with bad behavior, but at the same time I wanted to please everyone around me and I desperately longed for secure love and stability. I began to hate myself. I hated what I saw in the mirror and felt that I never measured up to my friends or family. School pictures were the worst; they reminded me of my pale complexion, red hair, and ugly teeth. As I grew older, I began to struggle with my weight. In middle school, I noticed (recognized?) that I wore a size bigger than my best friend and I was humiliated. My emotions carried me through as I sought out acceptance, approval, affection and love, turning to any boy that would give me the time of day. I may not have measured up my father, but I did find a way to pacify the wounds he left behind.

During the years that I had contact with my father, injury and heartache were a constant. He remarried several times, always searching for the one to make him happy. The first stepmother wanted nothing to do with my sisters and me and we were not allowed to visit when she was home. Even though her daughters were our age, and attended the same school, we were not encouraged to play together. One weekend, in particular, comes to mind when I think about the insanely unhealthy relationship we had with her. My sisters and I went for a visit, and upon arrival noticed that our stepmother left food for us on the kitchen counter. Along with dinner was a note that read, *Feed them this.* The package of frozen hot dogs was the perfect expression of her feelings for us and how we were clearly not welcomed in her home. I found it amazing how the feelings of rejection and shame came flooding back into my thoughts as I wrote this and how fresh the wounds felt, even though forty years had passed.

It must have been during this same timeframe that the embarrassment of being my father's daughter sat in. Although, it was not always apparent to me, because I found that the less I knew him the more I wanted his love and approval. I thought that I needed this man to love me in order to be a whole person. I thought that I needed this man to be my dad, but in reality he did not even want to be part of my life. I hurt so much when my friends asked about my father because he was not around and they wondered why. Most of the time, I lied to them and created a fairy-tale version of his happy life with his new family and the lack of time he had for me. I included parts of the truth as I explained he was a well-respected, sought after business owner and because he was so busy, I understood the reasons he gave for not seeing me. None of my friends knew the real story and I felt it was safer this way. The fairytale eventually carried over into my own life, when I performed as a puppet, the incredible show of strength, courage, and happiness. I formed a habit of lying; expanding the truth and exaggerating how "perfect" my home life was. When I did see my father, I lied about my school, my friends and my personal life, longing for his approval and wanting him to be proud of me.

My father's first marriage, after my mama, did not last long and soon he was divorced again. A short time later he married his third wife. This time my sisters and I were invited to participate in family events and encouraged to get to know his wife and her son. I immediately felt a connection with her. She appeared to be a warm and caring person. I had fun with my stepbrother and felt comfortable in their home. A couple of years later, this marriage also ended and again I found myself searching for a way to deal with the feelings of abandonment and another loss.

It was not long until this fourth wife came along with her two young children. My father's plan to marry her was not all together shocking, but when he announced that he wanted to adopt her kids, I was speechless. This was certainly something that my sisters and I had not heard before. I remember thinking, what is going to happen to those kids when he decides to divorce their mother. I was so angry! How could he do this to us? To me? To them? He was supposed to be my father, not theirs! I did not understand what was going on with him. Why did he want more children when he did not want to be a father to the ones he had? I felt cheated. Part of me wanted to be happy for those kids—we were told that their own father had mistreated them, but I was still so angry and I found it difficult to accept. I put on a happy mask and I buried my feelings. I presented myself as though I was comfortable with the situation, knowing full well that deep inside I was hurting and felt extremely jealous. My father was choosing to be a daddy to kids he barely knew and at the same time he was choosing to let go of his own flesh and blood. He was severing what little connection we had left. This was his doing, yet I took on the responsibility and rejection. All too familiar feelings of abandonment welled up within me as I withdrew from wanting to even be near him. I didn't even know this man and I no longer wanted to like him. I no longer wanted to love him, but I did and I was angry about it.

Going back now to life with mama, she did not date much after the divorce. In fact, I only recall her bringing home two men. The first was nice, but not appear to be up for the challenge of a single woman with three daughters. The second man entered our lives and chose to stay. He was entertaining and charming. He made my mama smile and over time I grew to love him deeply, in fact this man eventually became the one I call Dad and I am truly blessed to have him in my life. Mama dated him for several years, as she moved our family from one rural Kansas community to another. Our new home was nestled in the quaint little town where she grew up, assuring that we would be surrounded by family. Not only did her parents, brothers and their families live within a couple of miles from town, but so did her extended family. Struggling with heartache, I said farewell to the only friends I had ever known. The friends who had invited me to slumber parties, shared in tumbling and baton lessons, enjoyed many experiences in 4-H club, and who had known me all my life. These were the friends who shared my childhood memories, on and off the playground. These were the friends I had to say goodbye to. Feelings of sadness and desertion flooded my soul.

My mama was the only daughter and was encircled by four brothers; two older and two younger. All my uncles were married and had several children—making our extended family fairly large. As lifelong members of the small community, my mother's family name was well known as it offered me a sense of belonging. Mama did her best to care for my sisters and I as she attended the community college in our small town. The one-bedroom home was a huge adjustment, but we managed. My older sister and I shared the tiny bedroom with a bunk bed. We learned early on to be careful when opening the bedroom door, as it would hit the bed and we would get into trouble. My younger sister slept on a small cot in the living room next to our mama, who slept on the pull-out couch. It was not much, but it was doable and it was home. I remember that money was very tight. Mama said that my father stopped paying child support. I realized that she was doing the best she could; the rent got paid and if she needed help, my sisters and I gave mama money we earned from babysitting or other odd jobs. Not too long afterward, mama began working in a nearby city—it was not long before she realized that it would be easier if she lived closer to work. With about six months of our parents' divorce, we packed our things again, said goodbye to our extended family and new friends, and moved to the city.

Our lives had already changed so much over the past year and now we found ourselves surrounded by tall buildings, multiple train tracks, and unsafe areas of town—way different than life in a small town. Living on a busy street, traffic buzzed by and sirens were heard from a distance. We were not allowed to roam the streets, we did not know our neighbors, and mama had to keep a more watchful eye on us as we transitioned into our new surroundings. I thought that another new school and new friends would be easy, but I was wrong. It proved to be much more difficult than expected. I did not know anyone and they did not know me and for quite some time, it seemed as if they did not want to. Mama tried to make the transition easier on us girls by enrolling us in a small private school, rather than the large public school. The class sizes were very small and held two grade levels per classroom. For instance, I entered the fifth grade and my class of ten filled one-half of the room while the sixth grade class of eight filled the other half. It was a bit strange at first and I was scared, but I set those feelings aside and seemed to settle in fairly quickly. Lucky for me, I have never had trouble making new friends. When the girls in my class found out that I too loved lip gloss and stuffed animals, they opened up and accepted me as a friend.

One thing I especially liked about this new city, was that we were closer to the family of mama's boyfriend. Several sweet old ladies, filled of love and joy—busting to get their hands on some girls. Mama's boyfriend had just graduated high school when his father died. He and his two younger brothers were loved and cared for by their mother, aunt, great aunts and cousins. Even the lifelong housekeeper become part of the family over the years and helped raise the boys. The ladies worked together, raising those boys and nurturing them into respectful young men. When my sisters and I entered the picture, there were not any grandchildren and the ladies embraced us with open arms and hearts full of love—they always tried to make us feel extra special and there is no doubt in my mind that they loved us as if we were their own.

Mama dated this man for several years before agreeing to marry him, and when she did I was so happy! I had come to love this man very much and was so excited that he would officially be my stepdad. He already partially filled the void in me, left by my father's abandonment, and I wanted him to complete our family and make us "whole" again. I remember thinking that when Christmas comes around this year, and we visit our grandparents' home on Christmas Eve, we will no longer be the only kids without a dad. We would finally be the same as all of my cousins. We would fit in and be normal.

Mama's family built a legacy of farming and caring for the land that surrounded their small community. When she married my "real" father, the carpenter, she married outside of the family business and it proved to be one more thing that separated her from her brothers. Their strained relationship fueled the fire that separated my sisters and me from our cousins. We were different. We were the city kids that came to the farm for a visit. We were set apart from being friends with our cousins; from the inside jokes and their small town secrets. Holidays and summer vacations were the most difficult.

Christmas Eve at my grandparents' farm was a magical time. It was the one day of the year that I looked forward to the most. I saw it as an opportunity to be accepted; or at least try to be. My immediate family generally arrived first to the small bungalow, perched on the hilltop. Anxiously awaiting the arrival of the family, I would sit with anticipation, peering through the dining room window, watching for car lights to emerge over the landscape and make their way up the long, dirt road. Part of the excitement was trying to guess who was coming next. The evening was filled with family, both young and old. Usually, my cousins and I made our way up the stairs to the large room that my two youngest uncles once shared. We played games, told secrets, and tried to get to know each other better. The holidays always brought amazing food, much more than we could eat. And after dinner we all sat around the living room to open gifts. Nothing topped the most important event of the evening, a photograph of all the grandchildren, wearing matching pajamas.

Thanks to our grandparents, picture time and matching pajamas had been an annual event, for as long as I can remember. Without fail, year after year, they purchased matching nightgowns for the granddaughters and pajamas for the grandsons. Together, we looked like we belonged on the front of the Sears and Roebuck's Christmas catalog. As soon as the packages were ripped opened, the girls shuffled in to the small bathroom quickly changing into the long flannel nightgowns. The boys ran to change in grandma and grandpa's bedroom, closing the door as best as they could. Grandpa hung his overalls from the door frame and this caused the door to gap, but it did not slow them down at all. Everyone in the house was excited! When all the children were dressed, we piled on the couch and posed for the annual photo. It usually was not an easy task with crying babies and squirming children, but it was always worth it. We laughed and giggled as the flashes went off. Moments in time, forever captured. Beautiful memories.

Christmas Eve was probably my favorite day of the year. I felt safe at my grandparents' home and I felt as if I belonged. It was the one place that had been constant throughout my life. The one place I found peace. However, after my parents' divorce, times changed and the magic of the evening came to a screeching halt when each year someone would announce my father was heading up the drive. My sisters had to leave. We were different. Since our parents were not together we had to leave the family fun and I hated it. I hated my father for making this happen and I hated the way it made me feel. I hated that I had to go with him to his apartment or home, wherever he was living at the time and pretend to enjoy myself. I hated that I had to say goodbye to the one place that made me feel most safe. I hated this transition and it only became more difficult with each passing year. As I grew older, I grew more resentful toward him and I realized that even when I was with him, I was alone.

Christmas Eve was magical, but it was not the only time I enjoyed visiting my grandparents. I looked forward to summertime, as my sisters and I were allowed to each spend a week with my grandparents on the farm. Each year I found a new sense of independence on the farm, unequivocal to anything I had yet experienced. The liberty to run barefoot, with my cousins, down the gravel road; the freedom I experienced as I trampled the stalks in my grandfathers' cornfield, forming roads along the way; perfecting the talent of building forts in the hayloft, unaware of snakes concealed in dark corners. There are many delightful memories I have from the time spent on my grandparent's farm. However, being on the farm also provided times of uncertainty and moments that added to my already low self-esteem.

I will never forget the time my cousins and I were playing around the hog pins and they provoked me to walk along the narrow planking that topped the fence, separating the pigpens. The pins were full of very large sows, coupled with litters of screaming piglets. I was so afraid that I would fall into one of the pins, even so at the urging of my cousins, I followed their lead. After triumphantly crossing the pin, I was sure that I had proven to them that even though I was a city girl, I was just as good as them. However, it did not seem to matter, the feelings of rejection and not belonging remained and I continued to long for their approval and acceptance.

One summer when I stayed at their home, my grandfather requested my assistance. I longed to be near him, so I jumped at the opportunity. I loved the time spent with my grandfather, and even if the work was hard and dirty, he always taught me something and I appreciated his humor. He was a hard worker and always allowed me to tag along. He taught me how to milk the cows and we laughed together each time the fresh milk squirted across the room. It was quite something the day that he asked me to help him clean a bounty of fish he and a buddy had caught. The two of us, together at the old sink in the barn, cutting away at the nasty parts of the smelliest fish imaginable. I recall Grandpa's belly jiggling as he laughed at the site and sounds of my continued gaging. It was a disgusting job, but I wanted so badly to be near him as I wanted his approval and his attention and therefore I hung in there.

I was eleven the summer I stayed at their home and remember him waking me up just before dawn. He was preparing for a long day in the field and requested that I go along. Even in the darkness, I sprung out of bed with excitement and quickly changed my clothes, for this was the first time grandpa wanted me to go with him to the field. For years I had dreamed of this day, tagging along beside him, witnessing for myself how it all came together. In my mind, this was going to be one of the best days of my life! That thought quickly came to an end the moment he told me to change out of my shorts and tank-top and put on jeans and a long-sleeved shirt. I thought to myself why on earth would he want me to wear jeans and long sleeves on a beautiful summer day? I obviously had no idea the plans he had in store for me, nor the expectations that I was about to be confronted with. I was not going to be a bystander that day just hanging out and playing; I was going to be a participant in manual labor . . . on a farm . . . where dirt and grime blew across the field straight into my squinting eyes and the blistering sun squelched my thirst and melted my clothes to the skin of my youth—all out in the middle of nowhere!

After driving down several dirt roads, for what seemed like an eternity, Grandpa turned into the field and headed toward a tractor parked on a nearby hill. Arriving at the spot where my torture would begin, I quickly reminded him that I was a city kid and was not sure I belonged here. Laughing, with a twinkle in his eye, he instructed me to jump into the seat of the old tractor and fire it up. The tractor was parked horizontally on the hill and appeared to be leaning at an unsafe angle. I looked at the tractor and thought he must be crazy if he thinks that I am going to get on that thing. I tried my hardest to talk him out of it, but he was determined that I was going to drive that tractor. He offered some assurance that I was not going to die and that the tractor was not going to tip over. His words were coupled with his joyous laugh and I was not sure I believed him. Reluctantly, I climbed up onto the tractor and sat down into the seat just as a couple of trucks pulled into the field. Several of my cousins and uncles emerged and I was never so glad to see them in all my life! I thought they had come to rescue me and as I began to make my way down from the seat of the tractor, Grandpa caught a glimpse of me and instructed me to stay put. I started to argue, but he quickly shut me down. Again, I found myself seated at the wheel of the large, unwelcoming machine. I was not sure what he had in store, but I did not want to disappoint him, so I waited.

After some discussion amongst the men, the focus returned to me when Grandpa told me to fire up the tractor. I attempted to explain that I did not know how to start a tractor when my uncle jumped up next to me and with a push here and a pull there and a turn of the key, the engine began to rev. My uncle looked at me with a grin and chuckled, "this is going to be fun!" Grandpa instructed me to drive the tractor over to the open field where my cousins had congregated. At that point they would attach a hay trailer to the tractor for me to tow as they loaded bales of hay onto the trailer. Obviously, my shocked reaction surprised them, as they began laughing and teasing me for crying like a girl. I was filled with anxiety, fear, embarrassment, and regret. Negative self-talk flooded my mind as my grandpa coached me to move the tractor. Again, reminding myself that I was on a slant, visions of tipping over and being crushed by this enormous machine filled my mind, but I slowly began to steer the tractor toward my cousins. They got the trailer hooked up and started throwing hay bales onto the trailer, which only created more anxiety as the trailer rocked side to side and jolted the tractor. That day was scary, but I did not tip the tractor over. However it was clear to me that through a lot of negative self-talk, that I did not fit in with my cousins and I did not belong on a farm. I knew that my grandpa was trying to teach me a lesson and that he wanted me to rise above my fear and have faith in trusting him, but the lesson proved to be very difficult and I do not know if I was ready for it at the time.

I have always longed for a healthy relationship with my cousins. They all grew up within a few miles of each other and lived very close to our grandparent's home. Most of them lived on farms and enjoyed the opportunity to have both parents raise them in a stable environment throughout their childhood. As children, they were not exposed to the pain of divorce and devastation of a broken family. I realize it was not their fault and I do not blame them for the pain I felt—they were doing the best they knew, but I was jealous of the stability they enjoyed. I understood they were not aware of how the experiences with my father affected me and how those experiences would one day complicate my life. I wanted only for them to like me and to allow me to be a part of their normalcy.

After my mama and stepdad married, we moved to a larger city, about an hour away. Again, I found myself saying goodbye to my friends and family. As difficult as it was, this move felt tolerable. There was excitement in the air and I thought it would be a good opportunity to present myself differently to my peers. I saw it as a chance to make another first impression; a new occasion to develop relationships—a chance for lasting happiness. The idea of moving was difficult, but it was becoming easier. Even though I held on to treasures from my past, I found a certain freedom, as I packed, to sort through my belongings and get rid of items that had little or no meaning. I reflected on the events that happened in the past and looked forward to the

possibilities that lay ahead in the future. This move seemed like a real opportunity for a new beginning. With a new dad in the picture, I had great
anticipation that our family would have a happily ever after.

As we settled in to our new surroundings, it was not long before I made
new friends. While walking to school on my first day of eighth grade, I met a
kind girl with beautiful long braids. She was funny and agreed to walk with
me the following day. She quickly became a very important part of my life
and we spent most of our free time together. Life in the big city was proving
to be harder than I had originally anticipated. The kids at my new school
were not as nice as those from the small towns and I experienced a great deal
of humiliation and embarrassment when they found out that my last name
was Cluck. Kids can be so mean and these kids certainly knew how to tease
and bully, stripping away any dignity I may have had. In the small towns I
came from, my last name was not a big deal. There were several families in
the area that shared the name and it was normal. However, the city kids made
a point of letting me know that they had never heard it and I became an easy
target for their jokes and ridicule. As I walked down the halls of my new
school I was asked to lay eggs as they called out my new nick-names "Cluck-
butt" and "Clucker-fucker." The boys would wave dollar bills in my face and
holler, "fuck Cluck for a buck!" I could have chosen to run away, but I did
not. Rather I faced their cruelty and played along with their comments, acting
as if it did not bother me. By high school I adopted the nickname, "Cluck-
butt," and displayed it proudly on the sleeve of my senior sweatshirt. I chose
to overcome their teasing, but realize now the negative effect it left on me.

Also, while in the eighth grade I had my eye on a tall, shy, handsome boy
who attended the same church as I. He was not involved in our youth group,
so I had to figure out how to meet him. Both of our families sat towards the
back of the small, but comfortable sanctuary. I generally found myself
watching him throughout the service. On one particular Sunday morning, I
caught him watching me as well! We exchanged smiles and then each looked
away. The innocent glances continued for several months before I had the
nerve to speak to him and asked if he would like to join the youth group in
playing softball that Sunday afternoon. He accepted the invitation and thus
was the beginning of a beautiful and sweet relationship. We were both very
nervous and hardly spoke, which was strange for me since I flirted with all
the other boys at church. He finally asked me out on a date, which I gladly
accepted. However, since I was only fourteen at the time, my mother considered me too young to date and she insisted that my older sister chaperone. I
was so embarrassed to be under her watchful eye, but did whatever it took to
be with him. The three of us went to football games and high school dances.
She was nearby when he first held my hand the first time he kissed me. He
was thoughtful and compassionate, and I found myself falling in love with
him. We dated for ten months before I allowed the influence of a new

girlfriend to persuade me in making a poor decision; I ended the relationship with the most caring boy I had known in order to please my new friend and began a journey of seeking love in all of the wrong places. I found myself bouncing from one guy to another, which ultimately led to years of hopeless, unhealthy and distressed relationships.

My new friend had quite an influence on me as I allowed her encouragement to dictate my decisions concerning all areas of my life. She was from a wealthy family as her parents owned a large, beautiful home with an in-ground swimming pool. She always wore high-quality, name-branded clothing, which she usually purchased at Macy's. She appeared to have it all together and since she wanted me to be her best friend, I threw away the other relationships in my life and followed her lead. My new friend introduced me to Friday night parties in local pastures, where I found myself drinking whatever alcohol I could get my hands on. I did not stop with one or two, I usually ended up so drunk that I would vomit before getting home. I began dating a new guy; one that she picked out for me. Little did I know that his intentions would be to expand my interest in sexual behavior; never taking the plunge, but teetering on the edge of a cliff was certainly a dangerous place. I skipped class and my grades suffered. Eventually, mama asked the school to stop calling her when I was absent. Even though I continued to attend church and was actively involved in the youth group, I knew I was dishonest and was living two separate lives.

My home life was nothing short of a chaotic mess. Stressed and overwhelmed, mama did her best to hold our dysfunctional family together and hide the pain from the outside world. I did my best to avoid mama when she was in one of her moods, certainly not wanting to push my luck. One wrong look or snotty reply and I found myself grounded . . . again. I was a mess and found myself grounded most of my high school years. I believed my mother had eyes in the back of her head and it seemed as if they were always focused on me. She caught me and my friends smoking cigarettes and drinking beer. She found me at parties and dragged me home. She expected me to behave a certain way, but I was bound and determined not to. I wanted to be my own boss. My sisters and I fought all the time. I mostly hated them and was jealous of something they had or got to do that I did not. Mama yelled and screamed at us a lot, pulling hair if she really wanted to get our attention. All while my stepdad steered clear of the chaos and "checked out" from time to time. There were happy times, like family vacations to the mountains of Colorado and the birth of my little brother, but for the most part I was dysfunctional and ignorant to the amount of pain my mama was experiencing. I was oblivious to the unhealthy behaviors of my stepdad and the pain that his actions caused.

Fast forward a couple of years after high school and I found myself on a roller coaster of my own unhealthy, intimate relationships with men who offered promises of attention and wonderful future. Unbeknownst to me, time would prove that the disease of alcoholism and drug addiction would leave a lasting impression on my scared life. I moved to south central Kansas and it was not long before I found myself in a bar, being pursued by a young man named Lee. There was something about him that I created a red flag, so I resisted his many attempts to be together. Not too long after I met him, I began to receive roses on nearly a weekly basis. He ordered them to be delivered to me at work and later admitted to arriving prior to the delivery time in order to watch my reaction as I received them. On one particular day, I received a dozen roses as I sat visiting with my current boyfriend. Shocked that the flowers had arrived at that particular moment, I got up to answer the phone when it rang. Lee was on the other end stating that he was watching me and wondered what I was telling my boyfriend about the delivery. Very disturbed by his actions, I asked Lee to leave me alone and to stop sending me flowers.

For a couple of weeks he honored my request, but then I saw him at that bar that my friend and I frequented. Without knowing who he was, I accepted a dance with his brother and then followed him to the bar for another drink. As we approached the bar, Lee was standing there and said to his brother, "that's the girl I've been telling you about!" My gut reaction was telling me that I needed to run, but they threw out some funny jokes and began to buy my girlfriend and I drinks, so I stayed. Lee began to reveal that he had seen me and my girlfriend at another bar recently. He went on to describe what I was wearing! I don't know if it was the alcohol persuading me or not, but I was pretty impressed by the persistence of this guy, so I decided to give him a chance. We agreed to go to dinner at the end of the week and from that point on, we spent most of our free time together. Being the end of summer, we enjoyed quiet evening walks by the river and talked about our plans for the future.

Toward the middle of October I was pregnant. The timing was not great as my parents were already dealing with my older sister, who was also single and pregnant and due in November. Not only was I afraid to tell my family, but also feared telling Lee. I remember vividly the moment I found the courage to share the news with him. He was housesitting for his grandparents when I showed up for a visit. Cuddling in his arms, I began to cry. He asked what was wrong and I told him everything. I told him that I had known for a couple of weeks that I was pregnant and I was afraid to tell both him and my parents. I shared with him my feelings of being scared and alone. With shock in his voice, he said, "We'll figure it out together."

The next few weeks were rough. Not only was I an emotional wreck, I was hiding my pregnancy from everyone I knew. One night after dinner Lee and I were talking about what we were going to do about the baby. With absolute in his voice he said, "You need to get an abortion and I'll pay for it."

(To this day the words continue to ring in my ears as I allow those thoughts and feeling to flow back in.) With tears in my eyes I looked at him and could not believe what I was hearing—I would not abort my baby, it was completely against my personal and spiritual beliefs and values. I loved Lee and I did not want to lose him. I knew I had gotten myself into this mess, but I did not know how I was going to get out. I waited for a few days before I spoke to him about it again. Reluctantly, wanting to secure our relationship, I agreed to the abortion and Lee set up an appointment for the following week. I was in a daze, knowing that I did not agree with my decision. I was so desperate for Lee to love me and was choosing him over my baby. Finally, the day before the appointment I found the courage to stand up and face Lee with determination, saying, "I don't want the abortion and I'm not going to have it, I'm going to keep the baby." Lee's response of leaving should have been a sign that he was not the right guy for me, but when he came back a couple of weeks later, I accepted him with open arms.

Living away from my family, I was able to hide my pregnancy from them for several months. It was February when we finally shared the news with both of our families and even though there was disappointment looming in the air, there was also celebration of new life to look forward to. My mama and stepdad surprised me as they offered encouragement and support. Having just gone through this with my older sister, I remember my mama saying, "There are much worse things in life than having a baby; babies are a blessing." It had been a while since I had spoken to my father, and I knew that the conversation of me having a baby was going to be difficult. When I called him, we spoke in a generic manner at first, until I mustered the courage and revealed my pregnancy. He appeared to take the news in stride and asked if he and his family could come for a visit soon. I was completely shocked by his concern and agreed to the visit. I had such high hopes for his approval and interest in my life and over the next week, as I prepared for his visit, I realized that I was twenty years old and my father had not been inside my home since I was a little girl. It had been twelve years since he had seen my personal belongings. Emotions of guilt, shame, lose, fear and abandonment flooded every inch of my being. I longed for my father's approval and now it was just a matter of time before he would be sitting in my living room and I was afraid.

My father's visit left me an emotional wreck. Both he and his wife pushed and prodded Lee and I as to when we were planning to get married. They hounded us about our decision to wait and by the time they left we were barely speaking. I had finally found my voice, when speaking to my father, and with Lee's support I was able to tell him how I felt. He did not like it, but I was not willing to back down. While Lee and I had talked about marriage, we realized that we were certainly not ready and had already agreed that we were not going to be forced into getting married, just because I was pregnant.

My father did not appreciate the response and it was a couple of months before I spoke to him again.

The lease on my apartment came due and I was no longer able to afford it, so Lee spoke to his parents about the two of us staying with them, fifteen miles away in a small town. They agreed to take us in and my life of "walking on eggshells" began. Due to complications with my pregnancy, I was placed on bedrest for several hours a day and was no longer able to work. I spent most of my days with his mother, waiting for Lee to return home from work. The days were long and I felt judged for being there, for being with Lee, and for being pregnant. Most of my decisions were questioned and it appeared as if I could do nothing right. She was a wonderful cook and her home was spotless. We were not allowed to use the shower in the main floor bathroom, because she wanted to be sure that it was clean if company arrived. With everything in its place, Lee and I were given a small bedroom to use and it became a haven for me as I attempted to escape the judgmental comments and disapproving eyes of his mother. I am not sure if she intended to portray that behavior on me, but it was my perception of how she felt about me and it became the foundation on which our relationship was built. Lee's father was friendly and appeared to welcome me to make the best of the situation. As awkward as it was, he generally included me in conversation and was always ready to share an inappropriate story or jokes with me. As time passed, I became more uncomfortable around him and I found it easier to just avoid them both.

Three months before my due date I was admitted to the hospital for an evaluation. Two days later, at twenty-seven weeks gestation, I gave birth via caesarian section, to a healthy baby girl. Weighing in at one pound, fourteen ounces, she was perfect. I, on the other hand, was not doing so well. My body was working overtime fighting a toxic level of protein and I found myself recovering in a dark secluded room, under constant supervision. In and out of consciousness for several days, the toxicity levels began to drop and my blood pressure normalized. Finally, released to a regular room, I was detoured to the Neonatal Intensive Care Unit (NICU) to see my daughter for the very first time. Stretched out naked on an opened diaper, wearing eye protection for the UV lights, tubes extending from her nose, head, arm and foot— she took my breath away. I touched her and I felt death. I looked at her and I saw death. She was the smallest baby I had ever seen. I could not imagine how she was going survive. As I sat in the wheelchair next to her, I felt a barrier rising between us. I did not want to fall in love with her if she was going to die and I did not believe that she was going to live. I requested to be taken back to my room. Later in the evening, at the request of my mama, I reluctantly agreed to visit her again. Seeing her lay there, helpless and frail— I realized that I did love her, but I was so afraid of losing her. About a week later, I was discharged from the hospital—without my daughter. She remained in the NICU for two months. We visited daily, she grew and finally met all of the requirements of the physician, who released her on my twenty-first birthday.

It was not long until Lee and I announced our engagement. We planned a small wedding to be held two months away. Two weeks prior to the wedding, I received a phone call from my older sister, announcing that our stepfather was on his way to detox. Still unaware of his addiction, and not understanding what detox was or why he needed it, I had many questions. My sister explained what she could and said mama would call me later to fill in the details. Apparently, my stepfather had been addicted to all kinds of drugs and alcohol for many years and had hit rock bottom when his world began to close in on him. Mama explained that he would be admitted to inpatient treatment for several weeks. Several weeks? My wedding was less than two weeks away! He was supposed to walk me down the aisle! What about me? What was I supposed to do now? I wanted to be compassionate about his situation, but I was also mad at him—feeling as if he was interfering with my happiness. Time went on and he was released to outpatient the day before the wedding. Still not fully understanding the entire situation, I thought he was fixed and I was moving full steam ahead with wedding plans and such, all the while remaining obliviously to the pain and suffering both he and my mama were experiencing.

Lee and I got married, bought a small house and life was going along smoothly for the first couple of years of our marriage. I was able to ignore and excuse the sexual innuendos that Lee assigned to nearly every situation, believing that it was innocent and he was just teasing like his dad. However, about three years into our marriage, when I was pregnant with our second child, the negative behavior reached a level that disturbed me enough and caused me to reach out to friends. I continued to excuse it as harmless and immature, but it made me uncomfortable and began to create unsettling emotions that I could not shake. In the summer of 1990, Lee and I purchased a two-story home that was built in the late 1800s. We spent the many months clearing out the contents and gutting the entire structure. As a way to save money, we decided to move into an overhead camper, parked on the driveway of the new property. For the next few seasons, the camper was home for Lee and I as well as our two-year-old daughter. Shortly after we moved in, I found out that I was pregnant with our second child and crawling up into the loft every night to sleep proved to be very difficult the farther along I got. We did not have a toilet, so we excused ourselves to the neighbor's home often, except during the night when we would relieve ourselves in the yard. Although we were in the middle of town, the darkness of the night camouflaged us enough that the neighbors could not see. Even throughout the cold winter we would trek outside under the moonlight to use the bathroom. Lying to our friends and family whenever they questioned our situation, I attempted to dismiss the inconveniences and tried to draw their attention away from the camper and onto the gutted structure that would one day be our finished home.

During the time that we lived in the camper, our daughter spent most of her days with her grandmother while I worked on the house. Using a pry bar I tore plaster and lathe off the walls and loaded it into a wheelbarrow. I hauled the rubbish to a pile in the backyard. As the pile grew larger, part of my job was to separate items to be burned and items to be thrown away. One day, while I was working in the backyard and Lee was working upstairs, I noticed a strange noise in a tree next to me. When I looked around to find the source, I saw that Lee was out on the second-story deck shooting nails from his nail gun toward me. He was purposely missing me and hitting the tree a couple of feet away. He laughed and laughed when he saw that I caught him and at first I laughed too, but when he began shooting the nails on the ground around me—chasing me around the yard, I was no longer laughing, I was crying, begging him to stop. Not only was it unsafe for me, but I was seven months pregnant and found his behavior to be very disturbing. Even though I knew his actions were not decent, I continued to cover them with excuses of his low self-esteem. Many times throughout our marriage I told myself that he did not mean to treat me so badly. However, I knew that if he did not get his way, he would get pissed off and turn it back on me somehow making his problem my fault.

In the beginning of our marriage, I learned very quickly that my words were no match for his when we fought. He remembered exact dates, times, and situations and eventually when we had disagreements I shut down. I was no match for his quick-witted words and sarcastic remarks. I refrained from saying anything in order to not regret what I might say. I understood that disagreeing is part of marriage, but I also recognized that the way we fought was not healthy. Long-term marriage was one of the most important things to me and I was determined to make my marriage work. I was adamant to not end up divorced like my parents. I longed for the longevity of a healthy and happy relationship—one that I believed my grandparents had. I even looked for similarities in our relationship with others in long-term marriages. I took these similarities as signs from God that we were supposed to be together, and I needed to do whatever I could to make it work.

Lee was a jokester and it was common for him to grab me inappropriately and fondle my breasts if my hands were full or if I was doing dishes. Lee would approach me from behind, reach around and grab my breasts, not letting go until I cried. He would laugh and piss me off—sometimes to the point that I would throw things at him. If I hit him and it hurt, I would be punished for not taking a joke or playing along. If I sat on the floor he would use it as opportunity to shove his crotch in my face. He would grab the back of my head and hold it while he humped my face. His actions disgusted me, but he also seemed to turn it around and somehow make it my fault, as if I was inviting him to behave in such a way. If I bent over and picked up something off the floor, he threw out comments like, "hey, while you're down there." This was his way of inviting me to give him a blowjob, since in his opinion I was in a position to do so. I tried to ignore him and even begged him to change his behavior, but he refused. The anger and resentment within me grew. I was embarrassed and angry about his ridiculous conduct, but eventually, grew angry enough at myself for allowing him to treat me the way he did. I realized years after our divorce that Lee's actions were considered abusive and my anger and resentment were justified.

Lee was good at relating sex to nearly anything. Even with my experience, I was I and Lee had me convinced that if a guy was not given an opportunity to release his sperm, he would actually get "blue balls" that would cause an infection. I believed him; I had no reason not to. I did not know any better, and I certainly was not going to ask anyone! So basically, from the beginning of our marriage if Lee wanted sex, he got it, even if I was not feeling well. Ever since I was in middle school I have suffered from migraine headaches. Doctors checked for tumors and found none. The migraines were just something I had to learn to live with, suffering from at least one headache per week. Some were worse than others, debilitating in fact, but for the most part I took prescribed medication and learned to function with them and worked through them as best I could. It seemed as if Lee never fully understood the severity of my headaches, especially how sick they made me. The migraines were so common, that when I resisted him sexually, he began accusing me of sleeping with other men, which was a constant battle for most of our marriage. He would say that since I was not getting sex at home I must be getting it somewhere else. I think that he truly believed I had multiple affairs during our marriage and the accusations added to my resentment and anger. I thought that if he understood how dedicated I was to him and how important this marriage was to me, he would change and be the man I needed him to be. I will never forget the night that Lee pushed and pushed me to have sex, as a way to relieve my migraine. He stated that he read an article that stated sex releases blood flow and reduces the pain of the headache. He told me that he wanted to help me feel better. As much as I resisted, Lee forced himself on me. With tears running down the sides of my face, Lee took advantage of me and caused the pain in my head to hurt much worse, and it was at this time that I realized how much my heart ached as well. All I wanted to do was get away from him. The sight of him made me sick, but I was so afraid to leave. He had threatened me before that if I ever left him, he would make my life a living hell and I certainly believed him. I had witnessed his vindictive behavior and had seen the way he treated the people he believed had done him wrong.

I was a housewife until our third child was in preschool, then I went to work part-time. The security of making money increased my self-esteem as I recognized my own abilities. Eventually, I was hired by the same company that Lee worked for and I excelled in my position. Shortly after I began, Lee was fired for being noncompliant. This had become a repeated action on his part and even though he had many jobs throughout our marriage, I did my best to support his endeavors by standing up for him when questioned by friends or family. Because I was doing so well at my job, and Lee was without one, we agreed that he would stay at home with the kids and allow me to support the family. When I came home with exciting news about closing another deal, Lee would generally respond with, "Who'd you have to sleep with for that one?" One time I brought home a $50 gift card that a client gave me as a thank you and Lee was convinced that I had slept with the guy in order to close the deal. Even though I was excelling in my new position, I was sinking deeper and deeper into a dark depression. I began to go to bed early and pretend to be asleep when Lee approached me. I visited my primary physician and my journey on antidepressants began as I put things in order to prepare to leave the unhealthy situation I was in.

No longer could I stomach the sight of him. No longer could I breathe under the weight of his abuse. Even after several years of marriage counseling, I knew in my gut that if I was going to survive, I needed to get out. I was afraid of him and what he might do to me. I reached out to my mama and stepdad, who encouraged me to do what I felt was best for me and the children. Not at all shaming me for my decisions, they offered their support and prayers as I took the necessary steps to free myself from this situation. Afraid to speak to Lee about it, unsure of how he would react and expecting him to be enraged, I quietly secured a one-bedroom apartment and secretly planned my escape. Only talking to my immediate family about my plans, I prepared to tell the children the weekend prior to the move. Naturally, they were upset and did not understand, but I held my ground and proceeded with caution. When I finally told Lee, he surprised me by acting as if he accepted the idea of a separation, even offering to help me move. He offered to contact mutual friends to assist in moving my things, and I was furious when he cancelled them at the last minute. He purposely sabotaged me—leaving me with no one to help me move. I lied to him about this move only being temporary and I just needed to clear my head. He finally came around, contacted the friends and asked them to come and help me move. They did and together we moved the three children and me into the tiny apartment.

During this time, childhood memories of my father's abandonment were ever present. I struggled between the decision of my own health and well-being and that of creating an even more dysfunctional upbringing for my children. At first Lee and I shared custody. Eventually, our oldest daughter was taking the brunt of my leaving and no longer felt safe in Lee's home, stating that her dad had thrown a bowl of hot cheese dip at her because she would not answer his question about me. In order to secure her safety, Lee and I came to an agreement; our oldest daughter would live with me full-time, our son would live with him full-time and our youngest daughter would go back and forth weekly. Focusing on my own happiness and the security of my oldest daughter, I failed to foresee that bouncing from house to house on a weekly basis would create such an unhealthy balance in the life of our youngest daughter. Eventually, I enrolled both of the girls and myself into individual counseling. I begged Lee to put our son in counseling, but he refused, saying that our son did not have any problems with the divorce.

Over the next ten years I formed a pattern of unhealthy decisions regarding both intimate relationships as well as friendships. I remarried and divorced, twice. I found myself in similar, yet different situations; similar abuse, different avenues. Life had not turned out the way I planned. I was not the mother I had always dreamed of being. Even though I consistently found peace in my spiritual relationship with my Higher Power, I was not able to transfer that peace into my own life. I felt empty and had nothing to give. I was financially desolate, emotionally exhausted and on the verge of homelessness. Terrified by my future and haunted by my past, I sought refuge one hundred and fifty miles away in my parents' basement. Even though my children were now grown, leaving them and my granddaughter behind was a difficult decision to make. But I knew that if I was going to survive, I had to leave the only place I knew as home I for the past twenty-five years.

Desperate for healing, I entered the rooms of Alcoholics Anonymous (Al-Anon). Completely shattered from my own behavior as well as the effects of the behaviors of others, I was lost, alone, and nearly destroyed. The support of my parents, my younger sister, and the individuals I met at the meetings, I began to find serenity. In the beginning, I attended the meetings because it was the only place I thought I could find help. Even though I did not have an active alcoholic in my life, I knew that I felt comfort in those rooms and the people there seemed to relate to different parts of my story. As time passed, I came to understand that by applying the principles of the Al-Anon program to every area of my life, I could enjoy healthy relationships and heal from the events in my past. Working with a sponsor allowed me to have a deeper understanding of my own hurts and she offered her continued support as I learned to live the Al-Anon way and practice the principles in all my affairs. I experienced healing in the relationships with both of my daughters, as I learned to create healthy boundaries. Due to unfortunate circumstances, the relationship with my son is nonexistent, but it is my hope and prayer that one day he would find his way back into my life. Until then, I continue to pray God's protection over him. The people in Al-Anon offered me their experience, strength and hope and helped me find restoration, peace, security, laughter, beauty, confidence, courage, happiness, and serenity.

I enrolled in a local university and continued my restorative journey. Even though negative self-talk continued, I began to realize that I was more valuable than I thought. It took many years to destroy my self-esteem and I knew that I would not heal overnight. However, I did not realize I would find healing in a classroom. During my third semester I was introduced to Dr. Diane McMillen, a professor in the Human Services Department at Washburn University. To say she is amazing does not begin to describe the beautiful spirit that flows from the center of her being. Under her supervision, I was introduced to the idea that *innate health* is the foundation of all human experience; an insightful spiritual experience that had been revealed years earlier to Sydney Banks, a self-disclosed average man. McMillen taught me that Banks believed everyone is born with *innate health*, but due to circumstances, environment and life events, their *innate health* is buried under hurtful words, rejection, abandonment, judgement, and so on. The understanding of *innate health*, also known as the Three Principles, has provided hope for countless of ordinary, suffering individuals, allowing them to find release in many areas of their lives—including addiction and mental anguish. Banks described the Three Principles as: *Mind, Thought*, and *Consciousness*. I was intrigued and wanted to come to a deeper understanding of these principles and was willing to experience the spiritual health they embodied. In the beginning I was vulnerable and guarded; not wanting to compromise my faith. I was fascinated by the idea that *innate health* is always present and that I can draw on it at any time. I did question the validity of the idea and thought that it seemed too simple. The abandonment of my father, my experience with men and my low self-esteem had all lead me to believe that if I had *innate health* then I was past the point of being able to harness the healing that McMillen described. I was in a fairly deep depression and felt unworthy of forgiveness. I struggled to believe that this idea could aid me in my journey to health.

As I learned more about *innate health* and the *Three Principles*, I began to understand the *Mind* as a divine source of energy—for me that is God, who allows me the wisdom to make healthier choices in my life and the ability to create healthy boundaries, which is how I responded to others and how I allow them to treat me. Developing healthy boundaries has allowed me the opportunity to make an informed decision about who I allow to share my personal space. I realized that it is a continued process, but I learned to be comfortable, accepting and valuing the quality relationships verses the quantity. *Mind* is the source of life that flows through me and allows me to enjoy being me. I no longer felt it necessary to be intimately involved with a man in order to feel complete. I am complete in myself and hope that someday I find a man to compliment my existence and travel with me on the rest of my journey. I believe that without *Mind*, there is no flow, no energy, and no enjoyment. Accepting the idea and principle called *Mind* has allowed me a deeper understanding of the importance of having a spiritual relationship with my higher power. I am more aware of how I treat others and how I allow others to treat me. In order to take the focus off of the chaos in my own life, I used to try and fix others or tried to solve their problems. I now focus on myself and enjoy the peace and understanding behind the principle *Mind*.

The next principle of *innate health* played a tremendous part in my serenity. *Thought* is my own thinking; what I think of, for and about myself, both positive and negative, as well as my perspective of the: who, what, how, when, where and why of any given situation. Dr. McMillen taught me that I have power over thought; that I have the ability to change my own thinking. Through further study of the *Three Principles*, I came to understand that my thinking is just my perspective of what has happened and I alone have the choice to allow this thinking or perspective to leave me in a negative state or allow it to pass through my being and enjoy the beauty that lies within. I have power over each thought and how it affects me. For many years I allowed the hurtful words, actions and opinions of others dictate my own thinking. At times I wondered, if I had known about the principle of *Thought* at an earlier stage in my life, might I have been able to evade years of unhappiness, depression and anxiety.

My history proves that I gave power to the thoughts of others and allowed their words to dictate who I became. This new understanding sparked a flame within me as I became more aware of my own thinking. Negative self-talk, low self-esteem, guilt, and shame were so embedded in me and I allowed the effects of my fathers' abandonment lead me down a path of hurt. Insanity overcame my dreams and the cycle of abusive relationships directed my steps. Being more aware of my own thinking gave me the opportunity to stop the negative self-talk in its tracks, allowing me the chance to replace negative thinking with positive and uplifting thoughts about myself and my situation. I took responsibility for my own thinking and I utilized the power within me—my *innate health*—to change the negative thinking into positive. When flashbacks of the trauma invaded my present thinking, I realized the thoughts are from the past and are not currently happening to me; therefore, they have no power over me. Just the opposite, in fact, I now had power over my thinking and a choice to stop it in its tracks.

Another part of understanding *Thought*, is realizing that the people who caused the trauma in my life were also dealing with their own thoughts and, just like me, were doing the best they could at the time. I came to understand that I played a role in each relationship I had and I no longer needed to place blame on others. Rather, I learned to accept that life is a journey filled with joy and regret. Putting into practice what I learned about my thinking has allowed me to accept that I am a wonderful person and I am deserving of great things. The power of *Thought* is amazing, and when directed in a healthy manner, has the ability to leave an everlasting sense of peace and joy.

The final of these principles is *Consciousness*. In my understanding, *Consciousness* is the actual energy of the *Mind* flowing within me, offering the comfort that allows me to find rest. When learning about the *Three Principles* and relating *Mind* to my higher power, God, it was only natural that I related *Consciousness* to the Holy Spirit; an omnipotent being that dwells within me and rises up to defeat the enemy—my unhealthy thoughts. I found comfort in thinking of *Consciousness* as a peaceful feeling or a voice within, guiding my thoughts, decisions and choices. It is, if you will, the little angel or devil propped upon my shoulders, whispering in my ear, waiting for me to make my next move. I am most aware of *Consciousness* when I am experiencing negative thoughts. I feel its power when I allow negative thinking to control my mood, actions, and words. I recognize the shift that takes place within me when I purposely change my thinking from negative to positive. There is a beautiful and overwhelming emotion that floods my soul when I realize I just changed the course of my journey, simply by changing my thoughts. *Consciousness* allows me the appreciation of how quickly I am able to return from an unhealthy state of mind and how important it is, for my well-being, that I continue to pay special attention to the still, small voice within.

When a person comes to understand *Mind*, *Thought* and *Consciousness*, and the importance of their own *innate health*, it is then that they are finally able to begin living the life they were intended to live. Pain and suffering, addiction and corrupt behavior are all part of life's experience, but they do not have the power to dictate how we experience life. In my profession, I am privileged to work with individuals suffering from substance use disorder and who are also on intensive supervised probation (ISP). Many of them, both men and women, also suffer from an underlying mental health diagnoses as well. Struggling to find balance, due to whatever their situation, many have turned to self-medicating by experimenting with non-prescribed drugs and dangerous chemicals, all of which offer a false sense of normalcy. By the time I have the pleasure of meeting these individuals they have been dragged through the mud and are barely holding on to what little hope they may have left. Their life experience has left them suspicious of anyone wanting to help, many of them are homeless, most of them are filled with despair. They come to me because their probation officer (PO) has sent them, and they are usually carrying a fairly heavy burden. Their main focus is to get off paper which means to successfully complete ISP, and the last thing they want is someone else telling them what to do or when to do it. Very few of the individuals are happy to meet me. However, most appear relieved when they come to understand it is my job to advocate for them and to not add to their already chaotic life. It is my goal to assist them in making sense of and organizing what is already on their plate, so that they can ultimately succeed ISP and become a healthy and productive citizen.

One of the first things I do is assist the individual with completing a Strengths Based Assessment—a tool used to identify strengths, as well as any barriers standing in the way of them meeting goals or accomplishing tasks to successfully complete ISP. For instance, when an individual suffers from an undiagnosed mental health problem, they may have a difficult time attending recovery related meetings, groups, or treatment and might be consistently late to appointments. Their PO does what they can to assist, but often times mental health diagnosis goes undetected, ultimately resulting in the individual receiving a sanction to jail or prison, if they are lucky, or failure to complete ISP all together. As I begin to work with these individuals and identify mental health problems as a barrier, I utilize their strengths and assist them in meeting the goal of obtaining a mental health evaluation. Many times I walk alongside them and meet them at their first appointment. I may even join them by riding public transportation as a way of providing support and assistance when learning a new skill. One of the most valuable moments with a client is when they begin to disclose the experiences that lead up to their current situation. They often express feelings of worthlessness, reveal lack of healthy social support, and expose frustrations due to homelessness or unemployment. Many of them share they feel alone and have never had anyone actually care for them. In fact, they often question why I do.

Sometimes it is difficult to find an entry point to introduce my clients to their own personal *innate health*, but when I do have the opportunity, I jump on it. Sharing the idea of the *Three Principles* is not only beneficial to myself, but also to others. Keeping these ideas in the forefront of my mind has allowed me to be a happier person, simply because I rely on my *innate health* to lead me through my decisions and my thinking. Teaching another person about this way of living is exciting. It is rewarding when I witness a person come to the understanding that they too have *innate health* within them. Joy comes alive in their eyes as they realize the potential they have to overcome negative thinking, negative self-talk, and negative actions. It is a delight to help them come to the understanding that they are worthy of positive changes and that they are the only one standing in their way. Before being introduced to the *Three Principles*, I was in a dark, depressive state, fearing relationships and unhappy with myself as a person. I was driven toward fixing other people's problems, honestly believing that I was helping, not realizing that I was hiding from my own. Now, with this new way of living, I understand that answers are present within each person and by drawing on their own *innate health* they can change the course of their life. By introducing other individuals to the *Three Principles* and walking alongside them on their path to health, I have experienced healing toward others and have found healing within myself. Life does not always go as planned; we experience bumps and bruises along the way, but understanding that we have the ability to change the course we travel—simply by changing our

Patricia McCourt

thinking—is much like a rainbow on a cloudy day, offering hope in the distance while we stand in the rain.

Chapter Thirteen

Redemption, Restorative Justice, and Rebuilding Communities

Lynne M. Woehrle

INTRODUCTION

Several times each day we come to a crossroads where we are called to decide: how should we respond? Our responses are shaped by a complex combination of norms and values that we have developed at both the personal and the societal levels. Sometimes the decisions are easy because all the messages we have learned match and the way seems clear. But sometimes we are faced by conflicting choices or no real sense of choice at all. If how we act at those moments breaks a rule, an act which breaks our positive connection with the social structure, we may face some form of punishment imposed by self or community. This chapter focuses on what processes we use to respond to norm violations, what the restoration of community looks like and how the concept of redemption might be necessary for sustainable peace in the modern society.

In redemption we find a process of restoration. The disruption that has happened is mended. The outcome may not look the same as before the break was made but the ability of the relationship to move forward and succeed is made possible again. Blumstein and Nakamura (2009) defined it as the point when someone who has broken a law becomes seen again as trustworthy. In their research they related that point to the period of pro-social, good behavior after incarceration. Whether it is criminal conduct or less significant rule-breaking (e.g., a family or school behavior rule) what seems to move a person or group towards redemption is the re-establishment of trust. If we look at redemption as a process, not an act, it becomes easier to see what it requires as well as why it is a positive opportunity for individuals and communities to approach conflict as a pivot point rather than as an intractable end of relationship (Kriesberg 2015; Lederach 1995).

Something that has been restored does not look or feel the same way as before it was harmed or disrupted. Within the fabric of restoration there are threads of emotion and trauma that cannot be completely forgotten. But while those experiences cannot be erased, they can be attended to and they can be healed. Again the concept of healing does not mean that the scar becomes absent, it means understanding the significance of the scar and how it has to be part of the story going forward. What becomes important in the redemption process is how that scar or break gets remembered and incorporated in the story of the person or the community.

Communities are a product of cooperation. Sociological insights into society focus on that community level. Individuals are necessary to build communities but our theoretical and applied interests are at the group level. These groups can be formal or informal and they can be of any size that is more than one person, though the term community tends to invoke the idea of multiple participants connected through networks and through formal organizations. Individual stories of redemption or "second chances" provide inspiration for the possibilities and data for assessing trends and outcomes, while scientifically they do not alone offer enough insight into a best practice. Hearing a story of successful or failed redemption provides a starting place for us to wonder what in our social responses toward conflict and harm moves us to constructively use the idea of redemption and where we might improve our social practices and norms around punishment and justice for victims and perpetrators of crime.

If you were stopped on the street today and asked to describe how we treat those who break the rules of our society, what would you say? Are our responses constructive? Do they create the desired outcomes? Do we use reflective opportunities to assess decisions? Do our responses engage the whole person; the whole community of impact from the harm done?

Our challenge is to determine what measures we wish to use to assess our answers to these questions. For example, is success measured by the rule breaker experiencing as much harm as the one who was hurt by the breaking of the rule? This would be the concept of retribution in which justice is achieved by creating equal levels of pain. Is success measured by the level of conformity to the rules that the former rule-breaker practices in future encounters? Society tends toward the preference for assimilation as it makes achieving cooperation a smoother process. Do we achieve success when the victim feels appropriate punishment has been invoked? The challenge here is to establish consistency because often victims differ over what will make them whole again. Does full reintegration of the perpetrator of the harm into society provide the best measure for successful closure? While successful reintegration feels like a large achievement, there are inconsistencies around class, race, ethnicity, religion, gender, sexual orientation and other power identity categories in who gets that opportunity to be fully restored to society after breaking rules. As a result, the lens of justice also needs to be applied not just to the outcome of any criminal justice case or conflict resolution, but also the means by which that outcome was achieved.

DEFINING THE CHARACTERISTICS OF REDEMPTION

In the late nineteenthth century Jane Addams and Ellen Gates Starr spurred forward the establishment and growth of the settlement house movement in the United States. The settlement house concept, as embodied by Hull House in Chicago (established by Addams and Starr in 1889) was that both individual and community success for immigrants hinged on not on how many of them could find some "bootstraps" to pull themselves up by, but rather on leveling the playing field through sharing knowledge and by building community. Rather than viewing successful immigrants as individual survivors of a vetting process, they were interested in preventing the harms that came in communities of immigrants who did not have enough "successful" members to develop neighborhoods that were safe and well resourced. The settlement movement created those social structures in challenged neighborhoods. In a grassroots way settlement houses worked to create positive relationships among neighbors and across social class divides. Addams and Starr used Hull House to provide a local "safety net" through education, employment services, day care, and opportunities for leadership development among the neighborhood residents (Jane Addams Hull House Museum). According to Addams in her book, *Twenty Years at Hull House*, the settlement movement was a means of giving action to principals that many young adults felt at the time as they searched for how to use their economic and social privilege to address social problems. She wrote, "the good we secure for ourselves is precarious and uncertain, is floating in mid-air, until it is secured for all of us and incorporated into our common life" as she discussed the reasons that settlement houses were needed in society (Addams, p. 112). Addams approached her work for economic justice as a project that enhanced both those that lacked social and economic power and those that held social and economic power. Her writings about the work of Hull House suggest that she saw social justice through the lens of mutual redemption. People with plenty did not merely hand out material goods or emotional help in pursuit of a constructive social structure. Rather people with plenty needed to change their living relationship with those who were poor.

In the 1940s, sociologist Robert Merton developed Strain Theory. He was searching for a way to explain why even when clear, social norms and laws are broken. His insights remain important to understanding the limitations of deterrence as a method of limiting criminal activity and rule-breaking. According to Merton (1938) the large social norms which shape our society can have a significant influence on behavioral choices. For example, Merton discussed that people in the United States grow up with very materialistic definitions of success. We also are encouraged to develop our self-concepts around power and control. Merton theorized that some people find it more difficult to achieve those norms of success than others. Some members of society can get success by following the rules and expectations but others might find that those rules and expectations actually limit their chances of achieving the metrics of success. For Merton, this was exemplified by the case of the drug dealer who could from a success standpoint be seen as an entrepreneur but from a legal perspective be seen as a rule-breaker (Merton, 1938). A contemporary example might be the norm of education and how students who can sit still and learn in the ways that we execute education are much more likely to have success. Those who learn differently might also find success but the path there may not be as tuned to the rules of achievement and may depend on the willingness of those in power to accept challenging behaviors in the classroom.

Addams and Merton each offer systemic analysis of how what is viewed as normal processes might actually be sources of conflict and rule-breaking. In other words, what we normalize may not be in the interests of all people in society. So when we think about restoring a harm done, it may be about multiple layers of harm rather than the simplistic model of victim and offender.

Moving redemption into a sociological perspective does not reject the self-work that anyone committing a serious crime must do to re-enter society. However, it does move the conversation to healing and changing relationships in the broader perspective rather than the personal religious or secular path seeking atonement and restitution.

Barbara Deming, a scholar of nonviolence and an activist on gender and sexuality equality issues, offered a model in the 1970s that spoke to an interconnected understanding of oppression and resistance to harm. Her "two-hand" model (Deming, 1982) provided deep sociological insight into the interconnectedness of the harmer and the harmed. In her model, those who are oppressed and injured resist people and institutions that hurt them while also pledging not to impose threats of violence in return. In many social movements this situation has meant cultural resistance through framing and ideological persuasion but it has also at times meant nonviolent tactics of boycott, physical protest, and institutional impediment such as work slow-downs or organized demands for information to purposefully overload a system.

Archbishop Desmond Tutu, an important participant in the Truth and Reconciliation Commission following the end of the Apartheid government in South Africa in 1994 strongly advocated for the importance of public means for processing trauma and forgiveness (Tutu 2000). There continues to be extensive debate about such commissions and their value in restoring community and achieving justice. These are necessary and important conversations and do not undercut the important insight that simply relying on adjudication of individuals who have caused harm during inter- or intranational conflicts is not adequate to achieving healing or redemption as a community. Robert Enright, founder of the International Forgiveness Institute (https://internationalforgiveness.com), would provide another example of a holistic understanding of healing from harm. Moreover his work shows the importance of teaching the skills of forgiveness. For resolution forgiveness needs to happen on multiple fronts, realized by both those who harm others and those who were harmed. Both the act of forgiving and the decision to seek forgiveness are processes that develop through phases of individual and group realization of what it might take to set right a wrong that has been done (Sutton, n.d.). To restore a community to where it can move forward requires society-wide measures along with individual opportunities.

An important example of the depth to which harms done both by and to individuals have wider sociological impact is represented in the enduring challenges that racial divisions, institutional and individual racism provoke in the United States in the twenty-first century. bell hooks (1996) raised scholarly understanding of the impact of everyday racism. That idea that daily experiences of harm from racial exclusion and racist interactions has become widely accepted. Researchers often look for ways to measure the impact of such harm, as exemplified by studies which show that racism plays a role in the unexpectedly high rate of premature births among black women (Nuru-Jeter, Dominguez, Hammond et al., 2009; Murell, 1996; Collins, David, Handler et al., 2011). As expanded on in the next section this approach to understanding the social context in which transgressions against laws and norms happen is an important part of determining how our society can more effectively open opportunities for individual, group, and institutional paths toward redemption. To maintain a relationship of harm is detrimental to all involved whether victim or perpetrator.

Ultimately what studying social movements and processes of social change shows us is that you really cannot decouple what is personal from what is social and political. Sociologists in general have shown this connection and feminist theory in particular has shed light on this insight over the years. Redemption, often classified as a very personal journey of self-change is in fact very much shaped, expanded or constrained by ideals that we have as a community, as a nation, and even as a global system about harm, punishment, reconciliation and healing.

EVIDENCE OF OUR FAILURES TO ACHIEVE
REDEMPTION AND RESTORATION

The last forty years have been characterized by the United States relying heavily on incarceration to "address" social ills and misconduct. While in many places alternatives to incarceration, or more judicious use of it has meant a reduction in the societal investment in prisons as a primary means of (re)socialization for those breaking laws. Author and attorney, Michelle Alexander, made the conversation around our norms of incarceration a more public and present discussion when she drew attention to the practice she named "mass incarceration" in her book *The New Jim Crow* (Alexander, 2010). An example of intensive use of incarceration exists in Wisconsin where Milwaukee accounts for 70 percent of the state's black population, resulting in a race-based, hypersegregated population. Much of the segregation was systematically driven by early/mid-twentieth century housing policies. Anyone who was not white found it difficult to adapt to economic opportunities because where they could live was restricted by ordinances and restrictive covenants. Even once those housing rules were forced out by the Fair Housing Act of 1968, residential practices in Milwaukee remained very racially driven. As economic stagnation surged in the 1980s and 1990s, urban dwellers increasingly struggled to find legitimate, as Merton would say, means of income. Today generations have grown up in the difficulties of poverty and unemployment rates, at times, over 50 percent. Illegal sources of income have increasingly provided sustenance to stressed communities, the truly disadvantaged as William Julius Wilson (1990) calls them.

Over a period of twenty years (1990–2012), 26,222 black men from Milwaukee county were incarcerated, that means that more than half of all African-American men in their thirtiess to early fortiess in the county were at some point incarcerated in state correctional facilities (2013 UWM study).

In the 2010 census Wisconsin at 12.8 percent had the highest incarceration rate of black males in the U.S. The national rate of incarceration was 6.7 percent at that same time. In 2010 only 1.2 percent of white men in Wisconsin were incarcerated. The data also shows 7.6 percent of Native American men and 1.7 percent of Hispanic men incarcerated (Sakala 2014). Several social problems intersect with high incarceration rates. One is the difficulty of gaining legitimate employment with a prison record (Pager, 2007). Another is the economic instability of families where one or more adults are incarcerated and not contributing to the household. As Desmond's (2016) study of eviction patterns in Milwaukee shows, homelessness is often triggered because rents require families to have at least two incomes for stability of place. Homelessness in turn leads to school attendance issues, and that can trigger long-term employment challenges as too much of the workforce is classed as unskilled.

Increasingly those who study economically depressed communities are interested in the impact of generational poverty and trauma as well as the way that highly concentrated poverty shapes not just individuals but communities as a whole. These places of hopelessness do include pockets of thriving joy, people and organizations making small changes. Yet the challenge of system-wide change seems difficult. Not only do individuals in these communities struggle to find redemption, the communities as a whole barely have time to imagine what redemption would look like because they are so often dismissed by outsiders as hopeless. Policies intended to change the opportunities are often seen as obstructions to profit and business, for example, ordinances which require developers and construction companies to hire from minority groups and provide a living wage. Robert Enright, a professor of psychology believes after years of research that the idea that forgiveness actually needs to be taught in our modern society (Oxenden 2017). This suggests that commitment to redemption may also take incentives and developing the will to see the value that practices of empathy and reconciliation bring to society.

WHEN RESISTANCE IS NECESSARY

Barbara Deming's (1982) "two hands" method of nonviolence offers a significant insight that often nonviolent change involves shifting the power structure that supports unjust behaviors and norms. Yes, what is proscribed as normal is not always inclusive and just. With the development of democracy in the eighteenth century came the emergence of large scale social movements. As politics moved more into the public space debates about policies and practices were opened to more people across class, gender and cultural lines. Also with the increased attention to individual rights in the Enlightenment Period and in the concept of human rights that grew in the late-ninteenth and early-twentieth century, collectively advocating for causes expanded in the environment of increased political opportunity and societal support. Deming pointed though to the idea that the means by which change is achieved matters. In other words, while I may act to restrict your unjust power it is the structure I wish to eliminate not the person. Therefore, in advocating for the change, the shift must consider what is reasonably just for all, not just change who is in charge.

Today we often look to insights from individuals, including Henry David Thoreau, Mahatma Gandhi, and Dr. Reverend Martin Luther King, Jr. for guidance on resisting unjust power structures. For each of these leaders they identified points at which their conscience separated them from the behavior and stance of the state. Conscientious objection became a recognized practice as democratic rule widened opportunities to resist. Gandhi, King and many others turned the intellectual idea of disagreeing with policies through public action and voice into broad-based movements. Fighting nonviolently for civil/political rights, resistance to war, and other issues of conscience has emerged as a powerful force for change. Through scientific research, Chenoweth and Stephan (2011) showed that nonviolence campaigns are more effective at achieving change than violent protests. They are also more likely to lead to sustainable democracies than those achieved through violence. They suggest that part of this is explained by the moral high ground achieved by nonviolent strategies. Or as Dr. King was known for saying, "the arc of the moral universe is long, but it bends towards justice" (King, 1958). Thus it remains accepted and even expected in most societies today that we do not always achieve just social systems without a lot of negotiating, conflict, and protest.

RESTORATIVE JUSTICE SEEKS AN ALTERNATE PATH

Restorative Justice grew out of concerns for victims who felt left out of the justice system but later grew to embrace the forgotten needs of both victims and offenders. Howard Zehr, a key figure in the theory and practice of restorative justice explained it well that punishment is not the key or only factor in repairing the harm done (Zehr, 2002). He observed that criminal justice asks has the law been broken, by whom, and what punishment do they deserve; while restorative justice asks: who has been harmed, what does the harmed need, and who is obligated to help the harmed? (Zehr, 2000, p. 20). Zehr argued that changing the focus to the harm instead of to the law broken is a game changer when it comes to deciding on how to best restore justice. The three pillars of restorative justice call us to see the harm, understand the obligations that the harm creates, and include all the stakeholders in deciding how to address the harm and hold the offender accountable (Zehr, 2002, pp. 21–23).

In educating communities about restorative justice, Zehr put a name onto many strategies in use to focus on collaborative solutions to conflict, difference, and injustice. He also worked to develop the moral basis for how to approach questions of injustice and harm. Some of the tools today used in restorative justice are based on ancient practices, such as listening/deliberation circles which pick up on tradition, First Nations peoples' practices for problem solving and conflict resolution. There are many approaches to practicing restorative justice, some teach very precribed and scripted processes; others focus more on the norms of interaction and values behind the communication leaving the facilitation method more open to adaptation for a given environment. But through all of it runs the idea that the harmed and the harmer need to discuss (with a facilitator's guidance) the situation and that the restoration is an important part of the outcome but so is the achievement of understanding. Restorative justice practices are impactful because they shift the lens of how the situation is viewed and also because they change how communication happens and who is included. Restorative justice is not a total solution for all situations of harm, but the ideas have broad applications and combined with more traditional adjudication methods. The practice as used, for example, in the Department of Corrections in Minnesota, can potentially open space for forgiveness, redemption and reconciliation.

Processes that lead to empathy, understanding and forgiveness are seen as integral to the achievement of justice. Circle processes are used regularly in schools and in community settings to work through a wide range of issues from truancy to neighborhood crime to racial justice, to community-police relations, and much more. Where public policy issues exist, circles are a mechanism to bring community input and responsibility to the table. A circle can be applied to nearly any conversation situation. As Kay Pranis (2005) explained, what it does is help communication happen in a non-adversarial way so that people can discuss what is important to them, not try to anticipate what others expect or want to hear. This has many applications but for our interests in this chapter the key idea in circles, that listening can lead to new understanding and possibly to healing is important to thinking about the means for actually achieving redemption.

Redemption seems to require effort by both the offender and the harmed person. The offender needs to seek the opportunity to be redeemed and the harmed person and its collective society need to be opened to the idea that harm while not forgotten can be healed and possibly forgiven with time, communication, and effort towards individual and institutional changes. Redemption opportunities also can be expanded or constricted by society and collective practices. Blumstein and Nakamura (2009) raised this important issue in regards to the increasing use and availability of background checks by employers. They argued that the electronic world has increased ease of access to criminal records. Their research investigated redemption from the standpoint of when can an offender reasonably be expected to not commit another offense. Thus they found that lower levels of recidivism open trust and opportunities for the community to support redemption for the formerly incarcerated. They also found that the more serious the crime the longer it takes for people (such as employers) to trust that the person is no longer a threat (Blumstein and Nakamura, 2009). Restorative justice has been found in several studies to slightly reduce the risk of recidivism, probably because the offender is more involved in the process of constructing the penalty and a wider support group is formed to help the offender change behaviors (Sherman and Strang, 2007).

Restorative justice began with the focus on alternative ways to address harm caused by individuals but there has also developed work on how restorative just can involve groups. Truth and reconciliation are one example. But circles are also being used at the community level in many post-conflict zones (or as prevention of violent conflict) to identify harm and also to bring together offenders with the harmed. Sierra Leone and the work of Fambul Tok International are a good example of this connection between restoration of individual and community and the role of redemption in that process (Fambul Tok International).

Opening space for redemption is also part of the work of ex-offender advocacy and support groups. Some organizations work specifically on support during incarceration and post-release, others are actually formed and led by formerly incarcerated people. In Belfast and Londonderry/Derry ex-prisoners who were part of violence have come together to educate the community about the conflict as well as to work for constructive re-integration of those who fought in the civil war (EPIC). In many communities in the United States, nonprofits work with released prisoners, not just to meet their daily needs but to help them reintegrate into communities and families harmed by their actions. The work also educates the wider community on the importance of supporting and working with released prisoners whether that is emotionally forgiving them, offering them sustaining jobs, or successfully accepting them as neighbors. As this chapter suggested early on, redemption is many-sided and involves all parts of the community being open to building a new, positive relationship post-conflict.

COMMUNITY BUILDING WITH PRINCIPLES OF JUSTICE AND PEACE

In many parts of our world there is a great need for the restoration of community and the rebuilding of trust. Looking at examples such as racial segregation in the United States and South Africa, ethnic conflict in Ireland, Sudan and Bosnia, and political divisions in North and South Korea or between former British and French Cameroons, we learn that the road to peace and rebuilt trust is very long and requires constant attention and effort. One part of that healing process is to make space for those who have harmed others to seek redemption. In many societies those who break rules or laws are punished and an outcast finds it difficult to re-enter society as a "normal" person.

Redemptive processes can take many forms, but dialogue and collaborative projects seem to be central to their implementation. Opening space and willingness to allow redemption take willingness to re-establish trust and take risks on people/groups that have lost our confidence through their actions.

The field of Peace Studies offers many insights that can help to construct pathways to redemption. One important skill is to be able to analyze and understand the multiple dimensions that lead to conflict. A second important skill is to develop a range of nonviolent interventions that either help heal the harms done, or even prevent them from happening in the first place. There are many scholars and activists that have contributed to explaining how and why nonviolence works and what it takes to develop a system and philosophy of nonviolence. A recent important example of nonviolent leadership is the Peace Day message on nonviolent action that Pope Francis delivered for January 1, 2017. Peace Studies also has long focused on the different ways that injustices impact violently on people's daily lives. This concept of structural violence is intricately connected to understanding the need for a restorative approach to criminal justice questions.

The role of redemption is key in utilizing practices and principals of restorative justice. It is also central to the achievement of social equity. Taken together empathy, forgiveness, reconciliation and redemption provide a pathway to inclusive peacemaking and the establishment of personal relationships and social systems that are based on equity and justice. This chapter has laid out that these goals are processes and that the means are without a doubt integral to the ends. Strong communities are bound by cooperation and respect, not so much by commonality. Difference and conflict are necessary parts of a healthy social system, but how we treat people and groups with whom we differ impacts the quality of the entire community.

REFERENCES

Addams, Jane (n.d). *Twenty Years at Hull House by Jane Addams.* New York: The MacMillan Co., 1912.) Distributed online by A Celebration of Women Writers, edited by Mary Mark Ockerbloom; pdf ebook no date, accessed August 18, 2017. http://www.fulltextarchive.com/pdfs/Twenty-Years-At-Hull-House.pdf.

"About Jane Addams and Hull House," Jane Addams Hull House Museum, accessed August 18, 2017, http://www.hullhousemuseum.org/about-jane-addams/.

Blumstein, Alfred, and Kiminori Nakamura. 2009. Redemption in the Presence of Widespread Criminal Background checks. *Criminology*, 47(2): 327–355. DOI: 10.1111/j.1745-9125.2009.00155.x.

Collins Jr., James, W.; David, Richard J.; Arden, Handler; Wall, Stephen and Andes, Steven. 2011 (2004). "Very Low Birthweight in African American Infants: The Role of Maternal Exposure to Interpersonal Racial Discrimination" *American Journal of Public Health.* Published online October 10, 2011. Accessed August 18, 2017, http://ajph.aphapublications.org/doi/full/10.2105/AJPH.94.12.2132.

Deming, Barbara. 1982. *On Anger/New Men New Women: Some Thoughts on Nonviolence.* Philadelphia: New Society Publishers.

Desmond, Matthew. 2016. *Evicted: Poverty and Profit in the American City.* Crown Publishers.

Ex Prisoners Interpretive Center (EPIC), "Welcome to EPIC," accessed August 18, 2017 http://www.epic.org.uk/.

Fambul Tok International. Accessed August 17, 2017. http://www.fambultok.org.

hooks, bell. 1995. *Killing Rage: Ending Racism.* New York, New York: Henry Holt.

King, Jr., Martin Luther. 1958. 1958 February 8, *The Gospel Messenger, Out of the Long Night* by Martin Luther King, Jr., Start Page 3, Quote Page 14, Column 1, Official Organ of the

Church of the Brethren, Published weekly by the General Brotherhood Board, Elgin, Illinois. Accessed August 17, 2017, https://archive.org/details/gospelmessengerv107mors.

Kriesberg, Louis, 2015. *Realizing Peace: A Constructive Conflict Approach*. Oxford: Oxford University Press.

Lederach, John Paul. 1995. *Preparing for Peace*. Syracuse, NY: Syracuse University Press.

Levine, Marc. 2012. Race and Male Employment in the Wake of the Great Recession. Working Paper, Center for Economic Development, University of Wisconsin-Milwaukee. https://www4.uwm.edu/ced/publications/black-employment_2012.pdf.

Merton, Robert (1938). Social Structure and Anomie. *American Sociological Review* 3(5): 672–682. doi:10.2307/2084686.

Murrell, N.L. 1996. Stress, self-esteem, and racism: relationships with low birth weight and preterm delivery in African American women. *Journal of National Black Nurses' Association* 8(1):45–53.

Nuru-Jeter, Amani; Parker Dominguez, Tyan; Powell Hammond, Wizdom; Leu, Janxin; Skaff, Marilyn; Egerter, Susan; Jones, Camara P.; and Paula Braveman. It's The Skin You're In": African-American Women Talk About Their Experiences of Racism. An Exploratory Study to Develop Measures of Racism for Birth Outcome Studies. *Maternal and Child Health Journal* 13: 29. https://doi.org/10.1007/s10995-008-0357-x

Oxenden, McKenna. 2017. Is there a better response to injustice? Pioneering UW professor teaches forgiveness? *Milwaukee Journal Sentinel*. Accessed August 17, 2017, http://www.jsonline.com/story/news/education/2017/08/06/pioneering-uw-prof-has-radical-answer-injustice-forgiveness/435388001/.

Pager, Devah. 2007. *Marked: Race, Crime and Work in an Era of Mass Incarceration*. Chicago: University of Chicago Press.

Pope Francis. 2017. Nonviolence: A Style of Politics for Peace. Vatican. https://w2.vatican.va/content/francesco/en/messages/peace/documents/papa-francesco_20161208_messaggio-l-giornata-mondiale-pace-2017.html.

Pranis, Kay. 2005. *The Little Book of Circle Processes: A New/Old Approach to Peacemaking*. Intercourse, PA: Good Books Press.

Sakala, Leah. 2014. Breaking Down Mass Incarceration in the 2010 Census: State-by-State Incarceration Rates by Race/Ethnicity. Online briefing. Prison Policy Initiative, accessed August 17, 2017, https://www.prisonpolicy.org/reports/rates.html

Sherman, Lawrence and Strang, Heather. 2007. *Restorative Justice: The Evidence*. London: The Smith Institute. http://www.iirp.edu/pdf/RJ_full_report.pdf.

Sutton, Philip. N.d. The Enright Model of Psychological Forgiveness. (Unpublished essay). Accessed August 17, 2017, https://couragerc.org/wp-content/uploads/Enright_Process_Forgiveness_1.pdf.

Thoreau, Henry David. 1903. *On the Duty of Civil Disobedience*. E.C. The Simple Life Press. https://books.google.com/books/about/On_the_Duty_of_Civil_Disobedience.html?id=NbqObbBPUmoC&printsec=frontcover&source=kp_read_button#v=onepage&q&f=false.

Tutu, Desmond. 2000. *No Future Without Forgiveness*. New York: Random House.

Wilson, William Julius. 1990. *The Truly Disadvantaged*. Chicago: University of Chicago Press.

Zehr, Howard. 2002. *The Little Book for Restorative Justice*. Intercourse, PA: Good Books Press.

Chapter Fourteen

Transfiguration

Alfred T. Kisubi

It was a night bound with promise and play;
I couldn't forget it, because it was my aunt's birthday.
Now as I look back to life before,
I remember my mother's words as I walked out the door. . . .
"You're gonna go to Jail!"

Well, I was just pushing a little dope . . .
. . . . What the hell!

That's when all those good times
And being hard-headed came to an end
Because I was stuck-up by a so called friend
So as a young hood of the streets,
I couldn't allow him to get away,
For I had never been beat in any way

Now after looking at the ways of Black life
I knew calling the cops
Wouldn't get me justice that night
So as the anger and rage grew in my heart
My first and only thought was to go kill this narc.

As the events of the night came to pass
I grabbed my .44, because it was time to kick-ass.

Now true this choice was a bad one
But after the shootout, the guys and I felt it was fun. . . .
. . .. . .until the phone rang.
It was no longer a Jesse James dream
You see, my uncle was on the line

His voice sounded as if he was crying
He said . . .
. . . "Homeboy you got a murder case!"

Man, it hit me like a foot to a face!

Now from those words I knew things couldn't get much worse . . .
Well, time had come for me to get comfortable in the County Jail
Because I couldn't afford a $250.00 Bail
I sat and I sat, for 9 months
Seeing everyone through my cell window:
Snitches, pimps, thieves, punks and my victim's widow

Then that morning came, it was time to see the judge
I walked into the courtroom with a societal grudge.
All I could think about was the railroad that was going to take place
Even the jury saw through fear on my face that I'd budge.

Well, to make this long story short, I must admit guilt,
And for that I was given a semi-break in court.
Instead of banking me away for 25 years
The Judge gave me ten and that cleaned away my tears.
I guess by now I stood strong and didn't burst!
But, I just couldn't seem to quench my thirst

As I walked through the doors of Court House
I couldn't help but think how my out date was six years away.—
Man, this was going to be a road to hell!

Now I knew about the drugs in prison and gang ties
Male-to-male rape one couldn't escape
That's why I had to hide that fear my eyes.
So I kept my cool and blended right in
Ran into a few guys, some old school friends
Some I worked with as a bus boy at Days Inn

Well, time came and time passed
"It's been four years and I'm tired of sitting on my ass.
So I got some college, knowledge and some faith
But in my mind I still couldn't escape.
The stereotypes placed on inmates
It was my duty to show that as a Muslim
I was imbued with morale and moral fervor

I was truly tired of being a part of the curse
Remember, when society speaks of this curse
They aren't only speaking of drugs, and violence
But also of terrorism, jihad and intolerance

Which make the mind lose benevolence!

That's why in six weeks I go home
I'm not going to just speak to converse
I'm going to build a community Mosque
And as a Muezzin, I'll call folks to conform
I'm going to speak out loud and firm,
To get rid of the curse in our communities
For until we get our minds straight and away
From destruction of our community
We will never have, or give and get
Genuine humane human love and unity!

Index

Index

About the Contributors

Alfred T. Kisubi, PhD, is distinguished professor and alternate chair of the Human Services Leadership Department at the University of Wisconsin Oshkosh. Dr. Kisubi is also a poet and writer of socially significant stories with several books to his credit. He was born in Uganda and holds advanced degrees in political science, sociology and education from Makerere University (Kampala) and the University of Missouri–Kansas City. He started the annual Seminar on Globalization: Africa's Experience, which convenes for two weeks in Kenya every January and in Uganda every June: www.uwosh.edu/oie/abroad/destinations/coehs.php.

David Liners holds a BA from Marquette University (political science and theology, magna cum laude), a masters of divinity from Catholic Theological Union in Chicago and a doctor of ministry from St. Mary of the Lake University. He is executive director for WISDOM, a Wisconsin network of faith-based organizations, part of the international Gamaliel Foundation. WISDOM is a multi-issue, grassroots organization. It is best known for its work to end mass incarceration. Over the past thirteen years, Liners has overseen the growth of the statewide network from three to twelve diverse, interfaith local organizations in Wisconsin. His duties include leadership training, supervision of organizing staff, and work with local and state leadership groups to develop solid organizing plans. He has developed models for building new projects, for moving start-up projects into long-term stability, and reorganizing projects in need of revitalization. Liners lives in Milwaukee with his wife and two children. He is also an adjunct faculty member of the University of Wisconsin Milwaukee and Cardinal Stritch University.

Derek Dich, BS in human services leadership from the University of Wisconsin Oshkosh. An experienced respite worker, Mr. Dich currently works as claims representative at West Bend Mutual Insurance.

Diane McMillen, PhD, is a professor who has been teaching in human services for thirty-seven years. She began teaching at Washburn University in 1990, where she helped develop the baccalaureate degree in human services and most recently a masters of arts in human services. She received her doctoral degree from the University of Kansas, with a research focus in social action and community mental health. She has a longstanding interest in the field of prevention and has continued to research a new method of inside-out prevention. Diane continues to consult with and provide training for group homes, social service agencies and various community agencies and programs. She has given several keynote addresses and made numerous presentations at national, regional, and statewide conferences. She has served for a number of years on the national board for the National Organization of Human Services, both as a regional representative and as the membership chair. She remains actively involved in various community service and community development projects. Dr. McMillen's other great passions include a wonderful circle of friends, the multiple flower gardens planted across a ten-acre yard, indulgent bicycle rides down the country roads that surround her home on the outskirts of Baldwin, laughing with her husband of forty-four years, and the pack of domesticated animals that run the house.

Fonkem Achankeng, PhD, Hubert H. Humphrey International Fellow and a conflict scientist, is associate professor at the University of Wisconsin Oshkosh. Prior to joining the faculty at the University of Wisconsin Oshkosh, Dr. Fonkem taught at Marian University (2002–2006), University of Wisconsin Parkside (2005–2006) and the University of Wisconsin Fox Valley (1999–2004). He also served for a decade and a half as senior official in the Ministry of Foreign Affairs of Cameroon and was the founder and executive director of the Association for Nonviolence in Cameroon (1993–1998). Dr. Fonkem also earned his BA (summa cum laude) from the University of Benin, Benin City Nigeria, a master's degree from the University of Buea and another master's from Antioch University, Yellow Springs, Ohio. His research interests encompass peace and conflict studies; postcolonial nationalism and conflict; nonviolence; identity, culture and conflict; human and people's rights; international mediation; and crisis intervention. In addition to more than seventeen peer-reviewed articles and book chapters, Dr. Fonkem's recent books include *Nationalism and Intra-State Conflicts in the Postcolonial World*, Lexington Books, 2015; *British Southern Cameroons: Nationalism and Conflict in Postcolonial Africa*, FriesenPress, 2014; *Lefua in Lebialem: Decline or Transformation*, Nkemnji Global Tech, 2006. Dr.

Fonkem is currently a member of the executive council of the Wisconsin Institute for Peace and Conflict Studies (WIPCS) as the representative of the University of Wisconsin Oshkosh. He also serves on the global education and research team of the dignity and humiliation studies (DHS) and on the leadership and scientific committee of the Transnational Education and Learning Society (TELS).

John Paulson is assistant professor of social work at the University of Southern Indiana in Evansville, Indiana. He is a licensed clinical social worker and licensed clinical addiction counselor in the state of Indiana. John is recognized by the National Certification Commission for Addiction Professionals as a master addiction counselor. He is a member of the National Organization for Human Services and is recognized by the Center for Credentialing and Education as a human services-board certified practitioner. He is member of the National Association of Social Workers (NASW), is recognized as a member of the Academy of Certified Social Workers, and has served since 2014 as the elected Region 8 representative to the board of directors for the Indiana chapter of the NASW.

Janet Hagen, PhD, MBA, is chair of the Human Services Leadership Department at the University of Wisconsin Oshkosh. Her research agenda revolves around inclusion in communities and organizations. The specifics of her scholarship are mechanisms for inclusion.

Kendra Green is a graduate student at the University of Wisconsin Oshkosh where she earned her bachelor's in human services leadership. She earned her master's in educational leadership and policy in May 2017 with an emphasis in postsecondary, technical, and adult education.

Kevin Groves earned his bachelor of social work, master of social work, and master of public administration degrees from the University of Southern Indiana in Evansville, Indiana. He is a licensed clinical social worker and licensed addiction counselor in the state of Indiana. Mr. Groves currently works for Southwestern Behavioral Healthcare where he serves as a coordinator of addiction services. Mr. Groves was also the previous director of the Warrick County Drunk Driving and Drug Court Program in Boonville, Indiana.

Leslie A. Hagedorn earned her bachelor of social work and master of social work degrees from the University of Southern Indiana in Evansville, Indiana. She is a licensed social worker in the state of Indiana. She currently works as an addiction counselor at Counseling for Change in Evansville, Indiana.

Lynne M. Woehrle, PhD, is a faculty member in the Sustainable Peace-building Program, College of Nursing, University of Wisconsin Milwaukee. Her areas of interest include conflict and social change, social inequalities of race, class and gender, and environmentally sustainable communities. She has published broadly on social movements, gender and peace. Lynne Woehrle's books, include *Intersectionality and Social Change* (Emerald, 2014) and *Contesting Patriotism: Culture, Power and Strategy in the Peace Movement* (Rowman & Littlefield, 2008, coauthored with Patrick G. Coy and Gregory M. Maney). Dr. Woehrle is executive director of the Wisconsin Institute for Peace and Conflict Studies.

Mark Rice, a PhD candidate at UW-Milwaukee, is examining the emergence and evolution of efforts to end mass imprisonment in Wisconsin, and chairs the Post-Release Issues Workgroup of WISDOM, an organization that links communities across Wisconsin to work for justice. Mr. Rice works as a statewide organizer for EXPO (EX-Prisoners Organizing), a group of formerly incarcerated people who drive WISDOM's ROC (Restoring Our Communities) Wisconsin Campaign to end mass incarceration. In addition, he serves as a board member of Project RETURN, a nonprofit organization in Milwaukee that helps men and women leaving prison make a positive and permanent return to our community. Mark's experience with the state's punishment system inspired him to become a leader in the movement to transform this unjust system and help other people who have experienced incarceration.

Mark received a distinguished leadership award from the Milwaukee Inner-City Congregations Allied for Hope (MICAH) in 2016 and a certificate of special congressional recognition from Congresswoman Gwen Moore for his outstanding and committed work to end mass incarceration. He has contributed his expertise on issues like ban the box, rights restoration, and crimeless revocations to numerous news outlets in Wisconsin.

Melinda Kline, LMSW, works for Kansas Children's Service League as a family services supervisor. She supervises the statewide adoption exchange program (Adopt KS Kids), Adoption Search, and From Heart to Home (Domestic Infant Adoption). Melinda also serves as an adjunct professor for the Human Services and Social Work Departments of Washburn University. Melinda has a BA in human services from Ottawa University and a BSW and MSW from Washburn University. She is currently completing clinical hours towards her LSCSW with hopes of completing certification in 2016.

Melinda is a member of the National and Regional Organizations for Human Services (NOHS and MWOHS) and served as the secretary of MWOHS for four years. She has been a co-presenter in various workshops, regionally and nationally. She has more than thirty years of experience in human services. Nineteen years of service with social and rehabilitation services for the state of Kansas in various positions from disability examiner to human services specialist to social work supervisor with children and family services. She served for two years as the domestic violence child welfare specialist for the state of Kansas and worked in partnership with the Kansas Coalition against Sexual and Domestic Violence to develop curriculum and facilitate and present statewide training for child welfare workers in the area of child welfare and domestic violence. Most often she proclaims herself a "Joyologist."

Michelle Devine Giese has been on her recovery journey since 1995. Michelle is CEO of Apricity. She has a passion to promote recovery in the community. Michelle joined the staff at STEP Industries in 1996 and held the many positions, including operations manager, human resource manager, and president. In 2013, she had the opportunity to study different sober living models, which eventually lead to creating a program and starting three sober living houses in the towns of Neenah and Fox Crossing in Wisconsin. On January 1, 2018, STEP Industries merged with Mooring Programs, which provides residential treatment to men and women. The merged entity became known as Apricity—meaning the warmth of the sun on a cold winter day—which Michelle is now CEO. Michelle is a 1993 graduate of the University of Wisconsin Stout with a BS in business administration. She holds an AODA certificate from the University of Wisconsin–Madison and is a licensed substance abuse counselor in training. Vice president of the board for Solutions Recovery Inc. in Oshkosh, Michelle has also served on various boards and committees throughout the state of Wisconsin.

Patricia McCourt is a student at Washburn University seeking a degree in Human Services with a focus on mental health. Patricia holds two certificates, one for victim/survivor services and the second in Morita therapy. She works with individuals on intensive supervised probation as a care coordinator and is also Kansas-certified peer mentor for the Heartland Regional Alcohol and Drug Assessment Center. Patricia McCourt is a member of Washburn University's human service coalition, TUA—Human Service Honor Society, Phi Theta Kappa Honor Society, Phi Kappa Phi Honor Society, and Washburn University's Morita Study Group. She volunteers regularly through multiple community resources.

Pearl Wright earned her BA in religion and BS in human services degrees from the University of Wisconsin Oshkosh. She was one of several University of Wisconsin Oshkosh students in the Ronald E. McNair Post-Baccalaureate Achievement Scholars Program to travel to the nation's capital over the summer as part of a US Department of Education–sponsored delegation celebrating the fiftieth anniversary of "TRiO" programs and advocating for their future.

www.ingramcontent.com/pod-product-compliance
Lightning Source LLC
Chambersburg PA
CBHW022310280326
41932CB00010B/1055